Real-Time Rhythms: Navigating the Dynamics of Real-Time Systems in Operating Environments

Table of Content

Chapter 1: Foundations of Real-Time Systems

- Defining real-time systems and their critical role in time-sensitive applications.
- Exploring the historical evolution of real-time computing.
- Identifying key characteristics such as predictability and responsiveness.
- Understanding the importance of meeting stringent deadlines.
- Showcasing real-world examples of real-time systems in aerospace, healthcare, and manufacturing.
- Highlighting scenarios where real-time capabilities are indispensable.
- Exploring hardware requirements for real-time systems.
- Discussing the role of specialized components in ensuring timely task execution.
- Introducing software components essential for real-time operations.
- Discussing the role of operating systems in facilitating real-time computing.

Chapter 2: Types of Real-Time Systems

- Defining hard real-time systems and their strict deadline adherence.
- Exploring applications where failure to meet deadlines is critical.
- Introducing soft real-time systems with flexible deadline constraints.
- Examining scenarios where meeting deadlines is desirable but not mandatory.
- Defining embedded systems and their prevalence in real-time applications.
- Exploring the integration of real-time capabilities in embedded devices.
- Discussing the role of real-time systems in control applications.
- Exploring applications in robotics, automotive, and industrial control.
- Introducing distributed real-time systems spanning multiple nodes.
- Examining the coordination and communication challenges in distributed environments.

Chapter 3: Real-Time Operating Systems (RTOS)

- Defining Real-Time Operating Systems and their specialized nature.
- Discussing the critical features of RTOS, including deterministic scheduling.
- Exploring the architecture of RTOS with emphasis on task scheduling.
- Discussing the kernel's role in managing time-critical processes.
- Introducing scheduling algorithms tailored for real-time applications.
- Exploring Rate Monotonic Scheduling (RMS) and Earliest Deadline First (EDF).
- Examining memory allocation strategies in real-time environments.
- Discussing the challenges of dynamic memory allocation in time-sensitive tasks.
- Highlighting the prevalence of RTOS in embedded applications.
- Discussing the benefits of using RTOS in resource-constrained environments.

Chapter 4: Scheduling Algorithms in Real-Time Systems

- Emphasizing the central role of scheduling in meeting time constraints.
- Discussing the impact of scheduling decisions on system performance.
- Introducing the RMS algorithm and its principles.
- Discussing how RMS assigns priorities based on task execution rates.
- Exploring the EDF algorithm and its focus on meeting deadlines.
- Discussing how EDF dynamically adjusts priorities based on imminent deadlines.
- Introducing Deadline Monotonic Scheduling as an extension of RMS.
- Discussing its benefits in scenarios where deadlines are critical.
- Discussing practical challenges in implementing scheduling algorithms.
- Analyzing the impact of task arrival patterns on scheduling efficiency.

Chapter 5: Challenges and Solutions in Real-Time Systems

- Identifying hardware constraints that pose challenges to real-time systems.
- Discussing strategies to mitigate hardware-induced latencies.
- Addressing challenges arising from uncertainty in task execution times.
- Discussing methods for estimating and guaranteeing task execution durations.
- Introducing fault tolerance as a critical aspect of real-time computing.
- Discussing mechanisms such as redundancy and error detection for fault mitigation.
- Exploring power consumption challenges in real-time systems.
- Discussing strategies for optimizing power usage without compromising performance.
- Discussing adaptive strategies to dynamically adjust to changing conditions.
- Introducing machine learning applications in predicting and adapting to runtime variations.

Chapter 6: Real-Time Communication Protocols

- Emphasizing the critical role of communication in achieving synchronization.
- Discussing the impact of communication delays on real-time tasks.
- Introducing message queues as a mechanism for asynchronous communication.
- Discussing the benefits of publish-subscribe models in decoupled communication.
- Exploring the Precision Time Protocol for achieving precise time synchronization.
- Discussing its application in scenarios where accurate timing is crucial.
- Introducing MQTT as a lightweight messaging protocol for real-time communication.
- Discussing its efficiency in scenarios with constrained bandwidth and unreliable networks.
- Showcasing case studies of successful real-time communication protocol implementations.
- Discussing the considerations in selecting the appropriate protocol for specific applications.

Chapter 7: Applications of Real-Time Systems

- Showcasing applications of real-time systems in medical devices and patient monitoring.
- Discussing how real-time capabilities enhance diagnostic accuracy and treatment.
- Exploring the role of real-time systems in automotive safety and performance.
- Discussing applications in autonomous vehicles and advanced driver assistance systems.
- Showcasing real-time applications in industrial automation and control systems.
- Discussing how real-time capabilities optimize manufacturing processes and ensure efficiency.
- Exploring real-time applications in telecommunications and networked environments.
- Discussing the importance of low-latency communication in ensuring seamless connectivity.
- Highlighting the critical role of real-time systems in aerospace and defense applications.
- Showcasing examples in avionics, radar systems, and mission-critical defense operations.

Chapter 8: Future Trends in Real-Time Systems

- Exploring the synergy between real-time systems and artificial intelligence.
- Discussing how AI enhances decision-making and adaptability in real-time environments.
- Analyzing the role of edge computing in the evolution of real-time systems.
- Discussing how edge computing addresses latency challenges in distributed environments.
- Exploring the potential integration of blockchain technology in real-time systems.
- Discussing how blockchain enhances security and transparency in time-sensitive transactions.
- Analyzing ethical considerations in the deployment of real-time technologies.
- Discussing the societal implications of real-time systems in various domains.
- Exploring the implications of quantum computing on real-time processing.
- Discussing potential breakthroughs and challenges in leveraging quantum principles.

Introduction

In the dynamic landscape of modern computing, the rhythmic pulse of real-time systems orchestrates a symphony of instantaneous data processing, setting the tempo for technological advancement. "Real-Time Rhythms" serves as an inviting portal, ushering readers into the immersive realm where each tick of the clock resonates as a critical beat in this captivating symphony. As the guide unfolds, it embarks on a comprehensive journey, peeling back the layers of real-time systems to reveal the intricacies that shape their role in the contemporary digital landscape. The complexities, challenges, and innovations inherent in real-time systems become the focal points, guiding readers through a profound exploration of their significance.

The guide's narrative mirrors the metronomic precision of real-time systems, creating a harmonious flow that captivates both novices and seasoned professionals. Each chapter represents a distinctive movement in this symphony, shedding light on a specific facet of real-time systems. The symphony begins with an introduction that sets the tone, establishing the critical importance of real-time systems in the broader context of technological evolution. The subsequent chapters serve as movements, each delving into a different aspect, unraveling the layers that make up the intricate composition of real-time systems.

The significance of real-time systems is not merely discussed; it is illuminated through real-world examples, case studies, and practical applications across diverse industries. The guide's narrative prowess ensures that readers not only grasp the theoretical foundations but also witness the practical implications of real-time systems in action. From healthcare and automotive applications to industrial automation and telecommunications, the guide paints a vivid tableau of the pervasive influence of real-time systems in various domains.

As the exploration progresses, the complexities inherent in real-time systems come to the forefront. The challenges they face, from hardware limitations and uncertainties in task execution times to the need for fault tolerance and adaptive strategies, are dissected with precision. The guide, much like a skilled conductor, guides readers through these challenges, providing insights into the innovative solutions and strategies that maintain the rhythmic integrity of real-time systems.

Communication protocols, a vital component of the real-time symphony, are carefully examined. The guide navigates through message queues, publish-subscribe models, and precision time protocols, elucidating how these protocols contribute to seamless communication and synchronization in distributed environments. Real-world implementations serve as poignant notes in this symphony, showcasing the impact of communication protocols on overall system performance.

Applications of real-time systems emerge as powerful crescendos in the symphony, demonstrating their transformative influence in healthcare, automotive systems, industrial automation, telecommunications, and aerospace and defense. Through these applications, readers witness the tangible outcomes of integrating real-time capabilities, from enhancing patient care to optimizing manufacturing processes and ensuring the reliability of mission-critical defense operations.

The guide culminates with a forward-looking movement, exploring the future trends that will shape the evolving landscape of real-time systems. The integration of artificial intelligence, advance-

ments in edge computing, blockchain's potential, ethical considerations, and the intersection with quantum computing are all facets of
the symphony that portend the next chapters in the saga of real-time
systems.

"Real-Time Rhythms" is more than a guide; it is a melodic
odyssey through the beating heart of instantaneous computing. Its
pages resonate with the harmonious blend of theoretical insights,
practical applications, and forward-thinking perspectives. As readers
traverse this symphony of knowledge, they emerge not just informed
but equipped to navigate the complexities and innovations that define the captivating world of real-time systems within operating environments.

Chapter 1: Foundations of Real-Time Systems

Defining real-time systems and their critical role in time-sensitive applications.

Real-time systems stand as the linchpin within the intricate tapestry of modern technological landscapes, assuming a paramount role as the bedrock for time-sensitive applications across a myriad of domains. These systems, distinguished by their intrinsic capacity to swiftly process and respond to input within predefined temporal constraints, emerge as the vanguards of precision, ensuring that deadlines are met with unwavering accuracy. Their essence lies not merely in delivering correctness but in orchestrating timely outcomes, thereby rendering them indispensable in scenarios where the imperatives of time are absolute.

Among the myriad applications, the realm of industrial automation emerges as a primary domain where real-time systems wield indispensable influence. Manufacturing processes, robotics, and control systems rely intricately on the seamless coordination and synchronization enabled by the rapid decision-making and execution capabilities of real-time systems. In this milieu, where the timing of actions is of the essence, any delay may precipitate inefficiencies or, in dire circumstances, catastrophic consequences.

Transitioning to the domain of communication systems, real-time capabilities ascend to paramount significance in applications like voice-over-IP (VoIP) and video conferencing. The transmission and reception of audio-visual data hinge on minimal latency to sustain the natural cadence of communication. Real-time systems, with their instantaneous processing and delivery of data packets, become the linchpin ensuring a communication experience that is not just efficient but seamlessly immersive.

In the critical domain of healthcare, real-time systems play an instrumental role in monitoring and diagnostic applications. Devices for patient monitoring rely explicitly on real-time data processing to swiftly detect anomalies and trigger timely alerts. The repercussions of decisions made in this context are often life-critical, underscoring the indispensable nature of real-time systems and their pivotal role in ensuring responsiveness and reliability.

The automotive industry undergoes a transformative renaissance propelled by the integration of real-time systems, particularly evident in advanced driver assistance systems (ADAS) and autonomous vehicles. These systems necessitate instantaneous data processing for decision-making within dynamic and unpredictable driving environments. The ability to respond in real-time to changing road conditions and potential hazards becomes imperative for the safety and success of autonomous driving technologies.

Within the fast-paced crucible of financial markets, real-time systems are the unseen architects of efficacy, shaping the landscape of financial trading platforms. Split-second decisions in this milieu can wield substantial impact, and real-time data processing becomes the enabler for traders and financial institutions to execute trades, monitor market fluctuations, and manage risks with a swiftness that mirrors the velocity of market dynamics.

Beyond these realms, real-time systems extend their influence to diverse applications encompassing gaming, aviation, and emergency response systems. The underlying theme resonates with the criticality of time-sensitive operations, where the specter of delays looms large, bearing the potential for consequential outcomes.

Yet, attaining real-time capabilities is not devoid of challenges. System designers navigate the intricate terrain of determinism, grappling with the imperative that responses not only be rapid but also predictably consistent. The orchestration of hardware and software architectures becomes an art, meticulously crafted to meet stringent timing requirements, often necessitating the incorporation of specialized real-time operating systems (RTOS) and dedicated hardware components.

In conclusion, real-time systems emerge as the sine qua non of time-sensitive applications, permeating the multifaceted fabric of our technological landscape. From industrial automation to healthcare, communication to finance, the ability to process and respond in real-time emerges as the defining factor in the success and reliability of these systems. As the relentless march of technology persists, the role of real-time systems is poised to expand further, sculpting the contours of critical applications and augmenting our capacity to navigate a world that demands not just accuracy but the orchestration of timely precision.

Exploring the historical evolution of real-time computing.

The historical evolution of real-time computing traces a fascinating journey through the annals of technological progress, characterized by a relentless pursuit of precision and responsiveness. The roots of real-time computing can be discerned in early industrial automation endeavors during the mid-20th century, where the need for timely control of mechanical processes gave rise to rudimentary real-time systems. These initial forays set the stage for the subsequent exploration of real-time capabilities in various domains.

The 1960s witnessed a significant milestone with the advent of early real-time operating systems (RTOS). Innovations like the Dartmouth Time-Sharing System (DTSS) and the Real-Time System (RTS) paved the way for more sophisticated time-sharing capabilities, allowing multiple users to interact with a computer system simultaneously. These developments laid the groundwork for the expansion of real-time computing beyond industrial applications into emerging fields such as aerospace and defense.

In the realm of aerospace, the quest for real-time capabilities gained momentum during the 1960s and 1970s, driven by the imperatives of space exploration and military endeavors. The Apollo Guidance Computer, a marvel of its time, exemplified the integration of real-time computing in space missions, orchestrating complex maneuvers with precision. Concurrently, the defense sector embraced real-time systems for command and control applications, solidifying their role in mission-critical operations.

The proliferation of real-time computing in the following decades was propelled by the advent of microprocessor technology. The 1980s witnessed a surge in the development of embedded systems, where compact and specialized computing units found applications in diverse domains, including automotive control systems, medical devices, and consumer electronics. This era marked a democratization of real-time capabilities, as smaller-scale applications could now leverage the precision and responsiveness that were once the purview of large-scale industrial and military systems.

The 1990s brought forth a paradigm shift with the rise of networked and distributed real-time systems. The integration of real-time communication protocols and technologies facilitated the coordination of geographically dispersed computing resources, enabling collaborative real-time applications. This era also saw the emergence of the Internet of Things (IoT), where interconnected devices demanded real-time capabilities for seamless interaction and data processing.

As the 21st century unfolded, real-time computing continued to evolve in tandem with advancements in hardware and software technologies. Multi-core processors and parallel computing architectures became instrumental in enhancing the computational prowess of real-time systems, enabling them to handle increasingly complex tasks with precision. The integration of machine learning and artificial intelligence into real-time applications further expanded the horizons, imbuing these systems with adaptive and predictive capabilities.

The automotive industry became a focal point for real-time computing innovations, particularly with the advent of advanced driver assistance systems (ADAS) and the pursuit of autonomous vehicles. Real-time processing of sensor data, coupled with rapid decision-making algorithms, became imperative for ensuring the safety and efficiency of these evolving automotive technologies. Simultaneously, the healthcare sector witnessed the infusion of real-time computing in patient monitoring, diagnostics, and the management of medical devices, amplifying the potential for timely interventions and improved patient outcomes.

The contemporary landscape of real-time computing is characterized by a convergence of technologies such as edge computing, 5G networks, and the continued refinement of RTOS. Edge computing, with its emphasis on processing data closer to the source, aligns seamlessly with the requirements of real-time applications, reducing latency and enhancing responsiveness. The advent of 5G networks further catalyzes the potential for real-time communication, enabling a new era of interconnected devices and applications.

However, the journey of real-time computing is not without its challenges. The quest for determinism, wherein system responses are not only rapid but predictably consistent, remains a perpetual pursuit. Real-time systems must navigate the intricate balance between computational efficiency and temporal precision, often requiring specialized design considerations and trade-offs.

In conclusion, the historical evolution of real-time computing reflects a captivating narrative of technological progression, from its nascent applications in industrial automation to the contemporary ubiquity in diverse domains. The journey unfolds through epochs marked by the advent of RTOS, the miniaturization of embedded systems, the networking of real-time capabilities, and the infusion of advanced technologies in the 21st century. As real-time computing continues to shape the fabric of our technological landscape, its future promises further innovation, adaptation, and an enduring commitment to the quest for precision in the temporal realm.

Identifying key characteristics such as predictability and responsiveness.

At the core of real-time computing lie key characteristics that distinguish it from conventional computing paradigms, ushering in a realm where precision, predictability, and responsiveness take center stage. Predictability stands tall as a foundational pillar, encapsulating the assurance that system responses are not only swift but also reliably consistent. In the intricate dance of real-time applications, where temporal constraints are paramount, predictability becomes an imperative. This characteristic extends beyond mere speed, delving into the realm of determinism, where the outcome of system operations can be anticipated with a high degree of certainty. Achieving predictability in real-time systems involves meticulous orchestration of hardware and software components, navigating the intricate terrain where computational efficiency converges with temporal precision.

Responsiveness emerges as another cardinal characteristic, embodying the system's ability to promptly process and react to stimuli within defined timeframes. In the tapestry of real-time computing, responsiveness becomes the heartbeat that ensures the system not only meets deadlines but does so with a level of agility that aligns with the demands of the application. Whether orchestrating the control of industrial processes, navigating autonomous vehicles through dynamic environments, or facilitating instantaneous communication in critical domains, responsiveness is the linchpin that underpins the efficacy and reliability of real-time systems.

Determinism, an intrinsic facet of predictability, permeates the landscape of real-time computing. It entails the capacity to guarantee that a sequence of operations will produce consistent outcomes, irrespective of variations in external conditions or system loads. In the quest for determinism, system designers grapple with minimizing variability in execution times, ensuring that the temporal behavior of the system remains steadfast. This pursuit of determinism extends from the kernel of real-time operating systems to the design choices in hardware architectures, forging a path where the reliability of outcomes is not compromised in the face of dynamic and unpredictable environments.

Time is not an abstract concept but a tangible and quantifiable entity in the realm of real-time computing, giving rise to the characteristic of temporal precision. This precision dictates that operations occur within predefined timeframes, adhering rigorously to the temporal requirements dictated by the application. From microseconds in communication systems to milliseconds in industrial automation and beyond, real-time computing grapples with the challenge of temporal precision, where deviations from specified deadlines can yield outcomes ranging from inefficiencies to catastrophic failures.

Concurrency management stands as a critical characteristic, navigating the complexities introduced by simultaneous execution of multiple tasks within a real-time system. In scenarios where diverse operations vie for computational resources, effective concurrency management becomes paramount to prevent conflicts, prioritize critical tasks, and ensure that temporal requirements are met. Real-time systems grapple with the intricacies of concurrency, striking a delicate balance between parallel execution and the prevention of resource contention to uphold the responsiveness and predictability that define their essence.

Resource efficiency surfaces as an inherent characteristic, underscoring the imperative to accomplish tasks with minimal utilization of computational, memory, and communication resources. In the pursuit of efficiency, real-time systems optimize algorithms, streamline processes, and judiciously allocate resources to meet the dual objectives of meeting temporal constraints and conserving system resources. The efficiency imperative becomes particularly pronounced in embedded systems, where the constraints of size, weight, and power mandate a delicate equilibrium between performance and resource utilization.

Fault tolerance assumes heightened significance as a key characteristic, acknowledging the inevitability of potential failures within complex computing environments. Real-time systems must be endowed with mechanisms to detect and gracefully recover from faults, ensuring the continuity of critical operations. This characteristic becomes non-negotiable in applications where the cost of failure is prohibitively high, such as in medical devices, avionics systems, or industrial control systems.

Adaptability surfaces as a modern characteristic, reflecting the integration of real-time computing with cutting-edge technologies such as artificial intelligence and machine learning. Real-time systems are evolving beyond reactive responsiveness to embrace proactive adaptation, leveraging intelligent algorithms to anticipate changing conditions and dynamically adjust their behavior. This characteristic empowers real-time systems to navigate dynamic and unpredictable environments with a level of sophistication that transcends traditional deterministic approaches.

Networking capabilities weave into the fabric of real-time computing, as interconnected systems and devices become pervasive. The characteristic of networked real-time computing involves the seamless exchange of data and coordination across distributed computing nodes. In domains like the Internet of Things (IoT), where devices collaborate in real time, networking capabilities are integral to achieving cohesive and synchronized behavior. The challenges of network latency, reliability, and synchronization become focal points in ensuring the efficacy of real-time communication.

The evolution of real-time computing is inexorably intertwined with these key characteristics, each shaping the landscape in response to the demands of diverse applications. From the foundational principles of predictability and responsiveness to the nuanced intricacies of determinism, temporal precision, concurrency management, resource efficiency, fault tolerance, adaptability, and networking, these characteristics collectively define the essence of real-time computing. As the technological tapestry continues to unfurl, the interplay of these characteristics will shape the trajectory of real-time systems, ushering in an era where precision and responsiveness become not just benchmarks but the very fabric of computational reality.

Understanding the importance of meeting stringent deadlines.

The importance of meeting stringent deadlines permeates every facet of human endeavor, weaving a thread of urgency that binds together diverse domains and disciplines. At its core, the adherence to deadlines embodies a commitment to time as a finite and invaluable resource. In the realms of business and commerce, the significance of meeting deadlines is manifest in the orchestration of operations, project deliveries, and product launches. The intricate dance of supply chains relies on the synchronized meeting of deadlines, ensuring the seamless flow of goods and services. A delay at any juncture can trigger a cascading effect, disrupting the delicate equilibrium that underlies economic transactions.

In the crucible of project management, deadlines are the linchpin that governs the trajectory from ideation to execution. The ability to deliver projects on time is not merely a metric of efficiency; it reflects an organization's capacity to navigate complexity, allocate resources judiciously, and honor commitments made to stakeholders. A missed deadline in the project management landscape is not a mere temporal lapse; it reverberates with consequences ranging from cost overruns to a compromised reputation. The adherence to deadlines becomes a testament to an organization's reliability, professionalism, and its overarching commitment to delivering value in a timely manner.

In the realm of academia, the academic calendar is a tapestry woven with deadlines that delineate the progression of learning and research. Meeting deadlines for assignments, exams, and research submissions is a crucible where students hone their time management skills, a precursor to the demands they will face in their professional lives. For educators and researchers, the adherence to deadlines is pivotal in contributing to the collective knowledge base. Conference submissions, research papers, and grant proposals are governed by timelines that dictate the pace of scholarly advancement. A missed deadline can not only impede individual progress but also disrupt the broader cadence of academic discourse.

In the dynamic landscape of technology and innovation, where breakthroughs unfold at an accelerating pace, meeting deadlines is synonymous with staying relevant and competitive. Product launches, software releases, and technological advancements are driven by a relentless pursuit of timelines. In this arena, the proverbial "time to market" is not just a metric; it is a strategic imperative that defines success or failure. The ability to meet deadlines in technology is often the difference between being a trailblazer and a mere spectator in the ever-evolving landscape of innovation.

The healthcare sector provides a poignant illustration of the life-and-death consequences tied to meeting stringent deadlines. In emergency rooms, operating theaters, and critical care units, every moment is imbued with a sense of urgency. Timely interventions, accurate diagnoses, and prompt responses to changing conditions are predicated on meeting deadlines that transcend the conventional notion of time as a linear construct. A delay in administering medication, analyzing test results, or responding to an emergency can have profound repercussions on patient outcomes, underscoring the criticality of meeting deadlines in the realm of healthcare.

The interconnected nature of global systems, exemplified by financial markets and international trade, amplifies the consequences of failing to meet deadlines. In financial markets, where split-second decisions can shape fortunes, meeting deadlines for trade executions and financial reporting is not just a regulatory requirement but a fundamental pillar of market integrity. International trade hinges on the timely movement of goods across borders, and any disruption to this temporal flow can have ramifications that reverberate globally. The importance of meeting deadlines in these contexts is not confined to organizational efficiency; it is woven into the fabric of economic stability and international relations.

Furthermore, the societal fabric itself is interwoven with deadlines that govern legal processes, elections, and governmental functions. Legal proceedings are guided by deadlines that ensure due process and prevent undue delays in the administration of justice. Elections are orchestrated with precision deadlines, embodying the democratic rhythm of governance. Governmental functions, from budgetary allocations to policy implementations, are tethered to timelines that reflect the accountability of institutions to the citizens they serve. The repercussions of missed deadlines in these arenas extend beyond organizational or individual consequences to encompass the very foundations of societal order and governance.

The psychological dimensions of meeting deadlines are equally profound. Individuals and organizations that consistently meet deadlines cultivate a culture of discipline, responsibility, and trust. The fulfillment of commitments, whether to oneself or others, engenders a sense of accomplishment and builds a foundation of credibility. On the contrary, chronic failures to meet deadlines can erode trust, breed a culture of procrastination, and sow seeds of discontent.

The psychological impact of meeting or missing deadlines ripples through professional relationships, team dynamics, and personal well-being, shaping the ethos of individuals and organizations alike.

In conclusion, the importance of meeting stringent deadlines is a tapestry woven with threads of economic stability, professional credibility, societal order, and individual well-being. It is a testament to the value placed on time as a resource and underscores the imperative of honoring commitments made in various domains. Whether in the crucible of business, academia, technology, healthcare, or governance, meeting deadlines is not a perfunctory exercise; it is an embodiment of discipline, accountability, and the pursuit of excellence. As the world continues to evolve, the ability to navigate the cadence of deadlines remains a cornerstone of success, shaping the trajectory of individuals, organizations, and societies at large.

Showcasing real-world examples of real-time systems in aerospace, healthcare, and manufacturing.

In the aerospace industry, real-time systems represent a critical enabler for ensuring the safety, efficiency, and precision required for the complex operations in aviation and space exploration. One compelling example is the flight control systems employed in modern aircraft. These systems rely on real-time capabilities to process vast amounts of data from sensors and make split-second decisions to maintain the aircraft's stability and respond to dynamic flight conditions. Autopilot systems, a subset of flight control, showcase the intricacies of real-time processing, continuously adjusting control surfaces to keep the aircraft on its designated trajectory. Furthermore, in the context of space exploration, mission-critical tasks such as satellite navigation, orbital maneuvers, and interplanetary spacecraft operations heavily depend on real-time systems to ensure accurate and timely execution. The Mars rovers, for instance, exemplify the integration of real-time capabilities, enabling autonomous decision-making as they navigate the Martian terrain, analyze samples, and communicate findings back to Earth with minimal latency.

Within the healthcare sector, real-time systems play a pivotal role in monitoring, diagnostics, and patient care, demonstrating their indispensable nature in ensuring timely interventions and accurate assessments. One notable example is the use of real-time monitoring devices in intensive care units (ICUs). Patient vital signs, such as heart rate, blood pressure, and oxygen levels, are continuously monitored, and deviations from normal parameters trigger immediate alerts for healthcare professionals. This real-time monitoring allows for prompt responses to critical situations, enhancing patient safety and potentially saving lives. In the realm of diagnostic imaging, real-time processing is evident in technologies like ultrasound and magnetic resonance imaging (MRI), where the visualization of internal structures occurs in real-time, aiding physicians in making swift and accurate diagnoses. Surgical procedures, too, benefit from real-time imaging and guidance systems, enabling surgeons to navigate with precision and make informed decisions in the operating room.

In the domain of manufacturing, real-time systems form the backbone of industrial automation, optimizing processes, enhancing efficiency, and ensuring the quality of production. Consider the example of Programmable Logic Controllers (PLCs) embedded in manufacturing systems. These real-time controllers monitor and control machinery and processes on the factory floor, coordinating actions such as robotic assembly, material handling, and quality control in synchronization. The automotive industry provides another compelling illustration, where real-time systems are integral to the functioning of assembly line robots, precision machining tools, and quality assurance systems. Collaborative robots, or cobots, represent a more recent application, where real-time responsiveness allows these robots to work alongside human operators in tasks that require dexterity and adaptability. Furthermore, supply chain management in manufacturing relies on real-time tracking and coordination to ensure that materials and components are sourced, processed, and delivered with precision, minimizing delays and optimizing production schedules.

The aerospace, healthcare, and manufacturing examples underscore the diversity and criticality of real-time systems in various industries. These applications share common themes of precision, responsiveness, and the ability to handle dynamic and unpredictable environments. The integration of real-time capabilities in these sectors not only enhances operational efficiency but also plays a pivotal role in ensuring safety, reliability, and the ability to adapt to evolving demands.

In the aerospace sector, real-time systems are indispensable for the control and navigation of aircraft, ranging from commercial airliners to spacecraft. Flight control systems, autopilot mechanisms, and guidance systems rely on real-time data processing to ensure the safety and precision of air travel and space missions. For instance, the Airbus A380, one of the world's largest passenger aircraft, employs a sophisticated fly-by-wire system that translates pilot inputs into real-time adjustments of control surfaces, enhancing stability and responsiveness. In the context of space exploration, NASA's Mars rovers, including the Curiosity rover, utilize real-time systems to navigate the Martian surface, analyze soil samples, and transmit data back to Earth, demonstrating the crucial role of real-time capabilities in extraterrestrial missions.

In healthcare, real-time systems contribute significantly to patient care and medical diagnostics. Intensive care units (ICUs) leverage real-time monitoring systems that continuously track patients' vital signs, enabling healthcare professionals to respond promptly to any abnormalities. Monitoring devices, such as electrocardiograms (ECGs) and pulse oximeters, exemplify the application of real-time technology in capturing and analyzing physiological data. Additionally, medical imaging technologies like ultrasound and MRI often operate in real-time, providing immediate visualizations for diagnostic purposes. In the surgical domain, real-time imaging systems assist surgeons during procedures, enhancing precision and facilitating informed decision-making. Robotic surgery platforms, exemplified by the da Vinci Surgical System, integrate real-time control to enable surgeons to perform minimally invasive procedures with enhanced dexterity.

In manufacturing, real-time systems revolutionize industrial processes, optimizing production, ensuring quality control, and enabling adaptive automation. Programmable Logic Controllers (PLCs) serve as the nerve center of manufacturing machinery, orchestrating real-time control of processes such as assembly lines and robotic operations. Collaborative robots, equipped with real-time sensors and adaptive control systems, work alongside human operators, enhancing efficiency in tasks that require flexibility and agility. Advanced manufacturing technologies, including 3D printing and Computer Numerical Control (CNC) machining, leverage real-time feedback to achieve precision and consistency. Furthermore, supply chain management relies on real-time systems for tracking inventory, coordinating logistics, and responding dynamically to changes in demand, exemplified by Just-In-Time (JIT) manufacturing principles.

The common thread across these examples is the imperative for precision, responsiveness, and adaptability in the face of dynamic conditions. Real-time systems empower these industries to navigate the complexities inherent in their operations, ensuring not only efficiency and accuracy but also the capability to respond to unforeseen challenges in a timely manner. As technology continues to advance, the role of real-time systems in aerospace, healthcare, and manufacturing will likely expand, ushering in new possibilities and elevating the standards for safety, quality, and operational excellence in these critical sectors.

Highlighting scenarios where real-time capabilities are indispensable.

Real-time capabilities are indispensable in an array of scenarios across diverse domains, where the precision and immediacy of processing play a pivotal role in ensuring optimal outcomes. In the healthcare sector, real-time systems are crucial in critical care units, where patients' vital signs are continuously monitored to detect any deviations from normal ranges promptly. Immediate responses to changes in heart rate, blood pressure, or oxygen levels can be life-saving, underscoring the critical nature of real-time capabilities in this context. In surgical theaters, real-time imaging and guidance systems provide surgeons with instantaneous visual feedback, aiding in precise interventions and decision-making during procedures. The time-sensitive nature of healthcare demands the swift processing of information, making real-time systems integral to providing timely and effective patient care.

The aviation industry relies heavily on real-time capabilities to ensure the safety and efficiency of air travel. Flight control systems, autopilots, and navigation systems in aircraft are designed to process vast amounts of data in real-time, making split-second decisions to maintain stability and respond to dynamic flight conditions. In air traffic management, real-time tracking and communication are imperative to prevent collisions, ensure smooth air traffic flow, and manage airspace effectively. The repercussions of delays or inaccuracies in these real-time systems can have profound consequences, emphasizing their critical role in the aviation ecosystem.

Manufacturing processes, especially in industries embracing Industry 4.0 principles, leverage real-time capabilities to optimize production, quality control, and adaptive automation. Programmable Logic Controllers (PLCs) in manufacturing systems facilitate real-time control of machinery, orchestrating precise actions in assembly lines and robotic operations. Collaborative robots, equipped with real-time sensors and adaptive control systems, work alongside human operators, enhancing efficiency in tasks requiring flexibility and responsiveness. Supply chain management relies on real-time systems to track inventory, coordinate logistics, and dynamically respond to changes in demand, epitomized by the principles of Just-In-Time (JIT) manufacturing. The seamless synchronization of these processes hinges on the instantaneous processing of data, making real-time capabilities indispensable in modern manufacturing.

Emergency response systems, whether in law enforcement, firefighting, or disaster management, demand real-time capabilities to coordinate swift and effective responses. In law enforcement, real-time data analytics and communication systems are crucial for situational awareness, aiding in crime prevention and response. Firefighting operations require real-time monitoring of evolving situations to deploy resources strategically and mitigate risks promptly. Natural disasters and emergencies necessitate real-time communication and coordination among response teams to ensure a rapid and organized response. Delays or inefficiencies in these scenarios can have severe consequences, highlighting the vital role of real-time capabilities in safeguarding public safety and managing crises effectively.

Financial trading platforms operate in a high-stakes environment where split-second decisions can have significant financial implications. Real-time data processing is fundamental to executing trades swiftly, monitoring market fluctuations, and managing risks effectively. Algorithmic trading, which relies on complex algorithms and real-time analytics, epitomizes the intersection of finance and technology, where microseconds can determine trading success. The interconnected global financial ecosystem underscores the importance of real-time capabilities in maintaining market integrity, ensuring fairness, and responding to dynamic economic conditions with agility.

In the realm of communication systems, real-time capabilities are paramount for applications such as voice-over-IP (VoIP) and video conferencing. The transmission and reception of audio-visual data require minimal latency to maintain the natural flow of communication. Real-time systems facilitate the instantaneous processing and delivery of data packets, ensuring a seamless and immersive user experience. In scenarios where effective communication is essential, such as emergency services or military operations, the ability to transmit and receive information in real-time can be mission-critical. The demand for immediacy in communication extends to various sectors, including business, education, and healthcare, where virtual interactions rely on real-time technologies to bridge distances and facilitate collaboration.

Autonomous vehicles, representing a paradigm shift in transportation, heavily depend on real-time capabilities for safe and reliable operation. Advanced Driver Assistance Systems (ADAS) and self-driving cars require instantaneous data processing for decision-making in dynamic and unpredictable driving environments. Real-time sensors, such as lidar and radar, continuously scan the vehicle's surroundings, and the processing of this data in real-time allows the vehicle to respond swiftly to changing road conditions and potential hazards. The integration of real-time capabilities in autonomous vehicles is fundamental to achieving the safety standards required for widespread adoption and acceptance of these transformative technologies.

In the field of space exploration, real-time systems are indispensable for managing spacecraft operations and conducting missions beyond Earth. Autonomous decision-making, navigation, and communication with deep-space probes demand real-time capabilities to overcome the significant communication delays inherent in vast cosmic distances. The Mars rovers, such as Curiosity, exemplify the integration of real-time systems, enabling these robotic explorers to navigate the Martian terrain, analyze samples, and communicate findings back to Earth with minimal latency. The success of space missions relies on the ability of real-time systems to adapt and respond to unexpected challenges, ensuring the precise execution of mission objectives.

In the gaming industry, real-time capabilities are foundational to delivering immersive and interactive experiences. Video games, virtual reality (VR), and augmented reality (AR) applications require instantaneous processing to respond to user inputs and create a seamless and responsive gaming environment. Multiplayer online games rely on real-time communication and synchronization to ensure that players experience a consistent and cohesive virtual world. The competitive nature of gaming and the demand for realism in graphics and interactions underscore the importance of real-time capabilities in the gaming landscape.

In conclusion, real-time capabilities emerge as a linchpin across a multitude of scenarios, spanning healthcare, aviation, manufacturing, emergency response, finance, communication systems, autonomous vehicles, space exploration, and gaming. The common thread is the need for precision, immediacy, and adaptability to dynamic conditions. Whether in critical medical interventions, the control of aircraft, the optimization of manufacturing processes, emergency response coordination, financial trading, seamless communication, autonomous vehicle operation, space exploration, or gaming interactions, real-time systems play a pivotal role in shaping the efficacy and success of these diverse applications. As technology continues to advance, the relevance and indispensability of real-time capabilities will likely expand, shaping the landscape of industries and applications in an increasingly interconnected and fast-paced world.

Exploring hardware requirements for real-time systems.

The hardware requirements for real-time systems constitute a critical aspect of their design and functionality, encompassing a range of components and considerations to meet the stringent timing constraints inherent in real-time applications. Central to the hardware architecture of real-time systems is the processing unit, typically a microprocessor or microcontroller. The choice of processor is pivotal, as it determines the system's computational power and ability to execute tasks within predefined timeframes. In many cases, real-time systems demand processors with high clock speeds and multiple cores to ensure rapid and parallelized execution of tasks. Specialized processors, such as Digital Signal Processors (DSPs) or Field-Programmable Gate Arrays (FPGAs), find applications in scenarios where specific computational capabilities or reconfigurability are essential for meeting real-time requirements.

Memory architecture is another crucial facet of real-time systems' hardware, with considerations for both Random Access Memory (RAM) and non-volatile memory. RAM is pivotal for storing data and program code that is actively used during real-time operations. The speed and capacity of RAM impact the system's ability to swiftly access and manipulate data. Non-volatile memory, often in the form of Flash memory, is essential for storing the system's firmware, configuration settings, and persistent data. The efficiency of memory access and storage plays a significant role in meeting real-time deadlines, and designers must carefully balance the need for speed with the constraints of cost and power consumption.

Real-time systems often necessitate specialized input/output (I/O) interfaces to interact with the external environment or interface with sensors and actuators. These interfaces must be capable of swiftly capturing and delivering data in accordance with the system's temporal requirements. For instance, in industrial automation, the I/O interfaces must facilitate rapid communication with sensors and actuators on the factory floor to maintain precise control over machinery and processes. Similarly, in autonomous vehicles, the sensors providing real-time data, such as lidar and radar, demand high-speed interfaces for seamless integration into the system's decision-making processes.

Clock synchronization is paramount in real-time systems, and the choice of clocking mechanisms significantly influences the system's ability to maintain temporal precision. Many real-time systems rely on high-precision oscillators or clock generators to ensure accurate and consistent timing. Some applications, especially in distributed systems or communication networks, may necessitate synchronization protocols, such as Precision Time Protocol (PTP) or Network Time Protocol (NTP), to align the clocks across multiple nodes and maintain a cohesive temporal framework.

Real-time operating systems (RTOS) represent a critical layer in the software architecture of real-time systems, but their interaction with hardware is paramount. Real-time systems often require dedicated support from the hardware to implement features such as task scheduling, interrupt handling, and prioritized execution. Processors with built-in support for features like priority levels, interrupt controllers, and dedicated real-time clock (RTC) modules facilitate the seamless integration of real-time operating systems. Moreover, memory protection mechanisms and features like memory-mapped I/O contribute to the robustness and reliability of real-time systems by preventing unintended interference between critical processes and ensuring that the system operates within its specified temporal boundaries.

Hardware redundancy is a fundamental consideration in safety-critical real-time systems, where the failure of components could have severe consequences. Redundancy can be implemented at various levels, including processors, memory, and I/O interfaces, to provide backup mechanisms that can take over in the event of a failure.

This redundancy ensures fault tolerance and enhances the system's reliability. In aerospace applications, for instance, where real-time systems control critical functions in aircraft, redundancy is often incorporated in the form of dual or triple redundant systems to mitigate the impact of hardware failures.

Deterministic communication is essential in real-time systems, especially those involving distributed architectures or networked environments. The hardware must support communication protocols that prioritize low latency and predictable transmission times. In industrial automation, where real-time communication between devices is crucial for coordinated control, protocols like EtherCAT or PROFINET are employed to ensure timely exchange of data. Similarly, in vehicular communication systems or autonomous vehicles, the hardware must support communication protocols that guarantee low-latency and reliable data transfer for effective coordination and decision-making.

Real-time systems operating in dynamic or safety-critical environments often require hardware components that support fault detection and correction mechanisms. Error-correcting codes in memory modules, watchdog timers, and built-in self-test (BIST) capabilities contribute to the fault-tolerant nature of real-time systems. These hardware features enable the system to detect and, in some cases, correct errors that may occur during operation, preventing potential disruptions to real-time tasks.

Power consumption is a consideration that intertwines with the hardware requirements of real-time systems, particularly in applications where energy efficiency is paramount. Battery-powered devices, such as medical implants or portable real-time sensors, demand hardware designs that optimize power consumption without compromising processing capabilities. Low-power processors, power management units, and efficient voltage regulators contribute to achieving the delicate balance between meeting real-time constraints and conserving energy.

In safety-critical applications, the hardware architecture of real-time systems is often subjected to rigorous certification standards. Industries such as aerospace, automotive, and medical devices adhere to safety standards (e.g., DO-178C for avionics, ISO 26262 for automotive) that dictate the design, verification, and validation processes for hardware components. Hardware components must undergo extensive testing and documentation to ensure compliance with these standards, guaranteeing the reliability and safety of real-time systems in mission-critical applications.

The hardware requirements for real-time systems are multifaceted, encompassing considerations of processing power, memory architecture, I/O interfaces, clock synchronization, real-time operating system support, redundancy, deterministic communication, fault detection and correction, power consumption, and compliance with safety standards. The interplay of these hardware components is pivotal in crafting real-time systems that meet the stringent temporal constraints demanded by applications in domains such as healthcare, aerospace, manufacturing, and communication. As technology continues to advance, the evolution of hardware for real-time systems will likely involve innovations that enhance computational capabilities, energy efficiency, and integration with emerging technologies, further shaping the landscape of real-time computing.

Discussing the role of specialized components in ensuring timely task execution.

Specialized components play a pivotal role in ensuring the timely execution of tasks within real-time systems, contributing to the precision, responsiveness, and reliability demanded by applications across diverse domains. Central to this role are processors specifically designed for real-time applications, such as Digital Signal Processors (DSPs) and Field-Programmable Gate Arrays (FPGAs). DSPs excel in tasks involving signal processing, such as audio and video processing, due to their architecture optimized for mathematical computations and parallel processing. FPGAs, on the other hand, offer reconfigurability, allowing developers to tailor the hardware to the specific needs of real-time tasks. These specialized processors provide the computational muscle needed to meet the stringent timing requirements of real-time systems, ensuring that tasks are executed with the necessary speed and precision.

In the context of real-time operating systems (RTOS), specialized components play a critical role in task scheduling and execution. Real-time systems often require deterministic scheduling policies to ensure that high-priority tasks are executed within specified timeframes. Hardware components, such as timers and clock modules, are integrated into processors to facilitate precise timing and enable the RTOS to manage task execution with accuracy. Additionally, processors equipped with multiple cores and support for parallel execution contribute to efficient multitasking, enabling the system to handle concurrent real-time tasks without compromising responsiveness.

Memory architecture represents another realm where specialized components are instrumental in supporting timely task execution. In real-time systems, Random Access Memory (RAM) is a crucial resource for storing data and code actively used during execution. Specialized memory architectures, such as dual-port RAM or memory with low access latency, are employed to ensure that data can be swiftly retrieved and manipulated during real-time operations. The efficiency of memory access is paramount, as delays in accessing data can impede the system's ability to meet stringent deadlines.

Input/Output (I/O) interfaces with specialized components are essential for real-time systems that interact with the external environment or interface with sensors and actuators. These interfaces must be designed to capture and deliver data swiftly to meet the temporal requirements of the system. Specialized communication interfaces, such as those supporting high-speed serial communication or real-time fieldbuses, facilitate the seamless integration of sensors and actuators into the real-time system. In industrial automation, for instance, specialized I/O modules ensure rapid communication with sensors and actuators on the factory floor, enabling precise control over machinery and processes.

Clock synchronization is a critical aspect of real-time systems, and specialized components are employed to achieve precise and consistent timing. High-precision oscillators or clock generators provide the system with a reliable time base, ensuring that tasks are scheduled and executed with accuracy. Some applications, especially those in distributed systems, may require specialized components to implement clock synchronization protocols, such as Precision Time Protocol (PTP) or Network Time Protocol (NTP). These protocols enable multiple nodes in a networked environment to maintain synchronized clocks, crucial for ensuring cohesive temporal coordination across the system.

In safety-critical real-time systems, specialized hardware components contribute to fault detection and correction mechanisms, enhancing the system's reliability. Error-correcting codes in memory modules, watchdog timers, and built-in self-test (BIST) capabilities are examples of specialized components that detect and, in some cases, correct errors that may occur during operation. These components are crucial in mitigating the impact of hardware faults, ensuring that the real-time system continues to operate reliably even in the face of potential failures.

Redundancy, a fundamental aspect of safety-critical systems, is often implemented using specialized components. Redundant processors, memory modules, and I/O interfaces provide backup mechanisms that can take over in the event of a failure, ensuring continuity of operation. In avionics systems, for example, where real-time capabilities are paramount for flight control and navigation, dual or triple redundant systems are employed to safeguard against hardware failures that could compromise safety.

Deterministic communication is essential in real-time systems, particularly those involving distributed architectures or networked environments. Specialized communication components, such as real-time Ethernet interfaces or fieldbus controllers, prioritize low latency and predictable transmission times. In industrial automation, where real-time communication between devices is critical for coordinated control, specialized fieldbus protocols like EtherCAT or PROFINET are employed to ensure timely exchange of data. These components contribute to the deterministic nature of communication within the system, supporting precise coordination of real-time tasks.

Power consumption is a consideration that intertwines with specialized components, especially in applications where energy efficiency is crucial. Low-power processors, power management units, and efficient voltage regulators contribute to achieving the delicate balance between meeting real-time constraints and conserving energy. In battery-powered devices, such as medical implants or portable real-time sensors, specialized power-efficient components play a pivotal role in extending battery life without compromising the system's ability to execute tasks with the required timeliness.

Specialized components are integral to achieving deterministic behavior in real-time systems, and their role extends to ensuring that the hardware complies with safety standards. In safety-critical domains, such as automotive or avionics, compliance with standards like ISO 26262 or DO-178C necessitates the use of specialized components that have undergone rigorous testing and validation processes. Specialized safety mechanisms, such as hardware-based fault tolerance, are often integrated to meet the stringent safety requirements of these standards.

In conclusion, specialized components play a multifaceted and indispensable role in ensuring the timely execution of tasks within real-time systems. From processors and memory architectures to I/O interfaces, clock synchronization components, fault detection mechanisms, redundancy solutions, and power-efficient designs, each specialized component contributes to the overarching goal of meeting stringent timing constraints. The integration of these components into the hardware architecture is a delicate orchestration, balancing the need for speed, precision, and reliability in diverse real-time applications across healthcare, aerospace, manufacturing, communication systems, and beyond. As technology continues to advance, the evolution of specialized components for real-time systems will likely involve innovations that further enhance computational capabilities, energy efficiency, and integration with emerging technologies, shaping the landscape of real-time computing in the years to come.

Introducing software components essential for real-time operations.

Software components are the backbone of real-time systems, orchestrating the intricate dance of tasks, data processing, and communication with the precision and responsiveness demanded by time-sensitive applications across various domains. At the heart of real-time operations lies the Real-Time Operating System (RTOS), a specialized software layer that provides a framework for managing tasks and resources with deterministic timing. RTOS plays a pivotal role in ensuring that high-priority tasks are executed within specified timeframes, providing a cohesive and predictable environment for real-time applications. Task scheduling, a critical aspect of RTOS, involves allocating processor time to different tasks based on their priority levels and execution requirements. The RTOS scheduler facilitates the seamless execution of tasks, adhering to the temporal constraints dictated by the real-time system.

Task management within an RTOS involves the creation, scheduling, and termination of tasks. Real-time tasks are often categorized based on their criticality and timing requirements. High-priority tasks, such as control algorithms in industrial automation or sensor data processing in autonomous vehicles, take precedence over lower-priority tasks to ensure timely execution. Task management mechanisms in the RTOS enable developers to design systems where tasks can be created dynamically, ensuring flexibility and adaptability to evolving real-time requirements.

Interrupt handling is a fundamental aspect of real-time systems, allowing the system to respond swiftly to external events or hardware-generated signals. The RTOS provides mechanisms for managing interrupts, ensuring that high-priority interrupts can preempt the execution of lower-priority tasks to address time-sensitive events promptly. In scenarios where external inputs or sensor data must be processed without delay, the interrupt handling mechanisms of the RTOS play a crucial role in maintaining responsiveness and accuracy.

Communication between tasks and components is a cornerstone of real-time systems, and inter-task communication mechanisms are essential for facilitating seamless information exchange. Message passing, shared memory, and synchronization primitives are common components of real-time communication mechanisms. Real-time tasks often need to exchange data or synchronize their activities, and these communication mechanisms provide a structured and deterministic way to achieve coordination. For instance, in automotive systems, where control tasks must synchronize with sensor inputs and actuator outputs, well-defined communication channels within the RTOS ensure that information flows with precision and reliability.

Memory management in real-time systems is carefully orchestrated to meet the demands of timely task execution. Real-time tasks often have specific memory requirements, and the RTOS must allocate and deallocate memory in a deterministic manner. Memory protection mechanisms prevent tasks from unintentionally interfering with each other, contributing to the robustness and reliability of the real-time system. In safety-critical applications, where memory errors could have severe consequences, specialized memory management mechanisms are employed to ensure the integrity of data and code.

Clock management is a critical software component in real-time systems, ensuring that the system maintains accurate and synchronized timekeeping. The RTOS is responsible for managing system clocks, which are essential for scheduling tasks and enforcing timing constraints. Precise timing is paramount in applications such as medical devices, where sensor readings or therapeutic interventions must occur within predefined intervals. The RTOS provides APIs and services for managing time-related functions, allowing developers to design real-time applications that adhere to specific temporal requirements.

Real-time systems often rely on specialized algorithms and libraries tailored to meet the timing constraints of specific applications. Signal processing algorithms in digital signal processors (DSPs), control algorithms in automotive systems, or image processing algorithms in medical imaging devices are examples of software components that are finely tuned for real-time performance. These algorithms leverage mathematical models and optimizations to achieve the required level of accuracy and responsiveness within the constraints of the real-time environment.

In safety-critical applications, where the reliability and predictability of real-time systems are paramount, formal methods and verification tools become essential software components. Formal methods involve mathematical techniques for specifying and verifying the correctness of software designs. Model checking, theorem proving, and static analysis tools are employed to ensure that the software adheres to specified requirements and does not exhibit undesired behaviors. These software components contribute to the certification and validation processes necessary in domains such as aerospace, automotive, and medical devices.

Error handling and recovery mechanisms are integral software components in real-time systems, especially in safety-critical environments. The RTOS and application software must be equipped to detect and handle errors gracefully to prevent catastrophic consequences. Error detection mechanisms, such as checksums or redundancy checks, are implemented to identify potential faults. Error recovery mechanisms, such as task reinitialization or switching to redundant components, contribute to the fault tolerance of the system. These software components are designed to ensure that the real-time system can continue operating reliably in the face of unexpected events or hardware failures.

Middleware components are often employed in real-time systems to facilitate the integration of complex functionalities and support distributed architectures. Middleware provides services such as communication protocols, data distribution, and fault tolerance, enabling developers to build scalable and robust real-time systems. In distributed real-time applications, where tasks may be distributed across multiple nodes, middleware components ensure that data can be exchanged efficiently and reliably while maintaining the temporal coordination required by the system.

In the realm of graphical user interfaces (GUIs) or human-machine interfaces (HMIs), specialized software components contribute to the interactive and real-time nature of the user experience. Real-time graphics libraries, touch screen input processing, and event-driven programming paradigms are employed to create responsive and visually engaging interfaces. In applications such as automotive infotainment systems or medical device interfaces, these software components play a crucial role in ensuring that user interactions are processed with minimal latency.

Security considerations in real-time systems have become increasingly important, especially as these systems become more interconnected. Security software components, such as encryption algorithms, secure communication protocols, and intrusion detection mechanisms, are integrated into the software stack to safeguard real-time systems from malicious attacks. In industries like industrial automation or critical infrastructure, where the impact of security breaches can be severe, these software components contribute to the resilience and integrity of the real-time operations.

Software development tools tailored for real-time systems form another essential set of components. Integrated Development Environments (IDEs), compilers, and debugging tools designed for real-time applications provide developers with the necessary resources to design, implement, and analyze the performance of their real-time software. Profiling tools that analyze the execution time of tasks, memory usage, and system behavior are crucial for fine-tuning and optimizing real-time applications to meet stringent timing constraints.

In conclusion, the software components essential for real-time operations form a complex and interconnected ecosystem that drives the functionality and performance of real-time systems. From the foundational elements of the RTOS to task management, communication mechanisms, memory management, and specialized algorithms, each component contributes to the overarching goal of achieving precision and responsiveness in time-sensitive applications. As real-time systems continue to evolve and find application in an expanding array of domains, the ongoing advancements in software components will likely play a pivotal role in shaping the capabilities, reliability, and adaptability of these critical systems.

Discussing the role of operating systems in facilitating real-time computing.

Operating systems (OS) play a fundamental and multifaceted role in facilitating real-time computing, providing a crucial layer of abstraction between hardware resources and application software. At the core of real-time operating systems (RTOS) lies the commitment to ensuring that tasks are executed within well-defined and deterministic timeframes, distinguishing them from general-purpose operating systems designed for non-time-critical applications. The primary function of an RTOS is to manage and schedule tasks with precision, acknowledging the temporal constraints that are paramount in real-time systems. The scheduler within an RTOS is a key component, responsible for determining the order and timing of task execution based on priority levels and specified deadlines. This deterministic scheduling is essential for meeting the stringent timing requirements of real-time applications, where tasks must complete within predefined time intervals to ensure the system's reliability and effectiveness.

Task management is a pivotal aspect of the role played by operating systems in real-time computing. In a real-time environment, tasks are units of executable code representing specific functions or processes within the system. The OS, and specifically the RTOS, oversees the creation, scheduling, and termination of tasks, allocating processor time based on priority and executing them within specified time constraints. High-priority tasks, critical for timely decision-making or control actions, are given precedence over lower-priority tasks to guarantee that essential functions are performed within their designated timeframes. This meticulous task management is indispensable in applications such as industrial automation, aerospace systems, medical devices, and automotive control, where timely execution of tasks is paramount.

Interrupt handling is another critical function that operating systems perform to facilitate real-time computing. Interrupts are mechanisms that allow the processor to temporarily halt its current activities and address urgent tasks or events that require immediate attention. In real-time systems, timely response to external stimuli, sensor inputs, or hardware-generated signals is essential. The OS, including the RTOS, manages interrupt service routines (ISRs) to swiftly address these events, ensuring that high-priority tasks can preempt lower-priority tasks when time-sensitive events occur. This capability is particularly vital in applications like control systems, where rapid responses to changing conditions are imperative for maintaining stability and ensuring safety.

Communication mechanisms orchestrated by operating systems form a cornerstone in real-time computing. Real-time tasks often need to exchange data or synchronize their activities to achieve seamless coordination. The OS provides communication mechanisms such as message passing, shared memory, and synchronization primitives that enable tasks to interact in a structured and deterministic manner. In applications like collaborative robotics, where multiple tasks must coordinate their actions in real-time, these communication mechanisms are crucial for ensuring that data is exchanged with precision and reliability. Similarly, in distributed real-time systems, where tasks may be distributed across multiple nodes, the OS facilitates efficient communication to maintain temporal coordination across the system.

Memory management in operating systems contributes significantly to the efficiency and reliability of real-time computing. Real-time tasks often have specific memory requirements, and the OS, including the RTOS, is responsible for allocating and deallocating memory resources in a deterministic manner. Memory protection mechanisms prevent tasks from unintentionally interfering with each other, ensuring the integrity of data and code. In safety-critical applications, where memory errors could lead to catastrophic consequences, specialized memory management mechanisms are employed to enhance the robustness of real-time systems. Efficient memory utilization and protection mechanisms contribute to the reliability and stability of real-time applications.

Clock management is a critical aspect of real-time operating systems, ensuring that the system maintains accurate and synchronized timekeeping. The OS manages system clocks, which serve as the basis for scheduling tasks and enforcing timing constraints. Precise timing is paramount in applications such as medical devices, where sensor readings or therapeutic interventions must occur within predefined intervals. The OS provides services for managing time-related functions, allowing developers to design real-time applications that adhere to specific temporal requirements. Clock synchronization across distributed systems is particularly important in scenarios where multiple nodes must maintain synchronized clocks for cohesive temporal coordination.

Real-time algorithms and libraries, often integrated into operating systems, play a vital role in achieving the performance required by time-sensitive applications. These specialized software components are finely tuned for real-time responsiveness, leveraging mathematical models and optimizations to meet specific timing constraints. In applications like digital signal processing (DSP) or control systems, where algorithms must execute within stringent timeframes, the OS provides a platform for integrating these real-time algorithms seamlessly.

Error handling and recovery mechanisms are integral components within real-time operating systems, enhancing the reliability of the system in the face of unexpected events or hardware failures. The OS must be equipped to detect and handle errors gracefully to prevent catastrophic consequences. Error detection mechanisms, such as checksums or redundancy checks, are implemented to identify potential faults. Error recovery mechanisms, such as task reinitialization or switching to redundant components, contribute to the fault tolerance of the system. These mechanisms are particularly crucial in safety-critical applications, where the reliability and predictability of real-time systems are paramount.

Middleware components, often integrated into operating systems, facilitate the development of complex functionalities and support distributed architectures in real-time computing. Middleware provides services such as communication protocols, data distribution, and fault tolerance, enabling developers to build scalable and robust real-time systems. In distributed real-time applications, where tasks may be distributed across multiple nodes, middleware components ensure that data can be exchanged efficiently and reliably while maintaining the temporal coordination required by the system.

Security considerations have become increasingly important in real-time operating systems, especially as these systems become more interconnected. Security mechanisms, such as encryption algorithms, secure communication protocols, and intrusion detection systems, are integrated into the operating system to safeguard real-time systems from malicious attacks. In industries like industrial automation or critical infrastructure, where the impact of security breaches can be severe, these security mechanisms contribute to the resilience and integrity of real-time operations.

Development tools tailored for real-time systems form an essential part of the operating system ecosystem. Integrated Development Environments (IDEs), compilers, and debugging tools designed for real-time applications provide developers with the necessary resources to design, implement, and analyze the performance of their real-time software. Profiling tools that analyze the execution time of tasks, memory usage, and system behavior are crucial for fine-tuning and optimizing real-time applications to meet stringent timing constraints.

In conclusion, operating systems play a pivotal role in facilitating real-time computing by providing the essential infrastructure and services required for time-sensitive applications. From deterministic task scheduling, interrupt handling, and communication mechanisms to memory management, clock synchronization, real-time algorithms, error handling, middleware support, security mechanisms, and development tools, each facet of the operating system contributes to the overarching goal of achieving precision and responsiveness in real-time systems. As real-time computing continues to evolve and find application in an expanding array of domains, the ongoing advancements in operating system technologies will likely play a pivotal role in shaping the capabilities, reliability, and adaptability of these critical systems.

Chapter 2: Types of Real-Time Systems

Defining hard real-time systems and their strict deadline adherence.

Hard real-time systems represent a class of computing systems distinguished by their stringent requirements for deadline adherence, where meeting specified timing constraints is not just a performance goal but an absolute necessity. In the realm of hard real-time systems, the term "hard" emphasizes the inflexibility and criticality of temporal constraints imposed on the system's operation. These systems are characterized by tasks and processes with explicit and non-negotiable deadlines, and failure to meet these deadlines can have severe consequences, ranging from degraded performance to catastrophic outcomes. The defining feature of hard real-time systems is the deterministic nature of their response to stimuli or inputs, ensuring that tasks are executed within precise timeframes with minimal variability.

The foundation of hard real-time systems lies in the concept of determinism, a quality that sets them apart from systems where timing requirements are more relaxed. Determinism in hard real-time systems signifies the predictability and repeatability of their behavior, where the time taken to execute a task or respond to an event is not only known but guaranteed. This predictability is essential for applications where timing precision is critical, such as control systems in industrial automation, avionics in aerospace, or medical devices in healthcare. In these domains, deviations from specified deadlines could lead to unacceptable outcomes, emphasizing the non-negotiable nature of timing requirements in hard real-time systems.

One of the defining characteristics of hard real-time systems is their ability to provide guaranteed response times to external stimuli or events. In scenarios where tasks must react to changes in the environment or inputs from sensors within stringent time intervals, the predictability of response times becomes paramount. For instance, in automotive safety systems like anti-lock brakes or electronic stability control, hard real-time constraints dictate that the system must respond to sensor inputs within fractions of a second to ensure the effectiveness of these safety-critical features. The deterministic response times in hard real-time systems are achieved through meticulous task scheduling, where high-priority tasks are prioritized and executed within specified timeframes.

In hard real-time systems, meeting deadlines is not just a performance optimization but a fundamental requirement, often with zero tolerance for failure. The consequences of missing a deadline can vary based on the application domain. In avionics, a missed deadline in the execution of flight control algorithms could lead to instability or loss of control, posing a significant safety risk. Similarly, in medical devices such as infusion pumps or pacemakers, failure to deliver therapeutic interventions within prescribed timeframes could have life-threatening implications for patients. The severity of these consequences underscores the criticality of deadline adherence in hard real-time systems.

To ensure strict deadline adherence, hard real-time systems employ various techniques and mechanisms. Task scheduling is a critical aspect, with priority-based scheduling algorithms ensuring that high-priority tasks take precedence over lower-priority ones. These algorithms often follow fixed-priority or rate-monotonic scheduling schemes, where tasks with shorter deadlines or higher criticality are assigned higher priorities. Additionally, preemption is a common feature, allowing high-priority tasks to interrupt the execution of lower-priority tasks when necessary. This preemptive scheduling ensures that time-critical tasks can be initiated promptly, minimizing the risk of missing deadlines.

The design and analysis of hard real-time systems often involve worst-case execution time (WCET) analysis, a process that seeks to identify the maximum time a task or process could take to complete under the most unfavorable conditions. WCET analysis is crucial for determining whether the system can reliably meet its deadlines, and it involves considering factors such as processor speed, cache behavior, and memory access patterns. By accounting for these factors, designers can identify potential bottlenecks and optimize critical paths to enhance the system's ability to adhere to stringent deadlines.

Another key consideration in hard real-time systems is the avoidance of non-deterministic behavior, which could introduce uncertainty and jeopardize deadline adherence. Non-deterministic factors include unpredictable variations in execution times, such as cache misses, contention for shared resources, or interrupt latencies. Techniques such as cache locking, resource reservation, and minimizing interrupt latencies are employed to mitigate non-deterministic influences and enhance the predictability of system behavior. By minimizing these sources of variability, hard real-time systems can increase their assurance of meeting deadlines consistently.

Fault tolerance is another critical aspect in the design of hard real-time systems, especially in safety-critical applications where the consequences of failure are severe. Redundancy mechanisms, such as dual or triple modular redundancy, are employed to provide backup components or tasks that can take over in the event of a failure. These redundant elements contribute to the reliability of the system, ensuring that even in the presence of faults, the critical functions can continue to operate within specified deadlines. In aerospace applications, for instance, redundant flight control systems are implemented to maintain control in the face of hardware failures.

Hard real-time systems often require specialized hardware support to achieve the level of determinism necessary for deadline adherence. Real-time operating systems (RTOS) tailored for hard real-time applications provide services such as priority-based scheduling, precise timing functions, and minimal interrupt latencies. Some processors are designed with features specifically aimed at supporting hard real-time requirements, including deterministic instruction execution, predictable cache behavior, and support for high-precision timers. The choice of hardware components, including processors and peripherals, is a crucial consideration in the development of hard real-time systems, as it directly influences the system's ability to meet stringent timing constraints.

In safety-critical domains, standards and certification processes play a significant role in ensuring the reliability and adherence to deadlines in hard real-time systems. Industries such as aerospace (e.g., DO-178C), automotive (e.g., ISO 26262), and medical devices (e.g., IEC 62304) have established rigorous standards that mandate the certification of software and systems to meet specific safety and performance criteria. These standards often include guidelines for demonstrating the predictability and determinism of hard real-time systems, ensuring that they can reliably adhere to deadlines in the operational context.

While hard real-time systems excel in applications where deterministic responses are paramount, they also face challenges and trade-offs. The strict adherence to deadlines may limit the system's overall throughput, as resources are dedicated to ensuring timely execution of critical tasks. The complexity of analyzing and guaranteeing worst-case execution times introduces overhead in terms of design, validation, and testing. Additionally, the use of redundancy and fault-tolerance mechanisms, while crucial for safety, adds complexity and may impact the overall cost and resource utilization of the system.

In conclusion, hard real-time systems stand at the intersection of precision, predictability, and criticality, where meeting strict deadlines is not negotiable but a fundamental requirement. Deterministic scheduling, worst-case execution time analysis, fault tolerance mechanisms, and specialized hardware support collectively contribute to the ability of hard real-time systems to consistently adhere to specified timeframes. The consequences of failing to meet deadlines in these systems can range from compromised performance to life-threatening situations, underscoring the critical role they play in safety-critical applications. As technology continues to advance, the evolution of hard real-time systems will likely involve ongoing efforts to address challenges, enhance predictability, and broaden their applicability across diverse domains where precision and timing are of utmost importance.

Exploring applications where failure to meet deadlines is critical.

The consequences of failing to meet deadlines can be particularly severe in applications where timing precision is paramount, and deviations from specified timeframes can lead to significant disruptions, loss of life, or extensive economic repercussions. In the realm of aerospace, where safety is non-negotiable, failure to meet deadlines in systems such as flight control and avionics could result in catastrophic outcomes. For instance, a delay in executing critical control algorithms during an emergency situation might compromise the aircraft's stability, leading to a potential loss of control. The impact of missed deadlines in aviation extends beyond individual flights, affecting air traffic management systems where precise coordination is essential to prevent collisions and ensure the orderly flow of air traffic.

In the healthcare sector, failure to meet deadlines in medical devices or treatment delivery systems can have life-threatening consequences. For example, in the context of infusion pumps delivering medication to patients, a delay in administering a life-saving drug could worsen a patient's condition or lead to complications. Similarly, in radiation therapy for cancer treatment, the precise timing of radiation doses is critical to target tumors accurately while minimizing damage to healthy tissues. Failure to adhere to these deadlines could compromise the efficacy of treatments and jeopardize patient outcomes.

The automotive industry relies heavily on systems that demand strict adherence to deadlines, particularly in the context of advanced driver assistance systems (ADAS) and autonomous vehicles. In ADAS, features such as automatic emergency braking or collision avoidance systems require real-time responses to sensor inputs to prevent accidents. Failure to meet deadlines in these systems could result in delays in executing critical safety functions, compromising the ability to avoid collisions or mitigate the severity of accidents. In the case of autonomous vehicles, where split-second decision-making is essential, missed deadlines could lead to unsafe driving conditions and increase the risk of accidents.

Industrial automation represents another domain where the failure to meet deadlines can have far-reaching consequences. In manufacturing processes, robotics, and control systems, precise coordination and synchronization are imperative for efficient and safe operations. For instance, in a manufacturing assembly line, delays in the execution of robotic tasks could disrupt the entire production process, leading to inefficiencies and financial losses. In control systems for critical infrastructure, such as energy grids or water treatment plants, failure to meet deadlines could result in disruptions to essential services and potentially compromise the safety and well-being of communities.

The financial sector, particularly in high-frequency trading, is highly sensitive to timing precision, where split-second decisions can have substantial financial implications. In electronic trading platforms, failure to execute trades within extremely tight deadlines could result in missed opportunities or financial losses. The interconnected nature of global financial markets amplifies the impact of delays, as a delay in one part of the system can cascade through the entire network, affecting market stability and investor confidence.

Emergency response systems, including those in firefighting, law enforcement, and medical emergency services, rely on timely information processing and communication to save lives. For instance, in a fire detection and suppression system, delays in processing sensor data or activating sprinkler systems could allow a fire to escalate, causing greater damage and endangering lives. In law enforcement, the real-time analysis of surveillance data or emergency calls is critical for rapid response to incidents. Failure to meet deadlines in these systems could impede the effectiveness of emergency response efforts.

In the context of communication systems, particularly voice-over-IP (VoIP) and video conferencing applications, failure to meet deadlines can severely impact the quality of communication. In VoIP, delays in transmitting voice packets can result in poor call quality, making communication difficult or frustrating for users. In video conferencing, where real-time interaction is essential, delays in transmitting video and audio data can hinder the natural flow of communication, reducing the effectiveness of virtual meetings and collaboration.

In the gaming industry, especially in online multiplayer games, meeting deadlines is crucial for providing a seamless and immersive user experience. Delays in rendering graphics, processing user inputs, or synchronizing game states across multiple players can lead to lag and disrupt the fluidity of gameplay. In competitive gaming environments, where split-second reactions can determine success or failure, failure to meet deadlines could result in a subpar gaming experience and negatively impact player satisfaction.

In the domain of satellite communications and space exploration, adherence to deadlines is critical for mission success. Satellite systems, including those for Earth observation, weather forecasting, or communication satellites, rely on precise timing for data acquisition and transmission. Failure to meet deadlines in satellite operations could compromise the accuracy of data, disrupt communication links, or lead to mission failures. In space exploration missions, where coordination of spacecraft maneuvers and data collection is time-sensitive, missed deadlines could jeopardize the success of the entire mission.

In the field of cybersecurity, timely detection and response to security threats are paramount to prevent data breaches and protect sensitive information. Security systems that analyze network traffic, detect anomalies, and respond to cyber threats must operate within strict deadlines to identify and mitigate potential attacks. Failure to meet these deadlines could allow malicious actors to exploit vulnerabilities, compromise systems, and exfiltrate sensitive data, leading to significant security breaches and potential financial losses.

In conclusion, applications where failure to meet deadlines is critical span a wide range of industries and sectors, each with its unique set of challenges and consequences. From aviation and healthcare to automotive systems, industrial automation, finance, emergency response, communication, gaming, satellite operations, space exploration, and cybersecurity, the impact of missed deadlines can range from compromised safety and operational disruptions to financial losses and compromised data integrity. As technology continues to advance, the ongoing quest for precision and timing accuracy in these critical applications remains a central focus, driving innovations and advancements to ensure that systems can reliably meet their deadlines in the face of evolving challenges and complexities.

Introducing soft real-time systems with flexible deadline constraints.

Soft real-time systems represent a category of computing systems characterized by flexible deadline constraints, where meeting timing requirements is desirable but not necessarily mandatory. Unlike their hard real-time counterparts, which demand absolute adherence to deadlines, soft real-time systems operate in environments where occasional deviations from specified timeframes are tolerable, and the consequences of missing deadlines are less severe. These systems find application in a diverse array of domains where timing precision is valuable but not critical, allowing for a degree of adaptability to dynamic or unpredictable conditions.

The distinguishing feature of soft real-time systems lies in their ability to balance the pursuit of timing goals with a certain level of flexibility. This flexibility acknowledges the reality that not all tasks or processes within the system are equally time-sensitive, and occasional delays may be acceptable as long as they do not compromise the overall effectiveness of the system. In contrast to hard real-time systems, which prioritize deterministic responses and strict deadline adherence, soft real-time systems prioritize achieving satisfactory performance while recognizing that perfection in timing may not always be achievable or necessary.

One prevalent application domain for soft real-time systems is multimedia processing and content delivery. In streaming services, for example, delivering video or audio content with low latency is desirable to enhance user experience, but occasional delays in data transmission may be tolerable. Soft real-time constraints allow streaming platforms to optimize the quality of service without imposing rigid timing requirements. Similarly, in video conferencing applications, where real-time communication is essential, the flexibility of soft real-time systems accommodates variations in network conditions or processing delays without compromising the overall effectiveness of the communication.

In the realm of desktop computing and personal computing devices, soft real-time constraints come into play in various scenarios. User interface responsiveness, for instance, benefits from timely interactions between user inputs and system feedback. While efforts are made to minimize delays in responding to user actions, the soft real-time nature of these systems acknowledges that occasional delays, such as temporary freezes or lag in graphical rendering, may occur without severely impacting the user experience. This adaptability allows for more efficient resource utilization and responsiveness in scenarios where strict timing constraints may be impractical.

Soft real-time systems are prevalent in many automation and control applications, particularly those in industrial settings where tasks may have varying levels of criticality. In manufacturing processes, for instance, the coordination of robotic arms or automated assembly lines benefits from timely execution of tasks, but occasional delays may not disrupt the overall production workflow. The flexibility of soft real-time constraints in industrial automation systems allows for a balance between achieving efficiency and coping with variations in processing times or unexpected events.

Another significant domain where soft real-time systems find application is in automotive systems, particularly in infotainment and comfort features. In-vehicle entertainment systems, navigation, and climate control, while benefiting from responsive interfaces and timely updates, operate under conditions where occasional delays are acceptable. Soft real-time constraints in these systems allow for adaptability to changing priorities, such as prioritizing navigation updates over non-critical background tasks, without compromising the overall user experience.

Medical monitoring and diagnostic systems also leverage soft real-time constraints in scenarios where occasional delays are permissible without compromising patient safety. For example, in patient monitoring devices, the timely acquisition and display of vital signs are crucial, but the occasional delay in updating graphical displays may not have critical implications. This flexibility allows medical systems to balance the need for real-time data with the practical challenges of unpredictable conditions and varying processing workloads.

In the context of distributed systems and cloud computing, soft real-time constraints are prevalent due to the variability in network latencies and the dynamic nature of resource allocation. Cloud services that handle diverse workloads, such as data processing, storage, and virtual machine provisioning, often operate under soft real-time constraints. While minimizing response times is a goal, the adaptability of soft real-time systems allows them to handle fluctuations in demand, prioritize critical tasks, and manage resources efficiently without strict adherence to rigid timing requirements.

Soft real-time systems are integral to the functionality of modern telecommunications networks, where the timely processing of data packets is essential for maintaining network performance. In Voice over IP (VoIP) applications, for instance, minimizing latency is crucial for providing clear and natural communication, but occasional delays in packet delivery may be tolerated without significantly degrading the user experience. Soft real-time constraints in telecommunications systems allow for efficient data transmission while accommodating variations in network conditions.

The gaming industry is another domain where soft real-time systems play a crucial role. In online multiplayer games, achieving low latency and responsive gameplay is essential for providing an enjoyable user experience. While minimizing delays is a priority, the soft real-time nature of these systems allows for some flexibility in handling occasional network fluctuations or variations in processing capabilities, ensuring that the overall gaming experience remains engaging and satisfying.

Soft real-time constraints are also applicable in scientific computing and simulations, where the timely execution of computational tasks is desirable but not always critical. Simulations in fields such as weather forecasting, molecular dynamics, or fluid dynamics benefit from efficient processing, but occasional delays in computation may be acceptable without compromising the overall accuracy of the results. The flexibility of soft real-time systems allows scientists and researchers to balance computational efficiency with the practical challenges of complex simulations and varying computational workloads.

In the development of autonomous systems and robotics, soft real-time constraints are prevalent in applications where adaptability to changing environments is essential. For example, in autonomous vehicles, timely processing of sensor data and decision-making is critical for safe navigation, but occasional delays may be tolerated if they do not compromise overall safety. The flexibility of soft real-time constraints allows autonomous systems to adjust to dynamic conditions, prioritize critical tasks, and handle unexpected events without rigid adherence to deterministic timing.

The design and development of soft real-time systems involve considerations of trade-offs between performance, adaptability, and resource utilization. Unlike hard real-time systems, which prioritize deterministic responses and strict deadline adherence, soft real-time systems offer a more flexible approach to timing constraints. This flexibility allows for a pragmatic balance between achieving satisfactory performance and adapting to dynamic conditions, making soft real-time systems well-suited for applications where occasional deviations from timing requirements are acceptable without compromising the overall effectiveness and user experience. As technology continues to advance, the role of soft real-time systems is poised to expand further, contributing to the development of adaptive and efficient computing solutions across a wide range of domains.

Examining scenarios where meeting deadlines is desirable but not mandatory.

In numerous scenarios across various industries and domains, meeting deadlines is desirable for optimizing performance and ensuring efficiency, but it is not necessarily mandatory. One such context is found in the realm of software development, where project timelines often serve as a guide for planning and resource allocation. While adhering to deadlines can enhance project management and customer satisfaction, the dynamic nature of software development may lead to shifting priorities, unexpected challenges, or the discovery of additional requirements. In such cases, the flexibility to extend deadlines without severe consequences allows development teams to deliver higher-quality software, accommodate changes, and iterate on designs, fostering a more adaptive and customer-centric development process.

Similarly, in research and academic pursuits, meeting deadlines for project milestones, paper submissions, or grant proposals is highly valued for organizational purposes and academic rigor. However, the nature of research often involves uncertainties, unforeseen obstacles, or the need for additional experimentation. The ability to extend deadlines in academia acknowledges the complexity of scientific inquiry and encourages researchers to pursue thorough investigations, potentially leading to more robust and groundbreaking outcomes. Balancing the need for timely progress with the flexibility to accommodate unforeseen challenges is crucial for fostering innovation and intellectual exploration.

In the manufacturing sector, particularly in the production of complex products or prototypes, meeting deadlines is desirable for maintaining production schedules and customer commitments.

However, the intricate nature of manufacturing processes, supply chain dynamics, and quality assurance considerations may introduce variability. The ability to adapt timelines without severe consequences allows manufacturers to address unexpected issues, implement quality control measures, and ensure that the final product meets or exceeds specifications. This flexibility contributes to overall product quality and customer satisfaction, emphasizing the importance of achieving a balance between adherence to timelines and the need for adjustments.

In the context of infrastructure development and construction projects, meeting deadlines is often a priority to avoid budget overruns and ensure timely completion. However, factors such as adverse weather conditions, regulatory approvals, or unexpected site challenges can impede progress. Flexibility in project timelines allows construction teams to navigate these uncertainties, implement necessary safety measures, and maintain the integrity of the built environment. Striking a balance between adhering to schedules and adapting to unforeseen circumstances is crucial for delivering infrastructure projects that meet high standards of safety and quality.

Within the healthcare sector, where patient care is paramount, meeting deadlines is crucial for appointments, treatments, and interventions. However, the unpredictable nature of healthcare, including emergency situations, patient variability, and unexpected complications, may necessitate adjustments to timelines. The ability to accommodate changes without compromising the quality of care allows healthcare professionals to respond effectively to evolving patient needs, ensuring that medical decisions are made with thorough consideration and attention to individual circumstances.

In project management across diverse industries, such as marketing campaigns, event planning, or product launches, meeting deadlines is often a key success factor. However, the evolving landscape of markets, changing consumer preferences, and unexpected external factors can influence project trajectories. The ability to reassess and extend deadlines when necessary enables project managers to adapt strategies, incorporate new insights, and enhance the overall success of initiatives. This adaptability is particularly relevant in dynamic industries where staying ahead of trends and responding to market shifts are essential for sustained competitiveness.

In the context of information technology (IT) operations and system maintenance, meeting deadlines for routine tasks, updates, and security patches is desirable for ensuring the reliability and security of systems. Nevertheless, the occurrence of unforeseen issues, system vulnerabilities, or the need for additional testing may necessitate adjustments to maintenance schedules. The flexibility to extend deadlines in IT operations allows organizations to prioritize thorough testing, minimize the risk of disruptions, and maintain the integrity of critical systems. Striking a balance between timely updates and comprehensive testing is essential for mitigating potential risks in the rapidly evolving IT landscape.

In the field of education, particularly in curriculum planning and course delivery, meeting deadlines for academic schedules and assessments is important for maintaining order and consistency. However, educational institutions often encounter dynamic factors such as student needs, pedagogical innovations, or unforeseen disruptions. The ability to adapt and extend deadlines in education allows educators to tailor their approaches to student learning, address emerging challenges, and foster a responsive and inclusive learning environment. This flexibility contributes to the overall effectiveness of educational programs and supports diverse student needs.

In the competitive landscape of product development and innovation, meeting deadlines for product releases and feature launches is a common practice. Yet, the iterative nature of innovation, evolving market trends, and the need for user feedback may require adjustments to release timelines. The flexibility to extend deadlines in innovation processes allows development teams to refine product features, respond to user input, and ensure that the final product meets or exceeds user expectations. This adaptability is instrumental in delivering products that resonate with the target audience and stand out in dynamic market environments.

Within the creative industries, such as filmmaking, writing, or artistic endeavors, meeting deadlines is often important for project completion and commercial success. However, the creative process is inherently fluid, and artists may encounter inspiration, revisions, or unexpected challenges that influence their work. The ability to extend deadlines in creative pursuits allows artists to refine their creations, explore new ideas, and produce content that reflects their artistic vision. This flexibility contributes to the richness and authenticity of creative works, highlighting the delicate balance between structured timelines and the inherent unpredictability of the creative process.

In the domain of customer service and support, meeting deadlines for issue resolution and response times is crucial for maintaining customer satisfaction. Yet, the complexity of customer inquiries, the need for thorough investigation, or unexpected technical challenges may require additional time. The flexibility to extend deadlines in customer service allows support teams to provide comprehensive and accurate solutions, ensuring that customer concerns are addressed effectively. This adaptability contributes to positive customer experiences and fosters long-term customer loyalty.

Overall, examining scenarios where meeting deadlines is desirable but not mandatory reveals the importance of striking a balance between structured timelines and the need for flexibility. In dynamic and complex environments, the ability to adapt timelines allows organizations and individuals to navigate uncertainties, respond to changing conditions, and optimize outcomes without compromising quality or customer satisfaction. This nuanced approach recognizes that while deadlines provide a framework for planning and efficiency, the capacity to adjust timelines when necessary is essential for fostering resilience, innovation, and the ability to meet evolving challenges.

Defining embedded systems and their prevalence in real-time applications.

Embedded systems represent a ubiquitous and integral aspect of modern technological landscapes, playing a foundational role in a diverse array of applications across numerous industries. Defined as specialized computing systems designed to perform dedicated functions within larger systems or products, embedded systems are characterized by their integration into a host environment, often operating imperceptibly to end-users. Their prevalence stems from their ability to efficiently execute specific tasks with reliability and real-time responsiveness, making them indispensable in applications where timing precision is paramount.

One prominent domain where embedded systems demonstrate their significance is in real-time applications. These applications demand not only computational accuracy but also the ability to process and respond to input within stringent time constraints. Embedded systems excel in meeting these requirements, providing the necessary speed and reliability essential for tasks such as control systems, automation, and critical decision-making processes. The real-time capabilities of embedded systems find extensive use in areas like industrial automation, where machinery and processes require instantaneous responses to ensure seamless coordination and synchronization. In manufacturing environments, for instance, embedded systems govern robotic movements, monitor production parameters, and execute control algorithms with precise timing, contributing to the efficiency and reliability of the entire system.

In the context of automotive systems, embedded systems are fundamental to the operation of advanced driver assistance systems

(ADAS) and in-vehicle control systems. These applications demand real-time processing for tasks such as collision detection, adaptive cruise control, and emergency braking. Embedded systems enable the rapid interpretation of sensor data, facilitating split-second decision-making to enhance vehicle safety and driver assistance. The prevalence of embedded systems in automotive technology extends to the realm of autonomous vehicles, where the ability to process information in real-time is critical for navigating complex and dynamic driving environments.

Aerospace and avionics represent another domain where embedded systems are pervasive, contributing to the safety and functionality of aircraft. Flight control systems, navigation equipment, and communication systems rely on embedded systems to process data in real-time and execute precise commands. In aviation, where split-second decisions can have profound consequences, the deterministic nature of embedded systems is crucial for ensuring the reliability of critical functions. Whether in autopilot systems, cockpit displays, or communication protocols, embedded systems play a vital role in maintaining the integrity of aerospace operations.

The healthcare sector also benefits significantly from embedded systems, particularly in medical devices and diagnostic equipment. Patient monitoring systems, infusion pumps, and imaging devices leverage embedded systems to process real-time data and deliver timely information to healthcare professionals. The deterministic nature of embedded systems is crucial in medical applications where quick responses to changing patient conditions can be a matter of life and death. These systems contribute to the precision and reliability of medical interventions, reinforcing their role in enhancing patient care and safety.

Furthermore, embedded systems play a central role in communication networks and telecommunication infrastructure. From the real-time processing of data packets in networking equipment to the execution of protocols in telecommunications switches, embedded systems ensure the seamless flow of information across vast networks. Telecommunication applications, including voice-over-IP (VoIP) and video conferencing, rely on embedded systems for low-latency data processing, enabling clear and instant communication. The prevalence of embedded systems in communication technologies underscores their significance in sustaining the interconnected and rapidly evolving landscape of global information exchange.

The consumer electronics industry provides yet another arena where embedded systems are ubiquitous. Smartphones, smart TVs, and household appliances incorporate embedded systems to execute specific functions seamlessly. In smartphones, for example, embedded systems manage tasks ranging from processing touch input to executing applications with minimal latency. Similarly, the intelligent features of smart TVs, such as voice recognition and content recommendations, rely on embedded systems to provide a responsive and user-friendly experience. In household appliances like washing machines and refrigerators, embedded systems enhance functionality, optimize resource usage, and enable intuitive user interfaces.

The industrial Internet of Things (IoT) represents a paradigm where embedded systems are at the forefront, connecting physical devices and machinery to digital networks for enhanced monitoring and control. Embedded systems in IoT devices facilitate the collection and processing of sensor data, enabling real-time insights into industrial processes. In smart factories, for instance, embedded systems govern the operation of sensors, actuators, and control units to optimize production efficiency. The integration of embedded systems in the industrial IoT ecosystem contributes to the evolution of smart and connected manufacturing environments.

Despite their prevalence and diverse applications, defining embedded systems extends beyond their real-time capabilities. Embedded systems are characterized by their integration into larger systems or products, where their presence is often imperceptible to end-users. This integration involves a synergy between hardware and software components, tailored to meet specific requirements and constraints. The hardware components of embedded systems typically include microcontrollers or microprocessors, memory units, input/output interfaces, and often specialized peripherals. The software aspect encompasses the embedded software, which is designed to perform dedicated functions efficiently. Embedded systems differ from general-purpose computing systems by their specialized nature, tailored to address specific tasks rather than providing a broad range of functionalities.

One distinguishing feature of embedded systems is their reliance on real-time operating systems (RTOS) or real-time kernels. These specialized operating systems prioritize deterministic behavior, ensuring that tasks are executed within predefined time constraints. The use of RTOS in embedded systems contributes to the predictability and responsiveness required for real-time applications. Tasks in an embedded system, whether related to control, communication, or data processing, are scheduled and executed with precision, minimizing the variability in response times.

Embedded systems operate in diverse environments, ranging from resource-constrained devices with minimal computing power to sophisticated systems with advanced processing capabilities. The design considerations for embedded systems encompass factors such as power efficiency, size, and reliability, reflecting the diverse applications they serve. In resource constrained environments, embedded systems may employ lightweight architectures and optimizations to maximize efficiency. In contrast, high-performance embedded systems, such as those found in automotive control units or aerospace applications, leverage powerful processors and advanced hardware architectures to meet the demands of complex computations and real-time requirements.

The development of embedded systems involves a comprehensive engineering process, encompassing hardware design, software development, and system integration. Hardware engineers focus on selecting appropriate components, designing circuitry, and optimizing for efficiency. Software developers, on the other hand, create the embedded software, ensuring that it aligns with the hardware specifications and meets the real-time requirements of the application. System integration involves bringing together the hardware and software components, often requiring rigorous testing and validation to ensure the reliability and functionality of the embedded system.

Security is a critical consideration in embedded systems, especially as they become integral to the fabric of interconnected devices in the IoT era. The prevalence of embedded systems in critical infrastructure, healthcare, and industrial applications makes them potential targets for cyberattacks. Security measures, such as encryption, secure boot processes, and regular software updates, are implemented to safeguard embedded systems from unauthorized access and ensure the integrity of their operation. As embedded systems continue to evolve and become more interconnected, addressing cybersecurity challenges becomes imperative to maintain the trustworthiness of these systems.

In conclusion, embedded systems define a category of computing systems that have become pervasive in modern technological landscapes. Their prevalence is particularly evident in real-time applications, where their deterministic capabilities contribute to the efficiency, reliability, and safety of critical processes. From industrial automation and aerospace to healthcare and consumer electronics, embedded systems operate imperceptibly, executing specialized functions with precision. As technology continues to advance, the role of embedded systems is poised to expand further, driving innovation across industries and shaping the evolution of smart and interconnected systems.

Exploring the integration of real-time capabilities in embedded devices.

The integration of real-time capabilities into embedded devices represents a transformative advancement that has redefined the landscape of modern computing. Embedded devices, encompassing a wide array of systems from industrial controllers and automotive control units to medical devices and consumer electronics, have evolved beyond simple functionality to meet the growing demand for precise and timely responsiveness. This evolution is particularly evident in the seamless integration of real-time capabilities, allowing embedded devices to execute tasks with deterministic precision, respond to inputs instantaneously, and operate in synchronization with the time constraints imposed by their respective applications.

Real-time capabilities in embedded devices are paramount in applications where timing precision is critical, and deviations from specified deadlines can have significant consequences. In industrial automation, for instance, embedded controllers govern the movements of robotic arms, monitor production parameters, and execute control algorithms with real-time responsiveness. The ability to precisely coordinate these tasks in sync with the operational requirements of manufacturing processes ensures efficiency, reliability, and safety. Real-time capabilities in embedded controllers contribute to the seamless execution of tasks, preventing delays that could disrupt the production workflow and lead to inefficiencies or, in critical scenarios, pose safety risks.

The automotive industry represents another domain where the integration of real-time capabilities in embedded devices has revolutionized vehicle functionality. Advanced Driver Assistance Systems (ADAS) rely on embedded control units to process sensor data and make split-second decisions for features such as collision detection, adaptive cruise control, and emergency braking. The deterministic nature of real-time processing in these embedded systems is crucial for enhancing vehicle safety and assisting drivers in dynamic and unpredictable driving environments. The integration of real-time capabilities enables these embedded devices to operate with precision, contributing to the overall safety and efficiency of modern vehicles.

Medical devices, ranging from patient monitoring systems to infusion pumps, leverage real-time capabilities in embedded systems to ensure timely and accurate responses to patient needs. In patient monitoring, embedded devices process real-time physiological data and provide instantaneous feedback to healthcare professionals. The ability to detect anomalies and trigger timely alerts is critical in scenarios where patient safety is of utmost importance. Similarly, in infusion pumps delivering medication, real-time processing is essential to administer drugs at precise rates and respond promptly to changes in patient conditions. The integration of real-time capabilities in these medical devices enhances their reliability and effectiveness in delivering quality healthcare.

Consumer electronics, including smartphones, smart TVs, and smart home devices, showcase the pervasive integration of real-time capabilities in embedded systems. Smartphones, for instance, utilize embedded processors to handle touch input, execute applications, and manage various functions with low latency. The responsiveness of touchscreens, the smooth execution of applications, and the seamless operation of features such as voice recognition are all enabled by the real-time capabilities of embedded systems. In smart TVs, real-time processing ensures low-latency interactions with user input, enhancing the overall user experience. The integration of real-time capabilities in consumer electronics contributes to the fluidity and responsiveness expected by users in the era of interconnected and intelligent devices.

The industrial Internet of Things (IoT) represents a paradigm where the integration of real-time capabilities in embedded devices is fundamental. IoT devices, ranging from sensors and actuators to gateways and edge devices, operate in interconnected environments where data processing and decision-making must occur with minimal delay. In smart factories, for example, embedded devices with real-time capabilities facilitate the collection and processing of sensor data, enabling timely insights into industrial processes. The synchronization of tasks in real-time contributes to the optimization of production efficiency and the adaptive control of manufacturing operations. The integration of real-time capabilities in IoT devices is pivotal for the seamless functioning of interconnected systems in diverse industrial settings.

Aerospace and avionics applications underscore the criticality of real-time capabilities in embedded devices for ensuring the safety and reliability of aircraft operations. Embedded systems in avionics, including flight control systems, navigation equipment, and communication systems, operate in an environment where split-second decisions are imperative. The deterministic nature of real-time processing allows these embedded devices to execute commands, process sensor data, and communicate with precision. In flight control systems, for instance, the integration of real-time capabilities ensures that control inputs are processed instantaneously, contributing to the stability and safety of the aircraft. The reliability of embedded systems with real-time capabilities is paramount in aerospace applications where adherence to strict timing requirements is non-negotiable.

The integration of real-time capabilities in embedded devices involves considerations of both hardware and software aspects to meet the demands of specific applications. Hardware design for real-time embedded systems often involves the selection of appropriate microcontrollers or microprocessors, memory units, and peripherals optimized for deterministic processing. The architecture of the hardware components is tailored to support real-time requirements, considering factors such as clock frequency, bus speed, and input/output interfaces. In high-performance embedded systems, powerful processors and specialized hardware accelerators may be employed to handle complex computations and real-time tasks.

Software development for embedded systems with real-time capabilities is equally critical, requiring the design and implementation of embedded software that aligns with the hardware specifications and meets the timing constraints of the application. Real-time operating systems (RTOS) or real-time kernels are often employed to manage task scheduling, ensuring that critical tasks are executed within specified deadlines. The software architecture is designed to prioritize deterministic behavior, with careful consideration given to task prioritization, inter-task communication, and synchronization mechanisms. Programming languages suitable for real-time applications, such as Ada or Real-Time Java, may be chosen to enhance the predictability and reliability of the embedded software.

The development of real-time embedded systems involves a comprehensive engineering process that encompasses hardware design, software development, and system integration. Hardware engineers work on selecting components, designing circuitry, and optimizing for efficiency to meet real-time requirements. Software developers focus on creating embedded software that efficiently executes tasks, adheres to timing constraints, and ensures reliable performance. System integration involves bringing together the hardware and software components, often requiring rigorous testing and validation to guarantee the functionality and timing accuracy of the real-time embedded system.

Security considerations play a crucial role in real-time embedded systems, particularly as they become integral to critical infrastructure, healthcare, and industrial applications. The interconnected nature of embedded devices in the era of IoT introduces potential vulnerabilities that could be exploited by malicious actors. Security measures, including encryption, secure boot processes, and regular software updates, are implemented to safeguard real-time embedded systems from unauthorized access and ensure the integrity of their operation. The integration of robust security features is essential to maintaining the trustworthiness of embedded systems in applications where security is paramount.

The exploration of real-time capabilities in embedded devices extends beyond individual devices to the broader concept of real-time systems, where multiple interconnected embedded devices collaborate to achieve a common goal. Real-time systems, often found in applications such as distributed control systems or networked embedded devices, rely on precise timing and communication protocols to ensure coordinated operation. The integration of real-time capabilities in such systems enables tasks to be executed in synchronization, facilitating the seamless interaction of multiple embedded devices within a larger network.

In conclusion, the integration of real-time capabilities in embedded devices represents a paradigm shift that has elevated the functionality, reliability, and responsiveness of modern computing systems. From industrial automation and automotive control to healthcare devices and consumer electronics, embedded systems with real-time capabilities have become indispensable in applications where timing precision is critical. The deterministic nature of real-time processing enables embedded devices to execute tasks with precision, respond instantaneously to inputs, and contribute to the overall safety and efficiency of diverse industries. As technology continues to advance, the integration of real-time capabilities in embedded devices is poised to play a central role in shaping the future of intelligent, interconnected systems across a spectrum of applications.

Discussing the role of real-time systems in control applications.

Real-time systems play a foundational and indispensable role in control applications, where precision, responsiveness, and deterministic behavior are critical for ensuring the stability and efficiency of dynamic processes. The term "control applications" encompasses a diverse range of systems across various industries, from industrial automation and manufacturing to aerospace, automotive, and beyond. In these applications, real-time systems act as the nerve center, orchestrating the monitoring, decision-making, and actuation processes with split-second precision.

In the realm of industrial automation, real-time systems serve as the backbone of control applications governing the operation of machinery, production lines, and manufacturing processes. These systems are tasked with ensuring seamless coordination, synchronization, and control of diverse components within an industrial environment. The ability to respond in real-time to changes in parameters, sensor data, or external stimuli is paramount for optimizing production efficiency, preventing bottlenecks, and maintaining the overall reliability of automated systems. Real-time control systems in industrial settings contribute to the precise execution of tasks, minimizing delays, and enhancing the adaptability of production processes to dynamic conditions.

Manufacturing processes, characterized by intricate workflows and tight tolerances, rely heavily on real-time control systems to govern robotic movements, monitor quality parameters, and execute control algorithms with deterministic precision. For example, in a robotic assembly line, real-time control ensures that each robotic arm moves precisely, picks and places components accurately, and maintains synchronization with other elements of the production process. The stringent timing requirements in these environments demand swift decision-making and execution, preventing delays that could lead to inefficiencies or, in worst-case scenarios, catastrophic consequences. Real-time control applications in manufacturing exemplify the pivotal role of real-time systems in orchestrating complex and interconnected processes.

In the aerospace industry, real-time control applications are integral to the operation of flight control systems, navigation equipment, and communication protocols. Aircraft are equipped with sophisticated avionics that rely on real-time processing to maintain stability, respond to pilot commands, and navigate through dynamic and unpredictable environments. Flight control systems, for instance, require instantaneous processing of sensor data and precise execution of control algorithms to adjust control surfaces and ensure the aircraft's stability. Real-time systems in aerospace applications contribute not only to the safety of flight but also to the overall efficiency and reliability of avionics systems that govern critical aspects of aircraft operation.

The automotive sector represents another domain where real-time control applications are pervasive, influencing both traditional and emerging technologies. Advanced Driver Assistance Systems (ADAS) and in-vehicle control systems heavily rely on real-time capabilities to process sensor data, make split-second decisions, and execute control commands. In ADAS, features such as collision detection, lane-keeping assistance, and automatic emergency braking demand real-time responsiveness to enhance vehicle safety. In autonomous vehicles, real-time control is even more critical, as the vehicle must continuously interpret sensor inputs, make decisions, and control actuators to navigate safely through complex environments. The integration of real-time systems in automotive control applications underscores their role in shaping the future of intelligent transportation.

Within healthcare, real-time control applications are instrumental in medical devices and diagnostic equipment. Patient monitoring systems, for example, rely on real-time processing of physiological data to provide timely and accurate information to healthcare professionals. The ability to detect anomalies, trigger alarms, and respond promptly to changes in patient conditions is crucial in clinical settings. In medical imaging devices, real-time control is essential for tasks such as image acquisition, processing, and display, where precise timing is necessary to ensure the accuracy and effectiveness of diagnostic procedures. Real-time control applications in healthcare contribute to the reliability of medical interventions, supporting the delivery of timely and quality patient care.

The integration of real-time systems in control applications extends to the field of energy and utilities, where the precise control of power generation, distribution, and consumption is vital for grid stability and efficiency. Power plants leverage real-time control systems to regulate the generation of electricity, adjust parameters based on demand fluctuations, and respond to grid disturbances swiftly. Smart grids, which incorporate real-time control applications, enable the dynamic management of energy resources, optimize load balancing, and enhance the reliability of power distribution. The role of real-time systems in control applications within the energy sector is pivotal for achieving sustainability, minimizing wastage, and ensuring the stability of power networks.

In the context of transportation systems, real-time control applications are evident in traffic management, public transit, and intelligent transportation systems. Traffic signal control systems, for instance, utilize real-time capabilities to dynamically adjust signal timings based on traffic flow, minimizing congestion and improving overall traffic efficiency. Public transit systems leverage real-time control to optimize routes, monitor vehicle locations, and provide real-time information to commuters. Intelligent transportation systems integrate various sensors and control mechanisms to enhance safety, reduce travel times, and improve the overall efficiency of transportation networks. Real-time control applications in transportation underscore their role in shaping urban mobility and addressing the challenges of modern city living.

Financial trading platforms represent a domain where real-time control applications have a direct impact on economic activities. In the fast-paced world of financial markets, split-second decisions can make a substantial difference. Real-time control systems in trading platforms enable the rapid execution of trades, monitor market fluctuations, and manage risks swiftly and efficiently. The ability to process vast amounts of financial data in real-time contributes to the competitiveness and success of financial institutions and traders. Real-time control applications in finance exemplify the role of real-time systems in dynamic and high-stakes environments where timing precision is a decisive factor.

Real-time control applications are prevalent in scientific research and experimentation, particularly in fields such as physics, chemistry, and materials science. Experiments involving precise control of parameters, data acquisition, and feedback mechanisms rely on real-time systems to ensure accurate and repeatable results. Particle accelerators, for instance, utilize real-time control to adjust beam parameters, synchronize complex experiments, and maintain the stability of particle trajectories. Real-time control applications in scientific research contribute to the advancement of knowledge, enabling researchers to conduct experiments with a high degree of precision and control.

The overarching theme across these diverse domains is the critical role that real-time systems play in control applications. Real-time systems provide the temporal predictability and responsiveness required for tasks ranging from regulating industrial processes to ensuring the safety of flight, from optimizing traffic flow to executing high-frequency trades. The integration of real-time control applications involves the careful design of both hardware and software components to meet the specific requirements of the application.

Hardware components in real-time control systems are selected and designed with a focus on deterministic behavior, minimizing latency, and ensuring the timely execution of tasks. Microcontrollers or microprocessors, memory units, and specialized peripherals are chosen to support the real-time requirements of the application. The hardware architecture is tailored to facilitate rapid data processing, quick response to inputs, and precise control over actuators and sensors.

Software development for real-time control applications involves the creation of embedded software that aligns with the hardware specifications and meets the timing constraints of the system. Real-time operating systems (RTOS) or real-time kernels are commonly employed to manage task scheduling and prioritize critical tasks. The software architecture is designed to optimize for deterministic behavior, with considerations given to task prioritization, inter-task communication, and synchronization mechanisms. Programming languages suitable for real-time applications, such as Ada or Real-Time Java, may be chosen to enhance the predictability and reliability of the embedded software.

The integration of real-time control applications requires rigorous testing, validation, and verification processes to ensure that the system operates within specified timing constraints and meets performance requirements. Testing methodologies may include simulation, emulation, and hardware-in-the-loop testing to evaluate the real-time responsiveness and reliability of the control system. Verification processes often involve the analysis of worst-case scenarios, fault tolerance, and the assessment of system behavior under various conditions.

Security considerations are paramount in real-time control applications, especially as these systems become more interconnected and accessible. The potential impact of cyber threats on critical infrastructure, industrial control systems, and transportation networks necessitates robust security measures. Encryption, secure communication protocols, and intrusion detection systems are implemented to safeguard real-time control applications from unauthorized access, data tampering, and cyberattacks.

In conclusion, real-time systems play a pivotal role in control applications across diverse industries, providing the temporal precision and responsiveness required for tasks ranging from industrial automation and aerospace control to healthcare devices and financial trading platforms. The integration of real-time capabilities involves the careful design of hardware and software components, rigorous testing, and a steadfast commitment to security. As technology continues to advance, the role of real-time systems in control applications is poised to expand further, influencing the efficiency, safety, and reliability of systems that shape our daily lives and drive progress in various fields.

Exploring applications in robotics, automotive, and industrial control.

The integration of robotics, automotive technology, and industrial control exemplifies the transformative impact of advanced technological systems on various aspects of our daily lives and industrial processes. In the realm of robotics, applications span a wide spectrum, ranging from manufacturing and healthcare to exploration and service-oriented tasks. In manufacturing, industrial robots have become integral to automating repetitive and precision-oriented tasks, contributing to increased production efficiency and quality. These robots, equipped with sophisticated sensors and real-time control systems, operate seamlessly in industrial environments, handling tasks such as welding, assembly, and material handling with precision and speed. The precision and repeatability of robotic systems in manufacturing have led to significant advancements in industries ranging from automotive assembly lines to electronics manufacturing.

Automotive technology has undergone a revolutionary transformation with the advent of innovations such as Advanced Driver

Assistance Systems (ADAS), electric vehicles, and autonomous driving. ADAS, incorporating technologies like radar, lidar, and cameras, relies on real-time systems for processing vast amounts of sensor data and making split-second decisions to enhance vehicle safety. From adaptive cruise control to lane-keeping assistance, these systems leverage real-time control applications to respond to dynamic road conditions and potential hazards. In the pursuit of autonomous driving, automotive manufacturers are developing vehicles equipped with advanced sensors, machine learning algorithms, and real-time control systems. These systems enable vehicles to interpret complex environments, make decisions, and navigate safely without human intervention. The intersection of automotive technology with real-time control applications is shaping the future of transportation, emphasizing safety, efficiency, and sustainability.

Industrial control represents a domain where real-time systems play a central role in governing complex processes, ensuring precision, and optimizing efficiency. In industrial automation, control systems regulate the operation of machinery and processes, contributing to the seamless coordination and synchronization of diverse components. The integration of real-time control applications in industrial settings enables swift decision-making, precise execution of tasks, and adaptability to changing conditions. For instance, in a smart factory, real-time control systems govern robotic movements, monitor production parameters, and adjust processes in response to fluctuations in demand. The ability to respond in real-time to changes in parameters and external stimuli is paramount for optimizing production efficiency, preventing bottlenecks, and maintaining the overall reliability of automated systems.

Robotics, automotive technology, and industrial control converge in applications that require collaborative and autonomous systems. In manufacturing, collaborative robots, or cobots, work alongside human operators, leveraging real-time control systems to ensure safety and synchronization. These cobots are equipped with sensors and vision systems that allow them to adapt to dynamic environments, avoiding collisions and working in close proximity to humans. In the automotive industry, collaborative robots are employed in tasks such as assembly and quality inspection, contributing to flexible and adaptive manufacturing processes. The integration of real-time control applications in collaborative robots enhances their responsiveness and enables seamless human-robot collaboration.

The exploration of these technological intersections extends to applications in logistics and supply chain management. In warehouses and distribution centers, robotic systems equipped with real-time control capabilities automate tasks such as picking, packing, and sorting. Autonomous mobile robots navigate through warehouse environments, optimizing the movement of goods and minimizing response times. The real-time control systems in these logistics applications contribute to the efficiency of order fulfillment processes, reducing errors and enhancing the overall productivity of supply chain operations.

In the healthcare sector, robotics plays a crucial role in applications such as surgery, rehabilitation, and patient care. Surgical robots, guided by real-time control systems, assist surgeons in performing minimally invasive procedures with precision. These robots incorporate advanced sensing technologies to provide haptic feedback and enhance the surgeon's dexterity. Rehabilitation robots, designed to assist individuals in regaining motor functions, utilize real-time control applications to adapt to the patient's movements and provide tailored therapy. Additionally, robotic systems in healthcare contribute to tasks such as medication delivery, patient monitoring, and laboratory automation, enhancing the quality and efficiency of healthcare services.

The integration of robotics, automotive technology, and industrial control extends to applications in hazardous environments, where human presence may pose risks. In industries such as nuclear power, oil and gas, and mining, robotic systems equipped with real-time control capabilities are deployed for inspection, maintenance, and exploration tasks. These robots operate in environments with extreme temperatures, high radiation levels, or confined spaces, performing tasks that would be challenging or dangerous for humans. The real-time control systems in these applications ensure the adaptability and responsiveness of robots to unpredictable conditions, contributing to the safety and efficiency of operations in hazardous environments.

A notable frontier in the convergence of these technologies is the development of autonomous drones for various applications. In agriculture, drones equipped with real-time control systems and sensors monitor crops, assess field conditions, and optimize the application of fertilizers and pesticides. The real-time capabilities of these drones enable rapid decision-making, allowing farmers to respond to crop health issues promptly. In logistics, drones are explored for last-mile delivery, utilizing real-time control systems to navigate through urban environments and deliver packages with precision. The integration of autonomous drone technology showcases the versatility of real-time control applications in addressing diverse challenges across industries.

As these technologies continue to evolve, the role of artificial intelligence (AI) and machine learning (ML) becomes increasingly prominent in enhancing the capabilities of robotic, automotive, and industrial control systems. AI algorithms, trained on large datasets, enable robots and autonomous vehicles to recognize patterns, make informed decisions, and adapt to complex scenarios. The synergy between real-time control systems and AI/ML technologies amplifies the intelligence and autonomy of these systems, opening new possibilities in applications such as predictive maintenance, predictive analytics, and autonomous decision-making.

Challenges in the integration of real-time systems in robotics, automotive technology, and industrial control include addressing issues of safety, reliability, and cybersecurity. Ensuring the safety of robotic systems working alongside humans, validating the reliability of autonomous vehicles, and safeguarding industrial control systems from cyber threats require comprehensive solutions. The development of robust safety standards, validation methodologies, and cybersecurity measures is essential to foster trust in these technologies and promote their widespread adoption.

In conclusion, the exploration of applications in robotics, automotive technology, and industrial control unveils a landscape where real-time systems are instrumental in shaping the future of automation, transportation, and manufacturing. From collaborative robots enhancing industrial workflows to autonomous vehicles revolutionizing transportation, the integration of real-time control applications is driving innovation and efficiency across diverse industries. The convergence of these technologies not only enhances productivity but also opens new frontiers in addressing complex challenges, from hazardous environments to healthcare and logistics. As technology continues to advance, the synergy between real-time control systems and emerging technologies like AI/ML promises to redefine the possibilities and applications of intelligent, autonomous systems in our interconnected and dynamic world.

Introducing distributed real-time systems spanning multiple nodes.

The paradigm of distributed real-time systems marks a transformative shift in the landscape of computing, intertwining the principles of real-time processing with the distributed nature of networked architectures. Distributed real-time systems encompass a network of interconnected nodes, each equipped with computational resources, that collaborate to achieve common objectives while adhering to stringent timing constraints. This architectural paradigm is characterized by the distribution of tasks, data, and control across multiple nodes, enabling parallelism, fault tolerance, and scalability. At the core of distributed real-time systems is the imperative to process and respond to events or inputs within predefined time bounds, a crucial aspect that distinguishes them from conventional distributed systems.

The distributed nature of these systems offers a multitude of advantages, notably the ability to harness the collective computational power of multiple nodes to tackle complex tasks concurrently. This parallelism enhances the overall throughput and responsiveness of the system, making distributed real-time systems well-suited for applications demanding high computational loads or tasks with time-sensitive requirements. The nodes within the distributed architecture can range from traditional computing devices such as servers and workstations to more resource-constrained entities like embedded systems, IoT devices, or edge computing devices, reflecting the diversity of applications that can benefit from distributed real-time capabilities.

One prominent domain where distributed real-time systems find pervasive application is industrial automation and control. In manufacturing environments, distributed control systems (DCS) orchestrate the coordination of machinery, sensors, and actuators distributed across the factory floor. These systems ensure that manufacturing processes operate with precision and synchronization, minimizing delays and optimizing production efficiency. The distributed nature of the control system allows for modularization, where specific nodes focus on controlling individual components or subsystems, contributing to a scalable and flexible industrial automation ecosystem.

In the realm of telecommunications, distributed real-time systems play a central role in ensuring the seamless operation of communication networks. Telecommunication networks, ranging from traditional telephony to modern broadband and cellular networks, rely on distributed real-time systems for tasks such as call routing, resource allocation, and quality of service management. The distributed architecture allows for the efficient handling of dynamic network conditions, ensuring that communication services meet stringent latency requirements and providing a foundation for scalable and reliable telecommunication infrastructures.

The emergence of the Internet of Things (IoT) has further propelled the relevance of distributed real-time systems, as the interconnectivity of a multitude of devices necessitates decentralized processing and decision-making. In smart cities, for instance, distributed real-time systems manage diverse applications, including traffic control, environmental monitoring, and public safety. The ability to process data locally on IoT devices or at the edge of the network enables rapid responses to events, reducing latency and enhancing the overall efficiency of smart city systems.

Aerospace and avionics represent another domain where the distributed real-time paradigm is pivotal. In modern aircraft, distributed avionic systems comprise multiple nodes responsible for tasks such as navigation, flight control, and communication. These systems demand not only real-time responsiveness but also fault tolerance, as the reliability of avionic functions is critical for flight safety. The distributed architecture allows for the isolation of failures and the seamless integration of redundant components, contributing to the resilience and reliability of avionic systems in the face of challenging operating conditions.

The automotive industry has witnessed a paradigm shift with the incorporation of distributed real-time systems in Advanced Driver Assistance Systems (ADAS) and autonomous vehicles. In ADAS, sensors distributed throughout the vehicle generate real-time data, which is processed and analyzed locally to make split-second decisions for features such as collision avoidance and adaptive cruise control. The distributed nature of these systems allows for rapid sensor fusion and decision-making at the edge, contributing to enhanced safety on the road. In autonomous vehicles, distributed real-time systems play a central role in processing sensor inputs, executing control algorithms, and ensuring the coordination of various subsystems for navigation and safety.

Healthcare is yet another domain where the distributed real-time paradigm is making significant inroads. In the context of patient monitoring, for example, wearable devices equipped with sensors continuously gather physiological data, which is processed and analyzed in real-time to provide timely alerts for healthcare professionals. The distributed nature of these systems enables the seamless integration of data from various monitoring devices, fostering a comprehensive and real-time view of the patient's health. Additionally, in the field of telemedicine, distributed real-time systems facilitate the transmission and processing of medical data for remote consultations, enabling timely healthcare interventions regardless of geographical distances.

The financial sector relies extensively on distributed real-time systems for the operation of trading platforms, risk management, and transaction processing. In high-frequency trading, distributed systems process vast amounts of market data in real-time, executing trades with split-second precision to capitalize on market fluctuations. The ability to handle massive data streams and execute transactions in real-time is imperative for financial institutions to remain competitive in dynamic and fast-paced markets. The distributed architecture allows for the parallel processing of market data, ensuring low-latency responses and timely execution of trades.

Distributed real-time systems also play a crucial role in the realm of scientific research, particularly in experiments and simulations that require parallel processing and coordination across multiple nodes. Large-scale experiments in physics, climate modeling, and materials science often involve distributed computing architectures to handle computationally intensive tasks. The ability to distribute simulations across multiple nodes enhances the scalability and efficiency of scientific computing, enabling researchers to explore complex phenomena and analyze massive datasets with real-time responsiveness.

However, the adoption of distributed real-time systems is not without its challenges. The inherent complexities of managing communication, synchronization, and fault tolerance across distributed nodes demand sophisticated design principles and technologies. Ensuring temporal predictability and meeting stringent timing constraints in a distributed environment requires careful consideration of factors such as network latency, clock synchronization, and task scheduling. Additionally, fault tolerance mechanisms become paramount to maintain system reliability in the face of node failures or network disruptions. The development of distributed real-time systems necessitates a holistic approach that integrates real-time computing principles with distributed systems architecture, encompassing both hardware and software aspects.

From a software perspective, distributed real-time systems often leverage specialized middleware and communication protocols to facilitate inter-node communication and coordination. Real-time operating systems (RTOS) or real-time kernels play a crucial role in managing task scheduling and ensuring the timely execution of critical processes. Programming languages suitable for real-time applications, such as Ada or Real-Time Java, may be employed to enhance the predictability and reliability of the software components. Middleware solutions, such as the Data Distribution Service (DDS) for real-time systems, provide a standardized framework for data exchange and communication between distributed nodes.

The hardware architecture of distributed real-time systems involves considerations of node heterogeneity, communication interfaces, and synchronization mechanisms. Nodes may vary in computational power, memory capacity, and sensor capabilities, necessitating adaptive algorithms to efficiently utilize the available resources. Communication interfaces, such as Ethernet or fieldbus protocols, are chosen based on the specific requirements of the application, considering factors like latency, bandwidth, and determinism. Clock synchronization mechanisms, crucial for achieving temporal predictability, may involve protocols like the Precision Time Protocol (PTP) to align the clocks of distributed nodes.

Security considerations are paramount in distributed real-time systems, especially as they become integral to critical infrastructure, healthcare, finance, and other sensitive domains. The interconnected nature of distributed systems introduces potential vulnerabilities that could be exploited by malicious actors. Security measures, including encryption, secure communication protocols, and regular software updates, are implemented to safeguard distributed real-time systems from unauthorized access and ensure the integrity of their operation.

In conclusion, the introduction of distributed real-time systems spanning multiple nodes represents a paradigm shift that has redefined the capabilities and applications of computing architectures. From industrial automation and telecommunications to healthcare, aerospace, and finance, the distributed real-time paradigm has become instrumental in addressing the complexities of modern applications that demand not only parallel processing but also adherence to stringent timing constraints. The synergy of real-time principles with distributed systems architecture opens new frontiers for innovation, enabling scalable, fault-tolerant, and responsive solutions to challenges in diverse domains. As technology continues to advance, the integration of distributed real-time systems is poised to play an increasingly pivotal role in shaping the future of computing, connectivity, and intelligent systems.

Examining the coordination and communication challenges in distributed environments.

The coordination and communication challenges inherent in distributed environments form a complex tapestry of considerations that significantly influence the design, deployment, and operation of distributed systems. In these environments, where computational resources are spread across multiple interconnected nodes, achieving seamless coordination and effective communication becomes a critical aspect for ensuring the overall reliability, performance, and functionality of the system. One of the foremost challenges lies in managing the asynchronous nature of communication between distributed nodes. Unlike centralized systems where communication is inherently synchronous, distributed systems must contend with the variability in message transmission times, leading to potential delays and uncertainties. This asynchrony introduces challenges in maintaining a consistent and coherent view of the distributed state across all nodes, necessitating sophisticated synchronization mechanisms to reconcile differences and ensure a unified perspective.

The geographical distribution of nodes in a distributed environment adds an additional layer of complexity to coordination and communication. Nodes may be located in diverse physical locations, potentially spanning continents or even residing in remote and hostile environments. The latency introduced by geographical dispersion poses a formidable challenge, influencing the responsiveness of communication and coordination. Network latency, affected by factors such as transmission delays and packet loss, becomes a crucial consideration, particularly in applications where real-time responsiveness is essential. The need to minimize latency and optimize communication pathways becomes a central focus, leading to the exploration of techniques such as content delivery networks, edge computing, and efficient routing algorithms.

Another challenge arises from the heterogeneity of nodes in distributed environments. Nodes may vary significantly in terms of computational power, memory capacity, and network bandwidth. This diversity introduces challenges in resource allocation, load balancing, and task scheduling. Coordinating the execution of tasks across heterogeneous nodes requires adaptive algorithms that can efficiently utilize the available resources while accommodating the varying capabilities of each node. Load balancing mechanisms become instrumental in distributing computational workloads equitably, ensuring that no node is overwhelmed while others remain underutilized. The dynamic nature of resource availability further complicates coordination, requiring systems to adapt to fluctuations in node capabilities and gracefully handle failures or additions of nodes.

Ensuring fault tolerance and reliability in distributed environments represents a persistent challenge that directly impacts coordination and communication. The interconnected nature of distributed systems makes them susceptible to various types of failures, including node crashes, network partitions, and communication errors. These failures can disrupt the normal flow of communication and coordination, leading to inconsistencies and potential system-wide failures. Developing robust mechanisms for fault detection, isolation, and recovery becomes imperative to maintain the integrity of the distributed system. Consensus protocols, distributed algorithms, and replication strategies are employed to ensure that the system can continue functioning even in the presence of failures, albeit with degraded performance.

The challenge of achieving consensus among distributed nodes is a fundamental aspect of coordination in distributed systems. Consensus is the process of reaching an agreement among nodes regarding a shared state or decision. However, achieving consensus in the presence of failures, asynchrony, and varying latencies is a classic problem with no one-size-fits-all solution. Distributed consensus algorithms, such as the Paxos algorithm or the Raft consensus algorithm, provide approaches to handle these challenges. These algorithms involve intricate communication patterns and voting mechanisms to ensure that nodes converge on a consistent view of the system state. Coordinating the agreement on shared data or decisions across nodes becomes particularly critical in distributed databases, replicated storage systems, and distributed ledgers where maintaining data consistency is paramount.

Security considerations further compound the challenges of coordination and communication in distributed environments. The distributed nature of systems introduces new vulnerabilities and attack vectors that malicious actors may exploit. Ensuring the confidentiality, integrity, and authenticity of communication between nodes becomes a crucial aspect of system design. Encryption, secure communication protocols, and access controls are essential components of a robust security strategy. However, the distributed nature of systems also introduces challenges such as the secure distribution of cryptographic keys, protection against insider threats, and the need for secure bootstrapping mechanisms. Balancing the requirements of security with the demands of efficient coordination and communication adds layers of complexity to the design and operation of distributed systems.

The advent of microservices architectures and containerization technologies has further elevated the complexity of coordination and communication in distributed environments. Microservices, characterized by their modular and independently deployable nature, introduce challenges related to service discovery, load balancing, and inter-service communication. Coordinating the interactions between microservices while maintaining responsiveness and fault tolerance demands the implementation of service meshes, API gateways, and distributed tracing mechanisms. Container orchestration platforms, such as Kubernetes, provide solutions for deploying and managing containerized applications at scale. However, orchestrating the coordination and communication between containers across a distributed cluster involves addressing challenges related to networking, service discovery, and dynamic scaling.

The emergence of edge computing as a paradigm for processing data closer to the source of generation introduces new dimensions to the challenges of coordination and communication in distributed environments. Edge computing leverages computing resources at the periphery of the network, often in close proximity to where data is generated. Coordinating the communication between edge devices, cloud services, and centralized data centers becomes crucial for ensuring low-latency processing and real-time responsiveness. Challenges such as network congestion, intermittent connectivity, and dynamic edge device availability necessitate adaptive coordination strategies that can dynamically adapt to the changing conditions of the edge environment.

Distributed environments also face challenges related to data consistency and coherence. In distributed databases or storage systems, ensuring that multiple replicas of data are in sync and consistent poses a significant challenge. The trade-off between consistency and availability, as described by the CAP theorem, becomes a key consideration. Systems must choose whether to prioritize consistency, availability, or partition tolerance, recognizing that achieving all three simultaneously is inherently challenging. Coordination mechanisms, such as quorum-based approaches or eventual consistency models, provide ways to navigate this trade-off and maintain an acceptable level of data consistency in distributed systems.

The coordination and communication challenges in distributed environments are further amplified when dealing with dynamic and elastic workloads. Cloud computing platforms, which allow the dynamic allocation and deallocation of resources based on demand, introduce challenges related to auto-scaling, load balancing, and adaptive resource provisioning. Coordinating the scaling of services, ensuring proper load distribution, and adapting to fluctuations in demand without sacrificing performance require sophisticated orchestration mechanisms. Auto-scaling policies, predictive analytics, and self-healing mechanisms become integral components of a distributed system's ability to efficiently adapt to varying workloads.

Addressing these coordination and communication challenges in distributed environments often involves a combination of architectural choices, algorithmic solutions, and the use of specialized middleware. The design of distributed systems requires careful consideration of the trade-offs between consistency, availability, and partition tolerance. Coordination mechanisms, whether based on consensus algorithms, distributed transactions, or decentralized protocols, play a pivotal role in achieving agreement among distributed nodes. Communication patterns, such as publish-subscribe models, message queues, or remote procedure calls, influence the flow of information between nodes. Middleware solutions, including distributed databases, messaging systems, and communication frameworks, provide abstractions and tools to simplify the complexities of coordination and communication in distributed environments.

In conclusion, the coordination and communication challenges in distributed environments represent a multifaceted landscape that spans issues of asynchrony, geographical distribution, heterogeneity, fault tolerance, consensus, security, microservices, edge computing, and dynamic workloads. Navigating these challenges requires a holistic understanding of the system's requirements, careful consideration of trade-offs, and the adoption of appropriate architectural patterns and technologies. As distributed systems continue to evolve in response to the demands of modern applications, the exploration of innovative solutions and the development of best practices in coordination and communication remain essential for building robust, scalable, and responsive distributed environments.

Chapter 3: Real-Time Operating Systems (RTOS)

Defining Real-Time Operating Systems and their specialized nature.

Real-Time Operating Systems (RTOS) constitute a specialized class of operating systems designed to meet the stringent requirements of real-time computing applications, where timely and predictable responses to events are paramount. Unlike general-purpose operating systems, RTOS prioritize deterministic behavior, ensuring that tasks are executed within specific time constraints. The specialized nature of RTOS stems from their focus on providing temporal precision, reliability, and consistency, making them well-suited for applications where meeting deadlines is critical. RTOS find extensive use in diverse domains such as industrial automation, aerospace, healthcare, telecommunications, automotive systems, and more, where the consequences of delays can range from reduced efficiency to severe safety hazards.

The distinguishing feature of RTOS lies in their ability to guarantee the execution of tasks within predefined time frames, commonly referred to as deadlines. This deterministic behavior is crucial for applications with time-sensitive requirements, such as controlling industrial processes, regulating flight systems, or monitoring patient vital signs. The temporal predictability offered by RTOS ensures that critical tasks receive attention and resources in a timely manner, minimizing the risk of missed deadlines and providing a level of reliability essential for mission-critical systems.

One key characteristic of RTOS is their support for real-time scheduling algorithms. These algorithms determine the order in which tasks are executed, considering factors like task priority, deadlines, and dependencies. Common scheduling policies in RTOS include Fixed Priority Scheduling, Earliest Deadline First (EDF), and Rate Monotonic Scheduling (RMS). These policies allow system designers to allocate resources effectively, ensuring that high-priority tasks are executed ahead of lower-priority ones. The choice of scheduling algorithm depends on the specific requirements of the real-time application and the criticality of different tasks.

RTOS often exhibit a minimalistic kernel architecture to reduce overhead and enhance responsiveness. The kernel, responsible for managing system resources and scheduling tasks, is streamlined to prioritize real-time requirements. This lean design allows for faster context switching and reduced latency, critical factors in meeting the stringent timing constraints of real-time applications. The simplicity of the kernel facilitates rapid response times to external events, contributing to the overall efficiency of the real-time system.

To facilitate communication and synchronization among tasks, RTOS incorporate specialized mechanisms such as real-time inter-process communication (IPC) and synchronization primitives. These mechanisms enable tasks to exchange data, coordinate activities, and communicate in a manner that aligns with the temporal constraints of the application. RTOS provide semaphores, mutexes, message queues, and other synchronization tools to ensure that tasks collaborate effectively without compromising real-time responsiveness.

In the context of embedded systems, where resource constraints are common, RTOS are tailored to operate efficiently in environments with limited memory and processing power. Their footprint is optimized to conserve resources while delivering the necessary real-time capabilities. Embedded RTOS find applications in a myriad of devices, from microcontrollers in consumer electronics to complex embedded systems in automotive control units, ensuring that these systems can meet real-time requirements despite resource constraints.

Another characteristic of RTOS is their deterministic input/output (I/O) handling. Real-time tasks often interact with external devices, sensors, or networks, and the timing of these interactions is critical. RTOS provide mechanisms to manage I/O operations deterministically, allowing tasks to communicate with peripherals without introducing unpredictable delays. This capability is crucial in applications such as robotics, where precise control over sensors and actuators is essential for accurate and timely responses.

The robustness of RTOS extends to their ability to handle interrupts and prioritize them based on their urgency. Real-time systems often rely on interrupts to respond promptly to external events. RTOS manage interrupt handling in a way that aligns with the overall scheduling strategy, ensuring that critical interrupts take precedence over less time-sensitive ones. This capability enhances the responsiveness of real-time systems to external stimuli.

Security is a critical consideration in modern computing environments, and RTOS are designed to provide a secure foundation for real-time applications. As real-time systems become more interconnected and susceptible to cyber threats, RTOS incorporate security features such as memory protection, access controls, and secure boot mechanisms. These features safeguard the integrity of real-time applications and protect against unauthorized access or malicious attacks that could compromise the reliability and safety of the system.

RTOS are categorized into two main types: hard real-time and soft real-time. In hard real-time systems, meeting deadlines is not only desirable but imperative. Failure to execute a task within its specified time frame may lead to catastrophic consequences, making hard real-time systems suitable for safety-critical applications such as medical devices, avionics, and industrial control systems. Soft real-time systems, on the other hand, prioritize timely execution but allow for occasional deadline misses without catastrophic outcomes. Applications like multimedia streaming, where occasional delays are acceptable, benefit from the flexibility offered by soft real-time systems.

The development of real-time applications often involves the use of specialized development tools and programming languages. Real-time programming languages, such as Ada and Real-Time Java, provide constructs that facilitate the expression of timing constraints and support the development of predictable and reliable real-time software. Integrated Development Environments (IDEs) tailored for real-time systems offer features such as profiling, debugging, and analysis tools specific to the demands of real-time application development.

RTOS are commonly employed in safety-critical systems, where compliance with industry standards is essential. Standards such as DO-178C for avionics, ISO 26262 for automotive systems, and IEC 62304 for medical devices outline guidelines for the development and certification of safety-critical software. RTOS that adhere to these standards provide a framework for building reliable and certifiable real-time systems, instilling confidence in the safety and dependability of the applications they support.

The specialized nature of RTOS extends to their applicability in multi-core and multi-processor architectures. As modern computing systems embrace parallelism for improved performance, RTOS are designed to efficiently harness the capabilities of multiple cores or processors. Real-time task scheduling across multiple cores, inter-core communication mechanisms, and synchronization protocols are integral components of RTOS that support multi-core architectures. This enables the development of real-time applications that can leverage parallel processing without sacrificing timing predictability.

In conclusion, Real-Time Operating Systems represent a specialized class of operating systems uniquely tailored to meet the exacting demands of real-time computing applications. Their emphasis on deterministic behavior, real-time scheduling, minimalistic kernel design, and support for embedded and resource-constrained environments sets them apart from general-purpose operating systems. The application of RTOS spans a diverse array of industries, from aerospace and healthcare to industrial automation and automotive systems, where meeting deadlines and ensuring reliable and predictable responses are imperative. As technology continues to advance, the role of RTOS remains pivotal in shaping the landscape of real-time computing and contributing to the development of robust, responsive, and safety-critical systems.

Discussing the critical features of RTOS, including deterministic scheduling.

Real-Time Operating Systems (RTOS) encompass a set of critical features that distinguish them from general-purpose operating systems and render them well-suited for applications with stringent real-time requirements. One paramount feature is deterministic scheduling, a cornerstone of RTOS that ensures tasks are executed within predictable and precise time frames. Deterministic scheduling is imperative for real-time applications, where meeting deadlines is not merely desirable but essential. Unlike traditional operating systems, where task scheduling decisions are often influenced by factors such as process priority and system load, RTOS employ scheduling algorithms that prioritize time-critical tasks based on their urgency and deadlines. This ensures that high-priority tasks are executed in a timely manner, contributing to the overall responsiveness and reliability of real-time systems.

In the realm of deterministic scheduling, Fixed Priority Scheduling is a widely used approach in RTOS. This algorithm assigns priorities to tasks, and the scheduler ensures that higher-priority tasks are given precedence over lower-priority ones. The fixed nature of priorities facilitates predictability, as the scheduling order remains constant, allowing system designers to make accurate predictions about task execution times. This predictability is crucial for applications where timing constraints are stringent, such as in control systems or avionics, where the timing of responses directly correlates with system safety and performance.

Another deterministic scheduling algorithm employed in RTOS is Earliest Deadline First (EDF). In EDF, tasks are scheduled based on their absolute deadlines, ensuring that the task with the earliest deadline is given priority. This dynamic scheduling approach is particularly effective in scenarios where tasks have varying execution times and deadlines, allowing for optimal utilization of system resources. EDF is well-suited for applications where tasks exhibit dynamic behavior, and the scheduler must adapt to varying workloads and deadlines to meet real-time requirements.

Rate Monotonic Scheduling (RMS) is yet another deterministic scheduling algorithm commonly used in RTOS. In RMS, tasks are assigned priorities based on their rates of execution, with higher-priority assigned to tasks with shorter periods. This scheduling strategy is rooted in the concept that tasks with shorter periods inherently have higher urgency and, therefore, should be scheduled with higher priority. RMS is valuable in scenarios where periodic tasks dominate the workload, as it ensures that the most frequent and time-sensitive tasks are scheduled promptly.

The deterministic nature of scheduling in RTOS extends beyond algorithms to encompass mechanisms for task prioritization, preemption, and interrupt handling. Preemption, the ability to suspend the execution of a lower-priority task to allow a higher-priority task to run, is a critical feature for meeting real-time constraints. In RTOS, preemption is often implemented with minimal latency to ensure that high-priority tasks can interrupt lower-priority tasks swiftly. Task prioritization mechanisms, such as priority inheritance or priority ceiling protocols, are designed to prevent priority inversion, a scenario where a high-priority task is delayed by a lower-priority task holding a shared resource.

Interrupt handling in RTOS is tailored to prioritize and efficiently manage interrupts based on their urgency. Real-time systems often rely on interrupts to respond promptly to external events. RTOS incorporate mechanisms to manage interrupt handling in a way that aligns with the overall scheduling strategy, ensuring that critical interrupts receive expedited attention. The ability to prioritize and manage interrupts with deterministic characteristics is fundamental to achieving real-time responsiveness in applications such as industrial control systems, where timely response to external stimuli is crucial.

Beyond deterministic scheduling, RTOS exhibit features tailored to support real-time inter-process communication (IPC) and synchronization. These features enable tasks to exchange data, coordinate activities, and communicate in a manner that aligns with the temporal constraints of the application. RTOS provide a variety of synchronization primitives, including semaphores, mutexes, and message queues, which enable tasks to coordinate their execution and share data while adhering to real-time requirements. Real-time IPC mechanisms are designed to minimize latency and ensure that communication between tasks occurs within predictable time bounds.

The minimalistic kernel architecture is another critical feature of RTOS. The kernel, responsible for managing system resources and scheduling tasks, is streamlined to prioritize real-time requirements. Unlike general-purpose operating systems that may include a broad range of features and services, RTOS maintain a focused and efficient kernel design to minimize overhead and enhance responsiveness. The simplicity of the kernel architecture facilitates rapid context switching, reducing the time it takes to switch between different tasks, and contributes to lower overall system latency.

Resource management in RTOS is characterized by the efficient allocation of system resources to tasks based on their real-time requirements. RTOS provide mechanisms to allocate and deallocate resources with minimal overhead, ensuring that tasks receive the resources they need in a timely manner. Resource reservation mechanisms, such as fixed-priority scheduling with resource reservation, allow tasks to explicitly request and reserve resources, contributing to the predictability of resource allocation in real-time systems.

RTOS are adept at handling interrupts and exceptions in a manner that aligns with real-time constraints. Exceptions, which may arise from hardware faults or software errors, can impact the temporal predictability of a system. RTOS incorporate mechanisms to handle exceptions swiftly and deterministically, ensuring that the system can recover from faults or errors without compromising real-time responsiveness. The ability to manage exceptions with minimal impact on real-time tasks is crucial for applications where system reliability and availability are paramount.

Memory management in RTOS is designed to be efficient and deterministic. Real-time applications often operate in resource-constrained environments, and RTOS implement memory management strategies that minimize fragmentation and provide predictable memory allocation and deallocation times. Memory protection mechanisms are employed to isolate tasks and prevent unintended interference, contributing to the reliability and security of real-time systems.

RTOS are inherently designed to cater to embedded systems, where resource constraints are common. The specialized nature of embedded RTOS involves optimizing the operating system for deployment in environments with limited memory, processing power, and storage. The footprint of an embedded RTOS is tailored to conserve resources while delivering the necessary real-time capabilities. Embedded RTOS find applications in a diverse range of devices, from microcontrollers in consumer electronics to complex embedded systems in automotive control units, where meeting real-time requirements is essential despite resource constraints.

Security features are becoming increasingly integral to the design of RTOS as real-time systems become more interconnected and susceptible to cyber threats. RTOS incorporate security mechanisms, including memory protection, access controls, secure boot mechanisms, and encryption, to safeguard the integrity of real-time applications. These features are especially crucial in applications such as industrial control systems, healthcare devices, and automotive systems, where ensuring the security of the real-time system is paramount.

The versatility of RTOS extends to their applicability in multi-core and multi-processor architectures. As modern computing systems embrace parallelism for improved performance, RTOS are designed to efficiently harness the capabilities of multiple cores or processors. Real-time task scheduling across multiple cores, inter-core communication mechanisms, and synchronization protocols are integral components of RTOS that support multi-core architectures. This enables the development of real-time applications that can leverage parallel processing without sacrificing timing predictability.

In conclusion, the critical features of Real-Time Operating Systems collectively contribute to their specialized nature, making them indispensable for applications with stringent real-time requirements. Deterministic scheduling lies at the core of RTOS functionality, ensuring timely execution of tasks and meeting deadlines. The efficiency of real-time scheduling algorithms, preemption mechanisms, interrupt handling, and prioritization contributes to the predictability and reliability of real-time systems. Real-time IPC and synchronization mechanisms, a minimalistic kernel architecture, efficient resource management, and tailored memory handling enhance the responsiveness and efficiency of RTOS. The integration of security features, adaptability to embedded environments, and support for multi-core architectures further highlight the versatility of RTOS in addressing the diverse needs of modern real-time computing applications.

Exploring the architecture of RTOS with emphasis on task scheduling.

The architecture of Real-Time Operating Systems (RTOS) is intricately designed to prioritize the efficient execution of tasks within precise time constraints, making them well-suited for applications demanding deterministic behavior. At the heart of RTOS architecture lies the task scheduling mechanism, a critical component that ensures timely execution of tasks while adhering to predefined priorities and deadlines. The structure of an RTOS is tailored to provide a systematic framework for managing tasks, enabling them to share resources, communicate, and execute in a manner that aligns with the real-time requirements of the system.

The task scheduling architecture in RTOS is characterized by the utilization of specialized scheduling algorithms to determine the order in which tasks are executed. Fixed Priority Scheduling is a fundamental scheduling algorithm employed in many RTOS, assigning priority levels to tasks based on their criticality and urgency. Tasks with higher priorities are scheduled to run ahead of those with lower priorities, allowing the system to allocate resources and attention to critical tasks in a deterministic manner. This fixed priority approach simplifies the prediction of task execution times, a key consideration in meeting stringent real-time requirements.

Earliest Deadline First (EDF) is another prevalent scheduling algorithm in RTOS architecture, particularly suited for systems with tasks characterized by varying execution times and deadlines. In

EDF, tasks are scheduled based on their absolute deadlines, ensuring that the task with the earliest deadline is given priority. This dynamic scheduling approach adapts to varying workloads and deadlines, providing flexibility for real-time systems where tasks exhibit unpredictable execution times and temporal requirements.

Rate Monotonic Scheduling (RMS) is a scheduling algorithm rooted in the concept that tasks with shorter periods inherently have higher urgency. In RTOS architecture, RMS assigns priorities to tasks based on their rates of execution, with higher priority given to tasks with shorter periods. This approach ensures that the most frequent and time-sensitive tasks are scheduled promptly, enhancing the overall responsiveness of the system. RMS is particularly effective in scenarios where periodic tasks dominate the workload, aligning with the real-time nature of applications in fields such as industrial automation and control systems.

The scheduling architecture in RTOS also encompasses mechanisms to handle preemption, allowing the system to interrupt the execution of a lower-priority task to allocate resources to a higher-priority task. Swift and efficient preemption is crucial in meeting real-time constraints, and RTOS are designed to minimize the latency associated with task switches. Preemption mechanisms in RTOS are carefully orchestrated to ensure that high-priority tasks can interrupt lower-priority tasks with minimal delay, facilitating timely responses to external events and meeting critical deadlines.

To mitigate the challenges of priority inversion, a phenomenon where a higher-priority task is delayed by a lower-priority task holding a shared resource, RTOS often implement priority inheritance or priority ceiling protocols. Priority inheritance temporarily boosts the priority of a task holding a shared resource to that of the waiting task, preventing lower-priority tasks from delaying higher-priority ones. Priority ceiling protocols establish a maximum priority level that a task can inherit, preventing uncontrolled priority escalation and maintaining system stability.

Interrupt handling is a fundamental aspect of RTOS architecture, closely intertwined with task scheduling. Real-time systems frequently rely on interrupts to respond promptly to external events. The RTOS interrupt handling mechanism is designed to prioritize and efficiently manage interrupts based on their urgency. Critical interrupts receive expedited attention to ensure timely response, contributing to the overall real-time responsiveness of the system. The integration of interrupts into the scheduling architecture allows RTOS to seamlessly handle external stimuli while maintaining deterministic execution of tasks.

The kernel, the core component of an operating system responsible for managing system resources and scheduling tasks, plays a pivotal role in the architecture of RTOS. The kernel in RTOS is often minimalistic, emphasizing efficiency and responsiveness. Unlike general-purpose operating systems that may include a wide array of features, the kernel in RTOS is streamlined to prioritize real-time requirements. This simplicity contributes to faster context switching, reducing the time it takes to switch between different tasks, and minimizing overall system latency.

Real-Time Operating Systems often exhibit specialized memory management architecture to optimize resource utilization in resource-constrained environments. The memory management mechanisms in RTOS are designed to be efficient, deterministic, and predictable. Memory fragmentation is carefully managed to ensure that memory allocation and deallocation times remain consistent. Memory protection mechanisms are employed to isolate tasks and prevent unintended interference, contributing to the reliability and security of real-time systems. Efficient memory management is crucial in real-time applications, where predictability and determinism extend beyond task scheduling to encompass the entire system operation.

Resource management architecture in RTOS is geared towards efficiently allocating system resources to tasks based on their real-time requirements. RTOS provide mechanisms for task prioritization and resource reservation, allowing tasks to explicitly request and reserve resources to meet their temporal constraints. This resource management architecture ensures that critical tasks receive the resources they need in a timely manner, contributing to the predictability of resource allocation in real-time systems.

The architecture of RTOS extends to address the challenges of handling exceptions and errors in a manner consistent with real-time constraints. Exceptions, arising from hardware faults or software errors, can impact the temporal predictability of a system. RTOS incorporate mechanisms to handle exceptions swiftly and deterministically, ensuring that the system can recover from faults or errors without compromising real-time responsiveness. Exception handling is a critical aspect of the overall architecture, safeguarding the reliability and availability of real-time systems.

RTOS architecture is versatile, accommodating the demands of embedded systems where resource constraints are common. The specialized nature of embedded RTOS involves optimizing the operating system for deployment in environments with limited memory, processing power, and storage. The footprint of an embedded RTOS is tailored to conserve resources while delivering the necessary real-time capabilities. This architecture allows embedded RTOS to cater to a diverse range of devices, from microcontrollers in consumer electronics to complex embedded systems in automotive control units, ensuring that real-time requirements are met despite resource constraints.

Security features are integral components of RTOS architecture, reflecting the increasing interconnectedness of real-time systems and the corresponding rise in cyber threats. RTOS incorporate security mechanisms, including memory protection, access controls, secure boot mechanisms, and encryption, to safeguard the integrity of real-time applications. These features are crucial in applications such as industrial control systems, healthcare devices, and automotive systems, where ensuring the security of the real-time system is paramount.

The adaptability of RTOS architecture to multi-core and multi-processor architectures is another notable feature. As modern computing systems embrace parallelism for improved performance, RTOS are designed to efficiently harness the capabilities of multiple cores or processors. Real-time task scheduling across multiple cores, inter-core communication mechanisms, and synchronization protocols are integral components of RTOS that support multi-core architectures. This architectural flexibility enables the development of real-time applications that can leverage parallel processing without sacrificing timing predictability.

In conclusion, the architecture of Real-Time Operating Systems revolves around the central theme of efficient and deterministic task scheduling. The incorporation of specialized scheduling algorithms, preemption mechanisms, interrupt handling, and prioritization strategies defines the core of RTOS architecture. The kernel, memory management, resource allocation, exception handling, and security features are intricately woven into the architecture to complement the real-time demands of diverse applications. Embedded RTOS cater to resource-constrained environments, and the adaptability to multi-core architectures reflects the evolving landscape of modern computing. The architecture of RTOS, with its emphasis on precise and timely execution, stands as a testament to their indispensable role in applications where meeting deadlines is not just desirable but imperative.

Discussing the kernel's role in managing time-critical processes.

The kernel, as the core component of an operating system, plays a pivotal role in managing time-critical processes in Real-Time Operating Systems (RTOS). Its responsibilities extend beyond general-purpose operating systems, focusing on the efficient execution of tasks within precise time constraints, a fundamental requirement for real-time applications. The architecture of the kernel in RTOS is designed with a keen emphasis on providing a systematic framework for task scheduling, resource management, and overall system responsiveness to meet the stringent demands of time-critical processes.

Task scheduling is a cornerstone function of the kernel in RTOS, and it is specifically geared towards orchestrating the execution of tasks with utmost precision. Unlike general-purpose operating systems that may employ dynamic scheduling policies influenced by factors like process priority and system load, the kernel in RTOS implements deterministic scheduling algorithms. Fixed Priority Scheduling is a prevalent approach where tasks are assigned priorities based on their urgency and criticality. The kernel ensures that higher-priority tasks are scheduled ahead of lower-priority ones, allowing the system to allocate resources to critical tasks in a predictable and consistent manner. This deterministic scheduling is crucial for real-time applications where meeting deadlines is not just desirable but imperative.

In the context of time-critical processes, the kernel's role in preemption is equally critical. Preemption allows the system to interrupt the execution of a lower-priority task to allocate resources to a higher-priority task. The kernel in RTOS is designed to facilitate swift and efficient preemption to minimize the latency associated with task switches. Preemption is essential for ensuring that high-priority tasks can interrupt lower-priority tasks promptly, enabling the system to respond to external events in a timely manner. The seamless integration of preemption into the kernel's functionality contributes to the overall responsiveness of the real-time system.

Interrupt handling is another vital aspect of the kernel's role in managing time-critical processes. Real-time systems frequently rely on interrupts to respond promptly to external events. The kernel is responsible for prioritizing and efficiently managing interrupts based on their urgency. Critical interrupts receive expedited attention to ensure a timely response, aligning with the real-time nature of applications. The integration of interrupt handling into the kernel's architecture allows the system to handle external stimuli while maintaining deterministic execution of tasks, a key requirement for time-critical processes.

The minimalistic kernel architecture in RTOS is a defining characteristic that enhances its efficiency and responsiveness. Unlike the more feature-rich kernels found in general-purpose operating systems, the kernel in RTOS is streamlined to prioritize real-time requirements. The simplicity of the kernel architecture contributes to faster context switching, reducing the time it takes to switch between different tasks, and minimizing overall system latency. This lean design aligns with the specific needs of time-critical processes, allowing the kernel to swiftly and reliably manage the execution of tasks.

Memory management in the kernel is tailored to optimize resource utilization in the context of time-critical processes. The memory management mechanisms in RTOS are designed to be efficient, deterministic, and predictable. Memory fragmentation is carefully managed to ensure that memory allocation and deallocation times remain consistent. Memory protection mechanisms are employed to isolate tasks and prevent unintended interference, contributing to the reliability and security of real-time systems. Efficient memory management is crucial for time-critical processes, where predictability and determinism extend beyond task scheduling to encompass the entire system operation.

Resource management is a key function of the kernel in RTOS, ensuring the efficient allocation of system resources to tasks based on their real-time requirements. The kernel provides mechanisms for task prioritization and resource reservation, allowing tasks to explicitly request and reserve resources to meet their temporal constraints. This resource management architecture ensures that critical tasks receive the resources they need in a timely manner, contributing to the predictability of resource allocation in time-critical processes.

Exception handling is integral to the kernel's role in managing time-critical processes. Exceptions, arising from hardware faults or software errors, can impact the temporal predictability of a system. The kernel incorporates mechanisms to handle exceptions swiftly and deterministically, ensuring that the system can recover from faults or errors without compromising real-time responsiveness. Exception handling is a critical aspect of the overall kernel functionality, safeguarding the reliability and availability of real-time systems.

Security features are increasingly becoming integral components of the kernel's role in managing time-critical processes, reflecting the interconnected nature of real-time systems and the corresponding rise in cyber threats. The kernel incorporates security mechanisms, including memory protection, access controls, secure boot mechanisms, and encryption, to safeguard the integrity of time-critical processes. These features are crucial in applications such as industrial control systems, healthcare devices, and automotive systems, where ensuring the security of the real-time system is paramount.

The adaptability of the kernel to multi-core and multi-processor architectures is another notable feature. As modern computing systems embrace parallelism for improved performance, the kernel in RTOS is designed to efficiently harness the capabilities of multiple cores or processors. Real-time task scheduling across multiple cores, inter-core communication mechanisms, and synchronization protocols are integral components of the kernel that support multi-core architectures. This architectural flexibility enables the development of real-time applications that can leverage parallel processing without sacrificing timing predictability.

In conclusion, the kernel's role in managing time-critical processes in Real-Time Operating Systems is characterized by its central responsibility in orchestrating the execution of tasks with precision and determinism. The kernel's architecture, with its emphasis on deterministic scheduling, preemption, interrupt handling, and minimalistic design, defines its effectiveness in meeting the stringent requirements of time-critical processes. Memory management, resource allocation, exception handling, and security features further complement the kernel's role, ensuring the reliability, predictability, and responsiveness of real-time systems. The adaptability to multi-core architectures reflects the evolving landscape of modern computing, where the kernel remains a cornerstone in the quest for efficient and reliable time-critical processing.

Introducing scheduling algorithms tailored for real-time applications.

Scheduling algorithms tailored for real-time applications form the bedrock of Real-Time Operating Systems (RTOS), playing a pivotal role in orchestrating the execution of tasks within precise time constraints. The unique demands of real-time systems necessitate scheduling strategies that prioritize not only task completion but also adherence to stringent deadlines. One of the fundamental approaches is Fixed Priority Scheduling, where tasks are assigned priorities based on their urgency and criticality. The scheduling algorithm ensures that higher-priority tasks preempt lower-priority ones, allowing the system to allocate resources to critical tasks in a predictable and consistent manner. This fixed priority approach simplifies the prediction of task execution times, a key consideration in meeting real-time requirements, and finds application in scenarios where tasks exhibit well-defined priorities.

Earliest Deadline First (EDF) is another prominent scheduling algorithm tailored for real-time applications, particularly suited for systems with tasks characterized by varying execution times and deadlines. In EDF, tasks are scheduled based on their absolute deadlines, ensuring that the task with the earliest deadline is given priority. This dynamic scheduling approach adapts to varying workloads and deadlines, providing flexibility for real-time systems where tasks exhibit unpredictable execution times and temporal requirements. EDF is especially effective in environments where tasks have varying levels of urgency, allowing the scheduler to optimize for meeting imminent deadlines.

Rate Monotonic Scheduling (RMS) is rooted in the concept that tasks with shorter periods inherently have higher urgency. This algorithm assigns priorities based on the rates of execution, with higher priority given to tasks with shorter periods. RMS is particularly effective in scenarios where periodic tasks dominate the workload, ensuring that the most frequent and time-sensitive tasks are scheduled promptly. The simplicity of RMS makes it a popular choice for systems with periodic tasks, aligning with the cyclical nature of many real-time applications.

Deadline Monotonic Scheduling (DMS) is an extension of Rate Monotonic Scheduling, where tasks are assigned priorities based on their deadlines. The algorithm assumes that tasks with shorter deadlines are more critical and assigns higher priorities accordingly. This approach is well-suited for applications where meeting specific deadlines is paramount. The DMS algorithm complements the real-time nature of systems where tasks have distinct and critical temporal requirements, emphasizing the importance of timely task completion.

In addition to these fundamental scheduling algorithms, real-time systems often leverage Priority Inheritance and Priority Ceiling

Protocols to mitigate the challenges of priority inversion. Priority Inheritance temporarily boosts the priority of a task holding a shared resource to that of the waiting task, preventing lower-priority tasks from delaying higher-priority ones. Priority Ceiling Protocols establish a maximum priority level that a task can inherit, preventing uncontrolled priority escalation and maintaining system stability. These protocols are crucial for scenarios where resource sharing among tasks is prevalent, addressing priority inversion challenges that could otherwise compromise the predictability of task execution.

In the context of scheduling algorithms, the concept of Fixed Priority Preemptive Scheduling is fundamental in real-time systems. This approach allows higher-priority tasks to preempt lower-priority ones, ensuring that the most critical tasks receive immediate attention. The preemptive nature of the scheduling algorithm is essential for meeting real-time constraints, as it enables swift responses to external events and dynamic changes in task priorities. Fixed Priority Preemptive Scheduling is a cornerstone in many RTOS, providing a deterministic and efficient mechanism for managing time-critical tasks.

The challenges posed by sporadic and aperiodic tasks in real-time systems are addressed by algorithms like Earliest Deadline First with Server (EDF/S) and Least Laxity First (LLF). EDF/S extends the EDF algorithm to accommodate sporadic tasks by introducing a server task that executes during the slack time between sporadic tasks. This ensures efficient utilization of system resources and facilitates the integration of sporadic tasks into the real-time schedule. LLF, on the other hand, prioritizes tasks based on their laxity, which is the time remaining until a task's deadline. This approach is effective in scenarios where tasks have varying execution times and deadlines, providing flexibility in handling sporadic and aperiodic workloads.

A notable consideration in real-time scheduling is the trade-off between optimality and simplicity. Optimal algorithms like the Optimal Earliest Deadline First (O-EDF) algorithm aim to minimize the maximum lateness of tasks, ensuring an optimal schedule that meets all deadlines. However, optimal algorithms often come with higher computational complexity, making them less practical for real-time systems with limited processing resources. In contrast, heuristics such as the Deadline Monotonic Heuristic (DMH) strike a balance between optimality and simplicity, providing reasonably good schedules with lower computational overhead. The choice of scheduling algorithm depends on the specific requirements and constraints of the real-time application.

Multiprocessor scheduling in real-time systems introduces additional complexities, and algorithms like Global Earliest Deadline First (GEDF) and Partitioned Earliest Deadline First (P-EDF) are designed to address these challenges. GEDF extends the EDF algorithm to multiprocessor environments, ensuring that the task with the earliest deadline is scheduled across all processors. P-EDF, on the other hand, divides the set of tasks among processors, applying EDF scheduling independently on each processor. These multiprocessor scheduling algorithms are crucial for real-time systems that harness the capabilities of multiple cores or processors to meet computational demands.

In conclusion, scheduling algorithms tailored for real-time applications are diverse, each addressing specific challenges posed by the temporal constraints of time-critical processes. Fixed Priority Scheduling, Earliest Deadline First, Rate Monotonic Scheduling, and their variants provide foundational approaches, each suited to different characteristics of real-time workloads. Priority Inheritance and Priority Ceiling Protocols mitigate priority inversion challenges, ensuring stable and predictable execution in systems with shared resources. Fixed Priority Preemptive Scheduling caters to the preemptive needs of time-critical tasks, while algorithms like EDF/S, LLF, DMH, and O-EDF address the nuances of sporadic and aperiodic workloads. Multiprocessor scheduling algorithms like GEDF and P-EDF extend these principles to parallel computing environments. The selection of a scheduling algorithm depends on the specific requirements of the real-time system, striking a balance between optimality, simplicity, and the unique characteristics of the application's workload.

Exploring Rate Monotonic Scheduling (RMS) and Earliest Deadline First (EDF).

Rate Monotonic Scheduling (RMS) and Earliest Deadline First (EDF) stand as fundamental scheduling algorithms within the domain of Real-Time Operating Systems (RTOS), each strategically crafted to meet the distinctive challenges inherent in managing time-critical processes. At the core of RMS lies the premise that tasks with shorter periods exhibit higher urgency. RMS assigns priorities based on the rates of task execution, with the task possessing the shortest period being granted the highest priority. Consequently, tasks are scheduled in descending order of their execution rates, favoring the most frequent and time-sensitive tasks. This prioritization strategy proves particularly effective in scenarios where periodic tasks dominate the workload, aligning seamlessly with the cyclic nature of numerous real-time applications, including industrial control systems and embedded systems.

In stark contrast, Earliest Deadline First (EDF) embraces a dynamic scheduling paradigm by prioritizing tasks according to their absolute deadlines. In EDF, the task with the earliest deadline ascends to the highest priority, and tasks follow suit in ascending order of their deadlines. This adaptability to varying workloads and deadlines positions EDF as an ideal choice for real-time systems grappling with tasks characterized by unpredictable execution times and temporal demands. Its agility in adjusting priorities based on the urgency of each task makes EDF well-suited for environments hosting sporadic or aperiodic tasks, where the scheduling framework must dynamically adapt to meet impending deadlines. Applications such as multimedia systems and interactive user interfaces reap substantial benefits from EDF's capacity to navigate diverse task characteristics and deadlines with finesse.

The choice between RMS and EDF pivots on the specific characteristics of tasks within a given real-time system. RMS emerges as the preferred option when tasks exhibit well-defined and consistent execution rates, facilitating straightforward priority assignments. The simplicity inherent in RMS renders it an attractive solution for systems primarily comprising periodic tasks, where predictability in scheduling stands as a paramount consideration. On the flip side, EDF shines brightest in scenarios marked by tasks with variable execution times and deadlines. Its dynamic adjustment of priorities based on task urgency proves invaluable in environments characterized by unpredictable workloads, offering an efficient mechanism for handling sporadic and aperiodic tasks.

Despite their unique strengths, both RMS and EDF bear distinctive merits and shortcomings contingent upon the context in which they are employed. RMS excels in delivering a predictable and deterministic schedule, particularly when tasked with managing processes boasting fixed execution rates. This predictability facilitates a straightforward analysis of system behavior, ensuring deadlines are met with high certainty. Nevertheless, the rigid priority assignments of RMS may lead to suboptimal resource utilization, especially when tasks with longer periods are assigned higher priorities, even if their urgency is comparatively low. In contrast, EDF stands out for its prowess in optimizing resource utilization by dynamically assigning priorities based on impending deadlines. This adaptability heightens the system's efficiency in handling diverse workloads, albeit at the expense of challenges associated with predicting task execution times and meeting deadlines with absolute certainty.

Delving into the theoretical foundations of RMS and EDF provides valuable insights into their performance characteristics. The Rate Monotonic Theorem asserts that if a set of periodic tasks is schedulable under RMS, no other fixed-priority algorithm can surpass its ability to utilize the CPU. This theorem underscores the optimality of RMS in scenarios where tasks adhere to periodic and predictable execution patterns. Conversely, EDF claims its own realm of optimality in the context of uniprocessor scheduling for sporadic task systems. The EDF optimality theorem posits that if a set of sporadic tasks is schedulable, EDF can achieve equivalent results, underscoring its efficacy in managing sporadic and aperiodic workloads with finesse.

Multiprocessor scheduling introduces an additional layer of complexity, prompting adaptations of both RMS and EDF to address the challenges inherent in parallel computing environments. Global Rate Monotonic Scheduling (GRMS) extends the principles of RMS to multiprocessor systems, ensuring that the task with the shortest period is scheduled across all processors. This extension capitalizes on the simplicity and predictability of RMS while accommodating the parallelism inherent in multiprocessor architectures. Simultaneously, Global Earliest Deadline First (GEDF) extends the dynamic priority assignment of EDF to multiprocessor environments, ensuring that the adaptive scheduling framework is maintained across all processors. These adaptations strive to harness the inherent strengths of RMS and EDF in parallel processing scenarios, empowering real-time systems to scale their computational capabilities.

The practical implementation of RMS and EDF within an RTOS entails considerations that transcend their theoretical foundations. An integral aspect is the overhead associated with context switching and scheduling decisions. RMS, known for its simplicity, boasts low overhead owing to fixed priorities. Conversely, EDF may incur higher overhead, particularly in systems housing a multitude of tasks with dynamic priorities. The choice between RMS and EDF necessitates careful deliberation, weighing the trade-offs encompassing ease of analysis, predictability, and adaptability to varying workloads. Real-time system designers find themselves at the crossroads of evaluating task characteristics, system requirements, and hardware constraints to make judicious decisions concerning the selection of these scheduling algorithms.

In conclusion, Rate Monotonic Scheduling (RMS) and Earliest Deadline First (EDF) emerge as stalwart scheduling algorithms in the realm of Real-Time Operating Systems. RMS, with its emphasis on prioritizing tasks based on execution rates, crafts a deterministic and predictable schedule ideally suited for scenarios dominated by periodic tasks. In contrast, EDF, dynamically assigning priorities based on absolute deadlines, embodies adaptability to varying workloads and optimal resource utilization, especially in environments hosting sporadic or aperiodic tasks. The choice between RMS and EDF hinges on the unique characteristics of tasks within a system, the predictability requirements, and the system's efficiency in navigating dynamic workloads. Both algorithms enrich the toolkit available to real-time system designers, empowering them to tailor their scheduling approach to the nuanced demands of time-critical processes.

Examining memory allocation strategies in real-time environments.

Memory allocation is a critical aspect of real-time systems, where responsiveness and predictability are paramount. In such environments, where tasks must be executed within strict deadlines, efficient memory management becomes crucial to meet the system's real-time requirements. This discussion will delve into various memory allocation strategies employed in real-time environments, exploring their strengths, weaknesses, and implications for system performance.

At the heart of memory allocation lies the distinction between static and dynamic memory allocation. In real-time systems, static memory allocation is often favored for its determinism. Static allocation reserves memory at compile time, allowing for predictable memory access patterns during program execution. This predictability is essential in real-time applications where precise timing is imperative. However, static allocation comes with limitations, as it may not accommodate dynamic changes in memory requirements during runtime, posing challenges for systems with varying workloads.

In contrast, dynamic memory allocation provides flexibility by allowing memory allocation and deallocation during program execution. In real-time systems, dynamic allocation is typically managed through techniques such as heap allocation. While dynamic allocation offers adaptability, it introduces challenges related to fragmentation and non-deterministic behavior, which can jeopardize the predictability required in real-time applications.

A crucial consideration in real-time memory management is the choice between stack and heap allocation. The stack, a region of memory reserved for function calls and local variables, is often preferred in real-time systems due to its deterministic nature. Stack allocation and deallocation follow a last-in-first-out (LIFO) order, simplifying memory management and reducing the risk of fragmentation. However, the stack's fixed size can limit its suitability for applications with dynamic memory requirements.

Heap allocation, on the other hand, provides a more flexible memory management approach. Memory is dynamically allocated from the heap during runtime, allowing for efficient use of resources. However, heap allocation introduces challenges such as fragmentation, as memory blocks may be scattered across the heap, leading to inefficient use of available space. In real-time systems, heap allocation must be carefully managed to mitigate the risk of unpredictable delays associated with memory fragmentation.

In addition to stack and heap allocation, memory pools are a popular strategy in real-time environments. Memory pools involve preallocating a fixed-size block of memory and managing it as a pool of reusable blocks. This approach minimizes fragmentation and enhances predictability by allocating and deallocating fixed-size blocks in a controlled manner. Memory pools are particularly useful in scenarios where dynamic memory allocation must be avoided or minimized to meet real-time constraints.

One notable memory allocation strategy in real-time systems is the Fixed Block Memory Allocation (FBMA) approach. FBMA divides the available memory into fixed-size blocks and assigns each block to a specific task or component. This strategy enhances predictability by eliminating the risk of fragmentation and ensuring that each task has a predefined memory footprint. However, FBMA may be less efficient in scenarios where tasks have varying memory requirements, as it can lead to wasted memory if allocated block sizes exceed the actual needs of individual tasks.

An alternative to FBMA is Variable Block Memory Allocation (VBMA), which allows tasks to request variable-sized memory blocks based on their specific requirements. While VBMA provides greater flexibility, it introduces challenges related to fragmentation and can lead to non-deterministic behavior if not carefully managed. Striking a balance between flexibility and determinism is crucial when choosing between FBMA and VBMA in real-time systems.

Cache-aware memory allocation strategies are gaining prominence in real-time environments to exploit the hierarchical structure of modern processors' memory systems. Caches play a crucial role in improving memory access times, and cache-aware allocation aims to optimize memory usage to enhance cache locality. Techniques such as cache coloring, which assigns specific colors to memory regions to optimize cache usage, can significantly impact real-time system performance by reducing cache misses and improving overall responsiveness.

Real-time garbage collection is another area of interest in memory allocation strategies. Garbage collection involves reclaiming memory occupied by objects that are no longer in use. In real-time systems, traditional garbage collection mechanisms may introduce unpredictable delays, making them unsuitable for applications with stringent timing requirements. Real-time garbage collection algorithms aim to minimize pause times during memory reclamation, ensuring that the system remains responsive even during garbage collection activities.

Contiguous memory allocation is a fundamental concept in real-time systems, especially for applications with strict timing constraints. Contiguous memory allocation involves allocating a contiguous block of memory to a task or component, ensuring that all required memory is in close proximity. This approach minimizes access times and enhances determinism, making it particularly suitable for real-time applications where predictability is paramount. However, contiguous allocation may face challenges in scenarios with fragmented memory or varying task requirements.

Fragmentation, both internal and external, poses a significant challenge in real-time memory management. Internal fragmentation occurs when allocated memory includes unused space within allocated blocks, while external fragmentation arises when free memory is scattered across the heap or memory pool. Minimizing fragmentation is crucial for ensuring efficient use of memory resources and maintaining the determinism required in real-time systems.

One approach to address fragmentation is the use of memory compaction techniques. Memory compaction involves rearranging allocated memory to eliminate fragmentation and create larger contiguous blocks. While effective, memory compaction introduces challenges in real-time systems, as the compaction process itself may lead to unpredictable delays. Balancing the benefits of fragmentation reduction with the potential impact on real-time performance is a key consideration in implementing memory compaction in such environments.

Real-time operating systems (RTOS) play a pivotal role in memory management for real-time applications. RTOSes often provide specialized memory allocators designed to meet the specific needs of real-time tasks. These allocators may implement strategies such as fixed-size block allocation or priority-based allocation to ensure that critical tasks receive the necessary resources without compromising system responsiveness. The choice of RTOS and its memory management features can significantly influence the success of real-time applications.

The impact of memory allocation strategies on real-time systems extends beyond the traditional desktop or server environments to include embedded systems and Internet of Things (IoT) devices. In embedded systems, where resources are often constrained, memory efficiency becomes even more critical. Memory allocation strategies must be tailored to the unique requirements of embedded applications, balancing the need for determinism with the limitations imposed by resource constraints.

In the context of IoT devices, which may operate in dynamic and unpredictable environments, memory management strategies must account for variability in workloads and adapt to changing conditions. Dynamic memory allocation may be more prevalent in IoT scenarios, but careful consideration must be given to the potential impact on real-time performance, especially in applications where responsiveness is crucial, such as in smart grids or autonomous vehicles.

Security considerations also play a role in shaping memory allocation strategies for real-time systems. Memory-related vulnerabilities, such as buffer overflows or memory leaks, can have severe consequences in safety-critical applications. Memory protection mechanisms, such as memory regions with restricted access, are essential in preventing unauthorized access or modification of critical data structures. These security measures must be integrated with memory allocation strategies to create robust and resilient real-time systems.

In conclusion, memory allocation in real-time environments is a multifaceted challenge that requires a careful balance between determinism, flexibility, and efficiency. Static and dynamic allocation, stack and heap management, memory pools, and cache-aware strategies each have their merits and trade-offs. The choice of memory allocation strategy depends on the specific requirements of the real-time application, considering factors such as task predictability, resource constraints, and the need for adaptability to varying workloads.

The landscape of real-time memory management is continuously evolving, driven by advancements in hardware architectures, the proliferation of embedded systems and IoT devices, and the increasing demand for real-time responsiveness in diverse applications. As real-time systems become more pervasive and diverse, the exploration and refinement of memory allocation strategies will remain a critical area of research and development, shaping the future of reliable and predictable computing in time-sensitive domains.

Discussing the challenges of dynamic memory allocation in time-sensitive tasks.

Dynamic memory allocation poses significant challenges in the context of time-sensitive tasks, where meeting strict deadlines is paramount. While dynamic allocation offers flexibility in managing memory resources during program execution, its inherent characteristics introduce complexities that can impact the predictability and responsiveness required in time-sensitive applications.

One of the primary challenges associated with dynamic memory allocation in time-sensitive tasks is the potential for non-deterministic behavior. Unlike static memory allocation, where memory is reserved at compile time, dynamic allocation occurs during runtime, leading to uncertainties in the timing of memory operations. The unpredictability introduced by dynamic allocation can result in variable execution times for memory-related tasks, making it challenging to guarantee that critical tasks will complete within their specified deadlines.

Fragmentation is another critical challenge associated with dynamic memory allocation in time-sensitive applications. Fragmentation occurs when memory becomes divided into small, non-contiguous blocks over time, leading to inefficient use of available space. Both internal fragmentation, where allocated blocks have unused space, and external fragmentation, where free memory is scattered throughout the heap, can degrade system performance. In time-sensitive tasks, fragmentation becomes a concern as it can lead to increased memory access times and, consequently, unpredictable delays in task execution.

The memory management overhead introduced by dynamic allocation is a significant concern in time-sensitive systems. Allocating and deallocating memory dynamically involves additional processing steps, such as maintaining data structures to track allocated memory blocks and managing the heap. These overhead operations contribute to increased execution times, which can be detrimental in scenarios where even small delays can lead to missed deadlines. Minimizing the impact of memory management overhead is crucial for maintaining the efficiency of time-sensitive tasks.

Concurrency and race conditions present additional challenges in the context of dynamic memory allocation for time-sensitive applications. In multi-threaded or parallel processing environments, multiple tasks may concurrently access the heap for memory allocation or deallocation. Without proper synchronization mechanisms, race conditions can arise, leading to unpredictable behavior and potential data corruption. Coordinating memory access in a way that ensures consistency and avoids race conditions becomes a critical consideration in time-sensitive systems employing dynamic memory allocation.

Memory leaks pose a significant risk in time-sensitive tasks relying on dynamic memory allocation. A memory leak occurs when allocated memory is not properly deallocated, leading to a gradual consumption of system resources. In time-sensitive applications, where efficient resource utilization is crucial, memory leaks can have a cascading effect, eventually depleting available memory and causing system failures. Detecting and addressing memory leaks in real-time becomes challenging, as traditional debugging techniques may introduce additional overhead and disrupt the timing constraints of critical tasks.

Real-time garbage collection, a mechanism for reclaiming memory occupied by objects that are no longer in use, introduces its own set of challenges in time-sensitive applications. Traditional garbage collection algorithms often involve pause times during which the system is temporarily suspended to perform memory reclamation. These pauses can be unacceptable in scenarios where continuous, uninterrupted operation is essential. Developing and implementing real-time garbage collection algorithms that minimize pause times while effectively managing memory becomes a complex task in time-sensitive environments.

Resource contention is a challenge that arises when multiple tasks compete for access to limited memory resources dynamically. In time-sensitive systems, tasks may have varying memory requirements, and improper resource allocation can lead to contention, where critical tasks are impeded by others consuming excessive memory. Managing resource contention requires sophisticated memory allocation policies that consider task priorities, memory usage patterns, and overall system dynamics to ensure that time-sensitive tasks receive the necessary resources without compromising system responsiveness.

The impact of dynamic memory allocation on worst-case execution time (WCET) analysis is a significant concern in time-sensitive tasks. WCET analysis aims to determine the maximum time a task can take to execute, considering various factors such as processor speed, cache behavior, and memory access times. The non-deterministic nature of dynamic allocation makes accurately predicting WCET challenging. Variability introduced by dynamic memory operations can lead to conservative WCET estimates, potentially resulting in underutilization of system resources and missed opportunities for optimization.

Efficient memory utilization becomes a critical consideration in time-sensitive applications relying on dynamic memory allocation. In scenarios where memory is a constrained resource, effective strategies for allocating and deallocating memory dynamically are essential. However, the dynamic nature of memory allocation can lead to suboptimal memory usage patterns, such as fragmentation and inefficient block sizes. Balancing the need for adaptability with the imperative of efficient memory utilization becomes a delicate task in time-sensitive environments.

Addressing the challenges of dynamic memory allocation in time-sensitive tasks requires a multifaceted approach. One strategy involves the use of memory pools, where fixed-size blocks of memory are preallocated and managed as a pool of reusable blocks. Memory pools offer advantages such as reduced fragmentation and deterministic allocation times, making them well-suited for time-sensitive applications. However, choosing appropriate block sizes and managing pool configurations to accommodate varying memory requirements remain critical considerations.

Cache-aware memory allocation strategies can play a pivotal role in mitigating the impact of dynamic memory allocation on time-sensitive tasks. By optimizing memory usage to enhance cache locality, cache-aware strategies aim to minimize cache misses and improve overall system performance. Techniques such as cache coloring, which assigns specific colors to memory regions to optimize cache usage, can be particularly beneficial in real-time systems where memory access times directly impact task responsiveness.

The use of fixed-size block memory allocation (FBMA) is another approach to address the challenges of dynamic memory allocation in time-sensitive tasks. FBMA involves dividing the available memory into fixed-size blocks and assigning each block to a specific task or component. This strategy enhances predictability by eliminating the risk of fragmentation and ensuring that each task has a predefined memory footprint. However, FBMA may be less flexible in scenarios where tasks have varying memory requirements, necessitating careful consideration of task diversity.

In conclusion, the challenges associated with dynamic memory allocation in time-sensitive tasks are substantial and multifaceted. Non-deterministic behavior, fragmentation, memory management overhead, concurrency issues, memory leaks, real-time garbage collection concerns, resource contention, and the impact on WCET analysis all contribute to the complexities faced by developers and engineers working on real-time systems. Addressing these challenges requires a careful balance between the flexibility offered by dynamic memory allocation and the stringent timing constraints imposed by time-sensitive applications. Strategies such as memory pools, cache-aware allocation, and fixed-size block memory allocation offer potential solutions, but the choice of approach depends on the specific requirements of the application and the criticality of meeting time-sensitive deadlines. As real-time systems continue to evolve and become more pervasive, ongoing research and innovation in memory allocation strategies will be essential to ensure the reliability and predictability of time-sensitive tasks across diverse domains.

Highlighting the prevalence of RTOS in embedded applications.

Real-Time Operating Systems (RTOS) have become integral components in the landscape of embedded applications, playing a pivotal role in enabling real-time responsiveness and determinism. Embedded systems, characterized by their presence within various devices and machinery, often operate in environments with stringent timing constraints, requiring precise control and coordination. This discussion delves into the prevalence of RTOS in embedded applications, examining the unique challenges these systems face and the indispensable role RTOS plays in addressing these challenges.

Embedded systems, found in an array of everyday devices such as smartphones, medical devices, automotive control units, and industrial machinery, perform specific tasks within a defined scope. Unlike general-purpose operating systems, which cater to diverse applications and user interactions, embedded systems often prioritize specific functions and require deterministic behavior. The inherent limitations of embedded systems, including constrained resources and the need for real-time responsiveness, make the use of RTOS a natural fit.

One of the primary reasons for the prevalence of RTOS in embedded applications is the criticality of timing constraints. Many embedded systems operate in real-time environments where tasks must be executed within specific time frames to ensure proper functionality. RTOS provides mechanisms for precise task scheduling and guarantees timely execution, allowing embedded systems to meet the stringent timing requirements demanded by applications like control systems, robotics, and communication devices.

RTOS offers a deterministic execution environment, a crucial aspect in applications where predictability is paramount. Determinism ensures that the timing behavior of tasks is consistent and reproducible, enabling designers to analyze and guarantee the worst-case execution time (WCET). In safety-critical applications such as medical devices and automotive control systems, where the consequences of missed deadlines can be severe, the deterministic nature of RTOS is instrumental in ensuring reliability and safety.

The modularity and scalability provided by RTOS contribute significantly to its widespread adoption in embedded applications. Embedded systems often consist of diverse components with specific functionalities. RTOS allows for the modular design of applications, enabling developers to organize tasks into separate threads or processes. This modularity enhances maintainability, facilitates code reuse, and simplifies system integration, making RTOS a preferred choice in scenarios where resource efficiency and adaptability are crucial.

RTOS excels in managing concurrency, a common requirement in embedded applications with multiple tasks running concurrently. Concurrency arises in systems where various components or processes need to operate simultaneously, such as in communication devices handling data transmission and reception concurrently. RTOS provides mechanisms, like task prioritization and inter-task communication, to manage concurrent execution effectively. This capability is essential in embedded systems where efficient resource utilization and seamless coordination are critical for optimal performance.

Memory management is a key consideration in embedded applications, given the often limited resources available. RTOS offers memory management features tailored to the specific requirements of embedded systems. Memory protection mechanisms, efficient memory allocation strategies, and optimized memory footprint contribute to the efficient use of limited resources. These capabilities are crucial in applications such as IoT devices and wearables, where minimizing memory overhead is essential for extending battery life and ensuring optimal performance.

RTOS is adept at handling real-time communication require-ments, making it an ideal choice for embedded systems involved in networking and communication tasks. Many embedded applica-tions, including those in the IoT domain, require real-time commu-nication to exchange data with other devices or centralized systems. RTOS provides communication protocols and mechanisms for in-ter-device communication, ensuring that data is exchanged within predetermined time frames, contributing to the reliability of com-munication-intensive applications.

The prevalence of RTOS in embedded applications is also fueled by the need for power efficiency. Embedded systems often operate in resource-constrained environments where power consumption is a critical consideration. RTOS allows for fine-grained control over power states, enabling the system to switch between different power modes based on the current workload. This capability is particularly valuable in battery-operated devices, such as wearable health moni-tors and sensor nodes in industrial settings, where maximizing bat-tery life is essential.

Safety and reliability are paramount in many embedded appli-cations, especially those in automotive, aerospace, and medical do-mains. RTOS is designed with features to enhance the safety and re-liability of embedded systems. For instance, it supports mechanisms like watchdog timers, which can reset the system in case of a mal-function, preventing potential hazards. Additionally, RTOS facili-tates the implementation of fault-tolerant strategies, making it a pre-ferred choice in safety-critical applications where system failures can have severe consequences.

RTOS supports the development of real-time applications through a rich set of APIs and services. These APIs abstract low-level hardware details and provide standardized interfaces for tasks such as task scheduling, inter-task communication, and synchronization. This abstraction simplifies the development process, accelerates time-to-market, and enhances portability across different hardware platforms, contributing to the widespread use of RTOS in embedded applications.

RTOS also plays a crucial role in easing the challenges posed by the increasing complexity of embedded systems. As the functionality and sophistication of embedded devices continue to grow, managing the intricacies of system design, coordination, and resource allocation becomes more challenging. RTOS offers a structured and organized framework that simplifies the development and maintenance of complex embedded applications, making it an indispensable tool for embedded system developers.

The real-time nature of embedded applications in various domains, including automotive, healthcare, industrial automation, and consumer electronics, underscores the significance of RTOS in ensuring the reliable and timely operation of these systems. In the automotive sector, for example, RTOS is widely employed in Electronic Control Units (ECUs) to manage tasks related to engine control, braking systems, and advanced driver-assistance systems (ADAS). In healthcare, RTOS is utilized in medical devices for precise control of drug infusion, patient monitoring, and diagnostic equipment. The industrial automation sector relies on RTOS for controlling robotic systems, programmable logic controllers (PLCs), and other critical components of manufacturing processes.

The advent of the Internet of Things (IoT) further amplifies the role of RTOS in embedded applications. IoT devices, which connect and communicate with each other to enable intelligent automation and data exchange, often operate in real-time or near-real-time scenarios. RTOS provides the necessary infrastructure to manage the complexities of IoT applications, ensuring timely data processing, communication, and response to dynamic environmental changes.

Despite the prevalence and advantages of RTOS in embedded applications, it is crucial to acknowledge that selecting the appropriate RTOS for a specific use case requires careful consideration. Different RTOS implementations may have varying features, real-time capabilities, and resource requirements. The choice of RTOS depends on factors such as the nature of the embedded application, the criticality of timing constraints, resource constraints, and the desired level of determinism.

In conclusion, the prevalence of RTOS in embedded applications is a testament to its indispensable role in addressing the unique challenges posed by these systems. The deterministic nature, modularity, concurrency management, memory efficiency, real-time communication support, and safety features offered by RTOS make it well-suited for a wide range of embedded applications. As embedded systems continue to evolve and permeate various aspects of our daily lives, the significance of RTOS in ensuring the reliable, responsive, and efficient operation of these systems is poised to grow further. The symbiotic relationship between RTOS and embedded applications underscores the critical role that real-time operating systems play in shaping the future of smart and interconnected devices.

Discussing the benefits of using RTOS in resource-constrained environments.

The use of Real-Time Operating Systems (RTOS) in resource-constrained environments has become increasingly prevalent, driven by the need for efficient resource utilization, deterministic behavior, and precise control in applications where resources are limited. Resource-constrained environments, characterized by limitations in processing power, memory, and energy, pose unique challenges that demand specialized solutions. This discussion explores the benefits of employing RTOS in resource-constrained environments, shedding light on how these operating systems enhance the performance, reliability, and adaptability of embedded systems facing tight resource constraints.

One of the primary advantages of using RTOS in resource-constrained environments is its ability to provide deterministic behavior. Determinism ensures that the timing and execution of tasks are predictable and consistent, a critical requirement in scenarios where precise control is essential. RTOS achieves determinism by employing priority-based scheduling algorithms, allowing tasks with higher priorities to preempt lower-priority tasks. This deterministic behavior is crucial in applications such as industrial automation, where tasks must be executed within specified time frames to ensure the accuracy and reliability of control processes.

Efficient resource utilization is a key consideration in resource-constrained environments, and RTOS excels in optimizing the use of limited processing power and memory. RTOS employs lightweight task-switching mechanisms and minimal overhead, making it well-suited for environments where every computational cycle and byte of memory are valuable resources. This efficiency is particularly advantageous in applications like wearable devices and Internet of Things (IoT) sensors, where minimizing energy consumption and maximizing battery life are critical factors.

RTOS offers a modular and scalable architecture, allowing developers to tailor the operating system to the specific needs of resource-constrained applications. The modular design enables the inclusion of only essential components, reducing the overall footprint of the operating system. In situations where memory is scarce, this modularity allows for a fine-grained selection of features, ensuring that only the necessary components are included, thus conserving valuable resources in environments where every kilobyte matters.

Task scheduling is a fundamental aspect of RTOS that greatly benefits resource-constrained environments. RTOS employs scheduling policies, such as fixed-priority or rate-monotonic scheduling, to determine the order in which tasks are executed. This predictability in task scheduling enhances the system's overall responsiveness and ensures that critical tasks receive the attention they require. In applications with strict timing constraints, such as real-time control systems or communication protocols, RTOS scheduling mechanisms contribute to meeting deadlines and minimizing latency.

RTOS facilitates the effective management of concurrency, allowing multiple tasks to run concurrently without compromising determinism or causing resource conflicts. In resource-constrained environments, where efficient utilization of processing power is essential, concurrency management becomes a critical factor. RTOS provides mechanisms such as semaphores, mutexes, and inter-process communication, enabling seamless coordination among tasks without the risk of race conditions or resource contention. This concurrency management is particularly beneficial in applications like communication devices or embedded control systems.

Memory management in resource-constrained environments is a delicate balancing act, and RTOS offers strategies to optimize memory usage. RTOS employs efficient memory allocation and deallocation mechanisms, minimizing fragmentation and ensuring that memory is used judiciously. Techniques like fixed-size block memory allocation and memory pools are commonly employed in RTOS to enhance memory efficiency. This capability is crucial in scenarios where available memory is limited, such as in small-scale embedded systems or IoT devices with stringent resource constraints.

RTOS is designed to handle real-time communication requirements effectively, a valuable feature in resource-constrained environments where communication efficiency is essential. Many embedded applications, such as those in industrial automation or sensor networks, require real-time communication for timely exchange of data. RTOS provides communication protocols, message-passing mechanisms, and synchronization primitives that ensure data is transmitted and received within predetermined time frames, contributing to the reliability of communication-intensive applications.

Power efficiency is a paramount concern in resource-constrained environments, and RTOS plays a significant role in optimizing power consumption. RTOS allows for dynamic power management, enabling the system to transition between different power states based on the current workload. This adaptability is crucial in battery-operated devices, such as medical implants or IoT sensors, where extending battery life is a primary consideration. By intelligently managing power states, RTOS contributes to the overall energy efficiency of systems operating in resource-constrained environments.

RTOS supports the development of energy-aware applications by providing mechanisms for task suspension and low-power modes. In situations where certain tasks can be temporarily suspended to conserve energy, RTOS allows developers to implement power-aware strategies. For example, in scenarios where sensors can be periodically turned off to conserve energy and activated only when needed, RTOS facilitates the implementation of such power-saving schemes, contributing to the longevity of devices in resource-constrained environments.

Safety and reliability are paramount in many resource-constrained applications, particularly in domains such as automotive and healthcare. RTOS includes features and mechanisms to enhance the safety and reliability of embedded systems. For instance, it supports watchdog timers that can reset the system in case of a malfunction, preventing potential hazards. Additionally, the determinism provided by RTOS contributes to the predictability and reliability of safety-critical applications, ensuring that tasks critical for system safety are executed within specified time frames.

The adaptability of RTOS to diverse hardware platforms is another notable advantage in resource-constrained environments. RTOS provides hardware abstraction layers and standardized interfaces, allowing applications to be developed and ported across different embedded platforms seamlessly. This adaptability simplifies the development process, accelerates time-to-market, and facilitates the reuse of software components, particularly in environments where hardware heterogeneity is common due to variations in sensor types, communication protocols, or processing capabilities.

RTOS facilitates the development of firmware that is easy to maintain and update in resource-constrained environments. The modular architecture of RTOS allows developers to isolate and update specific components without affecting the entire system. This modular approach eases the integration of new features, bug fixes, or security patches, contributing to the longevity and upgradability of embedded systems operating in resource-constrained environments.

In conclusion, the benefits of using RTOS in resource-constrained environments are multifaceted and address the unique challenges posed by limitations in processing power, memory, and energy. The deterministic behavior, efficient resource utilization, modular design, concurrency management, memory efficiency, real-time communication support, power efficiency, safety features, and adaptability to diverse hardware platforms make RTOS a valuable choice in applications ranging from wearable devices and IoT sensors to safety-critical systems in automotive and healthcare. As resource constraints continue to shape the landscape of embedded systems, the role of RTOS in enhancing the performance, reliability, and adaptability of these systems is set to remain crucial in enabling innovative solutions across various domains.

Chapter 4: Scheduling Algorithms in Real-Time Systems

Emphasizing the central role of scheduling in meeting time constraints.

The central role of scheduling in meeting time constraints is a cornerstone principle in the design and operation of systems where timely execution of tasks is paramount. Scheduling, the process of determining the order and timing of task execution, is instrumental in orchestrating the utilization of computational resources and ensuring that tasks meet their specified deadlines. In a broad spectrum of applications, from real-time embedded systems to data centers and cloud computing, the effectiveness of scheduling directly impacts the system's responsiveness, predictability, and overall performance.

In the realm of real-time systems, where stringent timing requirements dictate the success of applications, scheduling takes on heightened significance. Real-time systems encompass a diverse array of applications, including control systems, medical devices, communication protocols, and industrial automation, where tasks must be completed within predetermined time intervals to maintain functionality and safety. The scheduling mechanism employed in real-time systems plays a pivotal role in determining whether critical tasks meet their deadlines, a factor that directly influences the system's reliability and suitability for its intended purpose.

One of the fundamental principles in scheduling is the allocation of priorities to tasks based on their criticality and timing requirements. Priority-driven scheduling is particularly prevalent in real-time systems, where tasks with higher priorities are granted precedence over lower-priority tasks. This approach ensures that critical tasks are scheduled and executed in a timely manner, reducing the risk of missed deadlines and ensuring the system's ability to respond to events or stimuli within specified time frames. Priority-driven scheduling is an essential strategy in meeting time constraints, as it aligns task execution with the criticality of the tasks themselves.

Fixed-priority scheduling is a commonly employed variant in real-time systems, where tasks are assigned static priorities that do not change during runtime. The predictability offered by fixed-priority scheduling is invaluable in scenarios where the worst-case execution time (WCET) of tasks can be accurately estimated. By adhering to a predetermined priority order, fixed-priority scheduling ensures that higher-priority tasks are consistently favored, minimizing the risk of unpredictable delays and contributing to the overall determinism of the system.

In contrast, dynamic-priority scheduling allows task priorities to be adjusted dynamically based on runtime characteristics. This adaptability is advantageous in scenarios where task execution times may vary, and dynamic adjustment of priorities can help optimize resource utilization. However, the challenge lies in maintaining predictability and meeting time constraints, as dynamic adjustments introduce uncertainties that can impact the timing behavior of tasks. Striking a balance between adaptability and predictability is a crucial consideration in selecting the appropriate scheduling strategy for a given real-time system.

Scheduling algorithms form the core of the scheduling mechanism, dictating how tasks are ordered and dispatched for execution. The choice of a scheduling algorithm profoundly influences the system's ability to meet time constraints. Classic algorithms such as Rate Monotonic Scheduling (RMS) and Earliest Deadline First (EDF) prioritize tasks based on their periodicity or deadlines. RMS assigns higher priority to tasks with shorter periods, while EDF prioritizes tasks based on their imminent deadlines. These algorithms provide effective means of meeting time constraints by ensuring that tasks critical to the system's operation are prioritized accordingly.

In scenarios where resources are shared among multiple tasks, the potential for contention arises, and scheduling must address the challenges posed by resource conflicts. Schedulers incorporating techniques such as the Priority Inheritance Protocol (PIP) or the Priority Ceiling Protocol (PCP) address resource contention issues by dynamically adjusting task priorities based on the resources they hold or request. These protocols prevent priority inversion, a situation where a lower-priority task holds a resource needed by a higher-priority task, thus ensuring that high-priority tasks are not unduly delayed by lower-priority tasks.

Scheduling is not confined solely to the domain of real-time systems; it plays a pivotal role in general-purpose operating systems and distributed computing environments as well. In these contexts, the focus extends beyond meeting strict timing constraints to optimizing overall system performance and resource utilization. Task scheduling in general-purpose operating systems involves considerations of fairness, responsiveness, and throughput. Schedulers aim to balance the competing goals of ensuring equitable access to resources for all tasks while maximizing system throughput, a delicate balancing act that becomes increasingly challenging in the presence of diverse workloads.

The complexities of modern computing environments, characterized by multi-core processors, distributed systems, and cloud computing, add layers of intricacy to scheduling strategies. Multi-core processors introduce parallelism, enabling concurrent execution of tasks across multiple cores. While this parallelism offers opportunities for improved performance, it also necessitates sophisticated scheduling algorithms that consider factors such as load balancing, affinity, and cache coherence. Efficiently harnessing the computational power of multi-core architectures requires scheduling mechanisms that exploit parallelism while mitigating contention for shared resources.

Distributed systems, where tasks are distributed across multiple nodes, introduce new challenges related to communication delays and network latency. Scheduling in distributed environments must account for these factors to ensure that tasks meet their inter-node communication deadlines. Coordination and synchronization mechanisms become crucial in achieving effective scheduling in distributed systems, where the timing behavior of tasks is influenced not only by local processing but also by the dynamics of communication across the network.

Cloud computing further transforms the landscape of scheduling by introducing virtualization and the dynamic allocation of resources based on demand. Cloud schedulers must consider factors such as resource provisioning, load balancing, and task migration to optimize the utilization of virtualized resources. Ensuring that applications hosted in the cloud meet their service level agreements (SLAs) requires adaptive scheduling mechanisms that can dynamically adjust to changing workloads and resource availability.

Meeting time constraints is not only a technical challenge but also a critical requirement in safety-critical systems. Industries such as aerospace, automotive, and healthcare rely on scheduling strategies to ensure that safety-critical tasks are executed within specified time frames. In avionics, for instance, where tasks related to flight control must be performed with precision, scheduling mechanisms are designed to prioritize safety-critical tasks and guarantee their timely execution, contributing to the overall safety and reliability of the system.

The real-world impact of scheduling on meeting time constraints is vividly demonstrated in mission-critical applications, such as space exploration missions or autonomous vehicles. In the realm of space exploration, where communication delays and limited resources are prevalent, scheduling strategies must accommodate the constraints imposed by space missions' unique operating environments. Similarly, in autonomous vehicles, where split-second decisions are required for safe navigation, scheduling mechanisms play a pivotal role in ensuring that perception, decision-making, and control tasks are executed in a coordinated and timely manner.

The role of scheduling in meeting time constraints extends beyond the traditional domains of computing and technology. In healthcare, for instance, scheduling is a critical component of medical procedures and treatments. Operating rooms, diagnostic equipment, and patient care tasks all require effective scheduling to ensure that medical procedures are conducted with precision and in accordance with patient safety protocols. In this context, scheduling contributes to optimizing the use of medical resources, minimizing patient wait times, and enhancing the overall efficiency of healthcare delivery.

In conclusion, the central role of scheduling in meeting time constraints is a pervasive and crucial aspect of system design and operation across diverse domains. From real-time systems and general-purpose operating systems to distributed computing, cloud computing, and safety-critical applications, the effectiveness of scheduling directly influences the responsiveness, predictability, and overall performance of systems. The intricacies of scheduling, encompassing priority assignment, scheduling algorithms, resource contention management, and adaptation to changing environments, underscore its significance in ensuring that tasks meet their specified deadlines. As computing environments continue to evolve, the ongoing refinement and innovation in scheduling mechanisms will remain essential in addressing the ever-growing demands for efficient, predictable, and timely task execution.

Discussing the impact of scheduling decisions on system performance.

The impact of scheduling decisions on system performance is a multifaceted and critical aspect that permeates various computing environments, influencing the responsiveness, efficiency, and overall effectiveness of systems. Scheduling decisions, which determine the order and timing of task execution, play a pivotal role in optimizing resource utilization, meeting timing constraints, and balancing competing objectives. This discussion delves into the intricate ways in which scheduling decisions impact system performance across a spectrum of domains, including real-time systems, general-purpose operating systems, distributed computing, and cloud computing.

In the realm of real-time systems, where meeting strict timing constraints is imperative, scheduling decisions have a direct and profound impact on the system's ability to guarantee timely task execution. Priority-driven scheduling, a prevalent approach in real-time systems, assigns priorities to tasks based on their criticality and timing requirements. The decision of priority assignment influences the order in which tasks are executed, with higher-priority tasks taking precedence. The impact is particularly evident in safety-critical applications, such as avionics or medical devices, where scheduling decisions dictate whether critical tasks meet their deadlines, contributing directly to the reliability and safety of the system.

The choice of scheduling algorithm is another crucial aspect influencing system performance in real-time environments. Algorithms like Rate Monotonic Scheduling (RMS) and Earliest Deadline First (EDF) prioritize tasks based on their periodicity or deadlines. RMS, for example, assigns higher priority to tasks with shorter periods, while EDF prioritizes tasks based on their imminent deadlines. The decision of selecting a specific scheduling algorithm affects the predictability, responsiveness, and efficiency of the system. In applications where task deadlines are stringent, the right choice of algorithm can mean the difference between meeting or missing critical timing requirements.

The impact of scheduling decisions extends to considerations of fairness and responsiveness in general-purpose operating systems. In these environments, where diverse workloads and user interactions coexist, scheduling decisions must balance the goals of providing equitable access to resources for all tasks while maximizing overall system throughput. Scheduling algorithms, such as the Completely Fair Scheduler (CFS) in Linux, aim to distribute CPU time fairly among competing tasks. The decision of how to allocate CPU time influences user experience, responsiveness, and the perceived performance of the system, especially in scenarios where multiple applications or users share computing resources.

Task prioritization and time-sharing policies contribute to the responsiveness of general-purpose operating systems. User-facing tasks or interactive applications often receive higher priority to ensure a responsive and interactive user experience. The decision of how to allocate CPU time among tasks competing for resources influences the overall system performance and user satisfaction. In scenarios where background tasks or system maintenance activities coexist with user tasks, scheduling decisions become crucial in maintaining a balance that does not compromise user experience.

The impact of scheduling decisions becomes increasingly complex in the context of multi-core processors, where parallelism introduces new challenges and opportunities. Scheduling mechanisms must evolve to effectively utilize the computational power of multiple cores while addressing concerns related to load balancing, affinity, and cache coherence. Decisions on how to distribute tasks among cores, whether to exploit parallelism or maintain affinity to improve cache performance, significantly influence the overall throughput and efficiency of systems equipped with multi-core architectures.

In distributed computing environments, where tasks span multiple nodes and communication latency is a factor, scheduling decisions acquire a global dimension. The coordination of tasks across nodes, the allocation of resources in a distributed manner, and the synchronization of activities become critical aspects. Scheduling mechanisms must account for communication delays, network latency, and the dynamics of distributed systems to optimize overall system performance. Decisions related to task migration, load balancing, and inter-node communication greatly influence the efficiency and responsiveness of distributed computing environments.

The impact of scheduling decisions in cloud computing is particularly pronounced, given the dynamic nature of resource provisioning and the virtualized nature of computing resources. Cloud schedulers must make decisions on resource allocation, task placement, and load balancing in real-time, responding to changes in workload and demand. Decisions related to scaling resources up or down based on demand, optimizing virtual machine placement, and efficiently utilizing virtualized infrastructure directly impact the cost, reliability, and responsiveness of applications hosted in the cloud.

Efficient scheduling decisions in cloud computing contribute to the overall cost-effectiveness of cloud services. Dynamic resource provisioning allows for the scaling of resources based on demand, ensuring that applications have access to the necessary computational resources during peak periods while minimizing costs during periods of low demand. Schedulers must make decisions on when to allocate additional virtual machines, how to distribute tasks among available resources, and when to release resources to achieve optimal cost-performance trade-offs.

The impact of scheduling decisions on system performance is heightened in safety-critical applications, such as autonomous vehicles or medical systems, where the consequences of scheduling errors can be severe. Scheduling decisions directly influence the timing behavior of tasks critical to the safety and reliability of these systems. For example, in autonomous vehicles, the decision of when to prioritize perception tasks, decision-making tasks, and control tasks influences the vehicle's ability to navigate safely. Similarly, in medical systems, scheduling decisions affect the timing of diagnostic tasks, treatment planning, and patient monitoring, directly impacting patient safety and well-being.

Resource contention and the potential for bottlenecks introduce additional considerations in scheduling decisions. In systems where tasks compete for shared resources, such as access to a shared database or communication channels, schedulers must make decisions that mitigate resource contention. The choice of scheduling policies, such as the Priority Inheritance Protocol (PIP) or the Priority Ceiling Protocol (PCP), directly influences how tasks contend for and release shared resources, minimizing the risk of priority inversion or resource conflicts that could impact system performance.

The impact of scheduling decisions is further accentuated in scenarios where energy efficiency is a paramount concern. Schedulers must make decisions related to task suspension, dynamic voltage and frequency scaling, and power management to optimize energy consumption. In battery-operated devices, such as smartphones or wearable devices, decisions that efficiently manage CPU states, transition between power modes, and intelligently schedule tasks directly impact the device's battery life and overall energy efficiency.

Machine learning and artificial intelligence applications introduce new challenges in scheduling decisions, especially when dealing with deep learning tasks that require substantial computational resources. Schedulers must make decisions related to task prioritization, GPU allocation, and parallelism to efficiently utilize hardware accelerators. The impact of scheduling decisions on the performance of machine learning tasks is crucial for applications ranging from real-time image recognition to complex data analytics.

In conclusion, the impact of scheduling decisions on system performance is pervasive and profound, cutting across diverse computing environments and applications. Whether in real-time systems, general-purpose operating systems, distributed computing, or cloud computing, the effectiveness of scheduling directly influences responsiveness, efficiency, and overall system performance. The intricacies of task prioritization, scheduling algorithms, resource contention management, and adaptation to changing environments underscore the significance of scheduling decisions in achieving optimal system performance. As computing environments continue to evolve, the ongoing refinement and innovation in scheduling mechanisms will remain critical in addressing the ever-growing demands for efficient, predictable, and timely task execution.

Introducing the RMS algorithm and its principles.

The Rate Monotonic Scheduling (RMS) algorithm is a fundamental and widely used scheduling technique in real-time systems, designed to prioritize tasks based on their respective rates of execution. Rooted in the principles of priority assignment, RMS is particularly well-suited for environments where tasks have periodic patterns and stringent timing constraints. As one of the earliest and most established algorithms in the field of real-time systems, RMS offers a deterministic approach to scheduling that ensures tasks with shorter periods are assigned higher priorities. The essence of RMS lies in its simplicity and predictability, making it an attractive choice for applications where meeting deadlines is crucial.

At the core of the RMS algorithm is the principle of assigning priorities inversely proportional to task periods. In other words, tasks with shorter periods are granted higher priority, and those with longer periods receive lower priority. This priority assignment strategy aligns with the underlying philosophy that tasks with more frequent deadlines demand more immediate attention and, therefore, should be scheduled with higher priority. The inverse relationship between priority and period ensures that the task with the shortest period, and consequently the highest frequency of occurrence, is given the highest priority in the scheduling queue.

The RMS algorithm assumes a cyclic executive model, where tasks repeat their execution at regular intervals, known as periods. Each task is characterized by a fixed period, representing the time between successive instances of task activation. The algorithm requires knowledge of these periods during the system design phase, making it crucial for applications where the timing requirements are known in advance. The periodic nature of tasks in RMS aligns well with many real-time applications, such as control systems, where tasks must execute at regular intervals to maintain system stability and responsiveness.

The priority assignment in RMS inherently implies a preemptive scheduling policy, meaning that a higher-priority task can interrupt the execution of a lower-priority task. The preemption capability ensures that tasks with more immediate deadlines are given the opportunity to execute as soon as they become eligible, preempting lower-priority tasks if necessary. This preemptive nature contributes to the determinism of the system, allowing the scheduler to enforce strict priority-based control over the execution of tasks, crucial in scenarios where predictability is paramount.

One of the key advantages of the RMS algorithm is its simplicity, both in terms of conceptual understanding and implementation. The priority assignment is solely based on the periodicity of tasks, making it straightforward to determine the relative priorities of tasks during the system design phase. The simplicity of RMS lends itself well to scenarios where a clear understanding of task periods and deadlines is achievable, allowing for effective utilization of the algorithm's benefits without the need for complex computations or dynamic adjustments during runtime.

The predictability offered by RMS is a central feature that has contributed to its enduring popularity. The deterministic nature of the algorithm enables system designers to analyze and guarantee the worst-case execution time (WCET) of tasks. Knowing the maximum time a task requires for execution is critical in real-time systems, especially in safety-critical applications where missing deadlines could have severe consequences. The predictability of RMS facilitates the development of systems that can be analytically validated to ensure compliance with stringent timing constraints.

Despite its simplicity and predictability, the RMS algorithm has inherent limitations that must be carefully considered in its application. The most notable limitation is the implicit assumption that tasks are independent and have no dependencies on each other. In scenarios where tasks share resources or have inter-task dependencies, the priority assignment based solely on periods may lead to suboptimal scheduling decisions. Priority inversion, a phenomenon where a low-priority task holds a resource required by a high-priority task, can occur, potentially impacting the overall performance and meeting time constraints.

The assumption of known and fixed task periods is another limitation of RMS. In dynamic environments where task periods may vary or are not precisely known in advance, the rigid nature of RMS may pose challenges. In such cases, adaptive scheduling algorithms or those that can dynamically adjust priorities based on runtime conditions may be more suitable. RMS is most effective when applied to systems where task periods are relatively stable and can be accurately determined during the design phase.

An important consideration in real-time systems is the schedulability analysis, which involves assessing whether a set of tasks can be scheduled to meet their deadlines. RMS offers a straightforward schedulability analysis that involves comparing the total utilization of the system to a specific threshold. The utilization factor, calculated as the sum of the task computation times divided by their respective periods, provides a threshold beyond which the system becomes unschedulable. If the total utilization is below this threshold, RMS ensures that all tasks meet their deadlines. This analysis simplifies the evaluation of system feasibility and aids in determining whether additional tasks can be added without violating timing constraints.

The RMS algorithm finds application in a range of real-time systems, including aerospace, automotive, industrial control, and medical devices. In avionics, for example, where tasks related to flight control, navigation, and communication must adhere to strict timing requirements, RMS provides a deterministic scheduling approach. In automotive control systems, RMS is employed to ensure that tasks associated with engine control, braking systems, and safety-critical functions execute predictably. Similarly, in medical devices, where tasks involve precise control of drug infusion or monitoring vital signs, RMS aids in meeting critical timing constraints.

In conclusion, the Rate Monotonic Scheduling (RMS) algorithm stands as a foundational and widely adopted scheduling technique in real-time systems. Its principles of priority assignment based on task periods, simplicity, and deterministic nature make it an attractive choice for applications where meeting deadlines is of utmost importance. While the algorithm excels in scenarios characterized by known and fixed task periods, its limitations, such as the assumption of task independence and lack of adaptability to dynamic environments, should be carefully considered. As real-time systems continue to evolve, the enduring relevance of RMS lies in its ability to provide predictability and analytically guarantee the schedulability of tasks, contributing to the reliable and timely operation of systems across various domains.

Discussing how RMS assigns priorities based on task execution rates.

The Rate Monotonic Scheduling (RMS) algorithm, a fundamental approach in real-time systems, assigns priorities to tasks based on their execution rates, specifically their task periods. At the heart of RMS lies the principle that tasks with shorter periods are assigned higher priorities, creating a direct correlation between the rate of execution and the priority level. This priority assignment scheme is rooted in the understanding that tasks requiring more frequent execution demand more immediate attention to ensure timely completion. The inverse relationship between priority and period is a distinctive feature of RMS, reflecting a design philosophy that aligns with the criticality of meeting deadlines in applications where timing constraints are paramount.

The concept of task periods is foundational to how RMS assigns priorities. Task periods represent the time between successive instances of task activation or execution. In the RMS algorithm, each task is associated with a fixed and known period, signifying the regularity with which the task must be executed. The algorithm relies on the assumption that these periods are predetermined during the system design phase, allowing for a static and deterministic priority assignment. The periodic nature of tasks aligns well with real-time applications, such as control systems or communication protocols, where tasks must execute at regular intervals to maintain system stability and responsiveness.

The priority assignment process in RMS follows a clear and straightforward logic: the shorter the period, the higher the priority. This direct relationship is established to ensure that tasks with shorter periods, indicating a higher rate of execution, are given precedence in the scheduling queue. The priority assignment is based on the principle that tasks with more immediate deadlines must be scheduled with higher priority to meet stringent timing requirements. As a consequence, the RMS algorithm assumes a preemptive scheduling policy, allowing higher-priority tasks to interrupt the execution of lower-priority tasks, a feature essential for meeting real-time constraints.

The simplicity of the priority assignment in RMS contributes to its ease of implementation and conceptual understanding. System designers can readily determine the relative priorities of tasks during the system design phase by examining their periods. Tasks with shorter periods are granted higher priorities, and those with longer periods receive lower priorities. This straightforward relationship facilitates the analytical assessment of system behavior, making it easier for designers to predict how the system will respond to different task configurations. The simplicity of RMS is particularly advantageous in scenarios where a clear understanding of task periods is attainable without the need for complex computations or dynamic adjustments during runtime.

The deterministic nature of the RMS algorithm is a key factor in its enduring popularity. The priority assignment based on task periods enables system designers to analyze and guarantee the worst-case execution time (WCET) of tasks. Knowing the maximum time a task requires for execution is crucial in real-time systems, especially in safety-critical applications where missing deadlines could lead to severe consequences. The deterministic nature of RMS facilitates the development of systems that can be analytically validated to ensure compliance with stringent timing constraints. The predictability offered by RMS is invaluable in applications where the consequences of task execution delays can have significant real-world implications.

However, the simplicity and predictability of RMS come with certain assumptions and limitations that must be carefully considered in its application. One notable limitation is the implicit assumption that tasks are independent and have no dependencies on each other. In scenarios where tasks share resources or have inter-task dependencies, the priority assignment based solely on periods may lead to suboptimal scheduling decisions. Priority inversion, a phenomenon where a low-priority task holds a resource required by a high-priority task, can occur, potentially impacting the overall performance and the ability to meet time constraints.

Another critical consideration is the assumption of known and fixed task periods. In dynamic environments where task periods may vary or are not precisely known in advance, the rigid nature of RMS may pose challenges. The algorithm is most effective when applied to systems where task periods are relatively stable and can be accurately determined during the design phase. In situations where task periods are subject to change or variability, adaptive scheduling algorithms or those that can dynamically adjust priorities based on runtime conditions may be more suitable.

The schedulability analysis is a significant aspect of the RMS algorithm, involving the assessment of whether a set of tasks can be scheduled to meet their deadlines. The algorithm provides a straightforward analysis based on the utilization factor, which is calculated as the sum of the task computation times divided by their respective periods. This utilization factor serves as a threshold beyond which the system becomes unschedulable. If the total utilization is below this threshold, RMS ensures that all tasks meet their deadlines. This analysis simplifies the evaluation of system feasibility and aids in determining whether additional tasks can be added without violating timing constraints.

The application of the RMS algorithm extends across various real-time systems, including aerospace, automotive, industrial control, and medical devices. In avionics, for example, where tasks related to flight control, navigation, and communication must adhere to strict timing requirements, RMS provides a deterministic scheduling approach. The algorithm ensures that tasks with more immediate deadlines, such as those critical for flight safety, are given priority to meet stringent timing constraints. In automotive control systems, RMS is employed to schedule tasks associated with engine control, braking systems, and other safety-critical functions to ensure predictable execution.

In conclusion, the RMS algorithm's priority assignment based on task execution rates, specifically their periods, is a fundamental principle in real-time systems. The inverse relationship between priority and period aligns with the philosophy that tasks requiring more frequent execution should be assigned higher priorities to meet stringent timing requirements. The algorithm's simplicity and deterministic nature contribute to its enduring popularity, making it well-suited for applications where meeting deadlines is critical. While the assumptions of task independence and known, fixed periods should be considered, the RMS algorithm continues to be a foundational scheduling technique, offering predictability and analytically guaranteeing the schedulability of tasks in diverse real-time applications.

Exploring the EDF algorithm and its focus on meeting deadlines.

The Earliest Deadline First (EDF) algorithm represents a pivotal scheduling approach in the realm of real-time systems, placing a paramount focus on meeting deadlines. Unlike the Rate Monotonic Scheduling (RMS) algorithm, which prioritizes tasks based on their execution rates, EDF prioritizes tasks according to their imminent deadlines. This key distinction makes EDF particularly well-suited for scenarios where tasks have varying execution times and dynamic requirements, allowing it to adapt to changing workloads. At the heart of EDF lies the principle that the task with the earliest deadline is given the highest priority in the scheduling queue, ensuring that the most time-critical tasks are executed first. This emphasis on deadlines aligns with the critical nature of real-time systems, where timely task completion is essential for maintaining system reliability and responsiveness.

The fundamental principle of the EDF algorithm revolves around dynamic priority assignment based on task deadlines. In

EDF, each task is assigned a priority inversely proportional to its remaining time until the deadline. The task with the earliest deadline, meaning the one that must be completed soonest, is granted the highest priority. This dynamic priority assignment ensures that tasks with more immediate deadlines receive precedence in the scheduling queue, allowing them to be scheduled for execution ahead of tasks with later deadlines. As a result, EDF exhibits an inherent adaptability to the varying execution times and requirements of tasks, making it suitable for environments with dynamic workloads.

The concept of task deadlines in EDF is central to its operational logic. Each task is associated with a fixed deadline, representing the point in time by which the task must be completed to meet its timing requirements. The dynamic nature of EDF lies in continuously assessing the remaining time until each task's deadline during runtime. The task with the earliest remaining time is granted the highest priority, ensuring that it is scheduled for execution ahead of tasks with later deadlines. This emphasis on deadlines is particularly advantageous in real-time systems, where missing deadlines can lead to system failures or degraded performance, especially in safety-critical applications.

The adaptability of EDF to varying task execution times is a notable strength. Unlike RMS, which assumes known and fixed task periods, EDF accommodates tasks with variable execution times and dynamic requirements. This adaptability makes EDF well-suited for environments where task characteristics may change during runtime or where accurate predictions of task execution times are challenging. In scenarios with a mix of short and long-running tasks, EDF excels by ensuring that tasks with imminent deadlines receive priority, regardless of their execution times, contributing to the system's flexibility and responsiveness.

The preemptive nature of EDF is another key aspect of its operational model. Preemption in EDF allows a higher-priority task to interrupt the execution of a lower-priority task if the higher-priority task has a more imminent deadline. This preemption capability ensures that tasks with more immediate timing requirements are given the opportunity to execute as soon as they become eligible, preempting lower-priority tasks if necessary. Preemption is a critical feature in real-time systems, where the ability to promptly respond to changing conditions and meet imminent deadlines is essential for maintaining system reliability.

The simplicity of EDF lies in its intuitive priority assignment based on deadlines. The algorithm's operational logic is transparent and easy to understand: the task with the earliest deadline receives the highest priority. This simplicity contributes to the ease of implementation and analysis, allowing system designers to readily comprehend how the scheduling decisions are made. The straightforward nature of EDF facilitates the design and validation of systems with predictable behavior, a valuable characteristic in safety-critical applications where the ability to meet deadlines is of paramount importance.

The schedulability analysis in EDF involves assessing whether a set of tasks can be scheduled to meet their deadlines. Unlike the utilization-based analysis of RMS, EDF relies on the concept of the "density" of tasks, calculated as the ratio of the task's computation time to its relative deadline. The density serves as a criterion for determining the feasibility of scheduling tasks without violating deadlines. If the sum of task densities is less than or equal to one, the set of tasks is deemed schedulable. This analysis aligns with EDF's focus on meeting deadlines and provides a means of evaluating system feasibility based on the inherent timing requirements of tasks.

While the EDF algorithm offers adaptability and a focus on meeting deadlines, it is not without its limitations. The primary challenge arises from the potential for task starvation, where a low-priority task may never get scheduled if higher-priority tasks with more imminent deadlines continuously arrive. This phenomenon, known as the "starvation problem," can impact the fairness of task execution, especially in scenarios with a constant stream of higher-priority tasks. Mitigating task starvation in EDF requires additional mechanisms, such as task aging or priority boosting, to ensure that lower-priority tasks eventually get scheduled.

Another consideration in EDF is the need for accurate and predictable estimates of task execution times and deadlines. The success of EDF relies on the ability to accurately assess the remaining time until each task's deadline during runtime. In scenarios where task execution times are difficult to predict or where variations in execution times are substantial, the effectiveness of EDF may be compromised. This consideration is crucial in applications where precise timing is essential, such as control systems or communication protocols, where inaccurate estimations can lead to missed deadlines and potential system failures.

The application of the EDF algorithm spans a range of real-time systems, including aerospace, automotive, multimedia processing, and industrial automation. In avionics, for instance, where tasks related to flight control, navigation, and communication require timely execution, EDF provides a scheduling approach that focuses on meeting the deadlines associated with critical tasks. In automotive control systems, EDF is employed to ensure the timely execution of tasks associated with engine control, braking systems, and other safety-critical functions, contributing to the overall reliability of the system.

In conclusion, the Earliest Deadline First (EDF) algorithm represents a significant scheduling approach with a central focus on meeting deadlines in real-time systems. The dynamic priority assignment based on the remaining time until task deadlines distinguishes EDF from other scheduling algorithms, providing adaptability to varying task execution times and requirements. The emphasis on deadlines aligns with the critical nature of real-time systems, where timely task completion is essential for maintaining system reliability and responsiveness. While EDF offers advantages in adaptability and simplicity, considerations such as the potential for task starvation and the need for accurate estimations of task execution times must be carefully addressed in its application. Despite these challenges, EDF continues to be a valuable scheduling technique in various domains, contributing to the development of reliable and responsive real-time systems.

Discussing how EDF dynamically adjusts priorities based on imminent deadlines.

The Earliest Deadline First (EDF) algorithm is a cornerstone in the field of real-time systems, renowned for its dynamic priority assignment based on imminent deadlines. This distinctive feature sets EDF apart from other scheduling algorithms and makes it particularly well-suited for environments where tasks have varying execution times and dynamic requirements. At the core of EDF lies a dynamic priority assignment mechanism that ensures the task with the earliest deadline is given the highest priority in the scheduling queue, fostering a focus on meeting deadlines and responding promptly to the timing requirements of tasks. This dynamic nature is instrumental in addressing the challenges posed by real-time applications, where the ability to adapt to changing workloads and prioritize tasks based on their urgency is crucial for maintaining system reliability and responsiveness.

The central principle governing EDF is the dynamic priority assignment that is inversely proportional to the remaining time until a task's deadline. Unlike traditional scheduling algorithms, such as Rate Monotonic Scheduling (RMS), which prioritize tasks based on their execution rates, EDF eschews a fixed priority scheme. Instead, it continuously assesses the urgency of each task by considering the time remaining until its deadline. The algorithm operates on the fundamental premise that the task with the earliest deadline deserves the highest priority. This dynamic priority assignment allows EDF to make scheduling decisions that align with the criticality of meeting imminent deadlines in a variety of real-time applications.

To delve into the operational dynamics of EDF, it's essential to understand the significance of task deadlines and how they drive the priority assignment. Each task in an EDF system is associated with a fixed deadline, representing the point in time by which the task must complete its execution to meet the specified timing requirements. The task's deadline is a critical parameter that guides the scheduling decisions made by EDF. The algorithm continuously evaluates the remaining time until each task's deadline during runtime, ensuring that it can adapt to changing conditions and prioritize tasks accordingly.

The dynamic priority assignment mechanism in EDF fosters adaptability to varying task execution times, making it particularly well-suited for scenarios where task characteristics may change during runtime. Unlike algorithms that assume known and fixed task periods, EDF accommodates tasks with variable execution times and varying timing requirements. This adaptability is crucial in applications where the predictability of task execution times is challenging, and the system must respond flexibly to dynamic workloads. By focusing on deadlines and dynamically adjusting priorities, EDF enhances the system's ability to respond promptly to the timing requirements of tasks, contributing to its versatility in real-world applications.

Preemption is a fundamental aspect of EDF that complements its dynamic priority assignment mechanism. Preemption allows a higher-priority task to interrupt the execution of a lower-priority task if the higher-priority task has a more imminent deadline. This preemption capability ensures that tasks with more immediate timing requirements are given the opportunity to execute as soon as they become eligible, preempting lower-priority tasks if necessary. The preemptive nature of EDF is crucial in real-time systems, where the ability to promptly respond to changing conditions and meet imminent deadlines is essential for maintaining system reliability.

The simplicity of EDF lies in its operational logic, which revolves around the intuitive concept of scheduling tasks based on their earliest deadlines. Unlike algorithms with complex priority schemes or fixed priority assignments, EDF's dynamic approach is transparent and easy to understand. The task with the earliest deadline is granted the highest priority, reflecting a clear and straightforward decision-making process. This simplicity not only aids in the ease of implementation but also facilitates the design and validation of systems with predictable behavior, a valuable characteristic in safety-critical applications where the ability to meet deadlines is of paramount importance.

Despite its advantages, EDF is not without challenges, and a notable consideration is the potential for task starvation. Task starvation occurs when a low-priority task may never get scheduled if higher-priority tasks with more imminent deadlines continuously arrive. This phenomenon, known as the "starvation problem," can impact the fairness of task execution, especially in scenarios with a constant stream of higher-priority tasks. To address this issue, additional mechanisms, such as task aging or priority boosting, may be employed to ensure that lower-priority tasks eventually get scheduled. The mitigation of task starvation is an ongoing area of research and development in real-time systems using EDF.

Another consideration in the application of EDF is the need for accurate and predictable estimates of task execution times and deadlines. The success of EDF relies on the ability to accurately assess the remaining time until each task's deadline during runtime. In scenarios where task execution times are difficult to predict or where variations in execution times are substantial, the effectiveness of EDF may be compromised. This consideration is crucial in applications where precise timing is essential, such as control systems or communication protocols, where inaccurate estimations can lead to missed deadlines and potential system failures. Balancing the benefits of adaptability with the challenges of accurate estimations is a delicate trade-off in the application of EDF.

The schedulability analysis in EDF involves assessing whether a set of tasks can be scheduled to meet their deadlines. EDF relies on the concept of the "density" of tasks, calculated as the ratio of the task's computation time to its relative deadline. The density serves as a criterion for determining the feasibility of scheduling tasks without violating deadlines. If the sum of task densities is less than or equal to one, the set of tasks is deemed schedulable. This analysis aligns with EDF's focus on meeting deadlines and provides a means of evaluating system feasibility based on the inherent timing requirements of tasks. The density-based analysis is particularly well-suited for dynamic environments where task periods may vary, and accurate predictions of task execution times are challenging.

The application of the EDF algorithm spans a diverse range of real-time systems, including aerospace, automotive, multimedia processing, and industrial automation. In avionics, for instance, where tasks related to flight control, navigation, and communication require timely execution, EDF provides a scheduling approach that focuses on meeting the deadlines associated with critical tasks. The adaptability of EDF to varying task execution times makes it well-suited for multimedia processing applications, where tasks may have dynamic requirements and variable execution times. In industrial automation, EDF's emphasis on meeting deadlines is crucial for controlling and coordinating tasks in real-time, contributing to the efficiency and reliability of automated systems.

In conclusion, the Earliest Deadline First (EDF) algorithm stands as a key scheduling approach that dynamically adjusts priorities based on imminent deadlines in real-time systems. The algorithm's distinctive feature of prioritizing tasks according to their remaining time until deadlines makes it adaptable to varying execution times and well-suited for dynamic environments. The focus on deadlines aligns with the critical nature of real-time systems, where timely task completion is essential for maintaining system reliability and responsiveness. While EDF offers advantages in adaptability and simplicity, challenges such as the potential for task starvation and the need for accurate estimations of task execution times must be carefully addressed in its application. Nonetheless, EDF remains a valuable scheduling technique, contributing to the development of reliable and responsive real-time systems across various domains.

Introducing Deadline Monotonic Scheduling as an extension of RMS.

Deadline Monotonic Scheduling (DMS) emerges as a noteworthy extension of the Rate Monotonic Scheduling (RMS) algorithm, introducing a refined approach to real-time task scheduling. Rooted in the principles of priority assignment, DMS builds upon the foundation laid by RMS, further emphasizing the importance of meeting deadlines in time-sensitive applications. This discussion delves into the intricacies of Deadline Monotonic Scheduling, exploring its conceptual framework, operational principles, advantages, and potential applications.

At its core, DMS shares the fundamental concept of priority assignment with RMS, prioritizing tasks based on their periods. However, DMS takes a step beyond RMS by incorporating the specific deadline information of tasks into the priority assignment mechanism. This extension refines the scheduling decisions, enabling the system to not only consider the frequency of task execution (as in RMS) but also the urgency implied by the task deadlines. The result is a scheduling algorithm that inherently values tasks with tighter timing constraints, aligning more closely with the critical nature of real-time systems.

The basic tenet of DMS is that tasks with shorter deadlines are assigned higher priorities. Unlike RMS, where priority is solely determined by the inverse of task periods, DMS introduces a prioritization mechanism that accounts for both the period and deadline of each task. This nuanced approach recognizes that in certain scenarios, tasks with shorter periods may have less stringent timing requirements, while tasks with longer periods and tighter deadlines demand immediate attention. By incorporating deadline information into the priority assignment, DMS strives to enhance the system's ability to meet critical timing constraints.

The integration of deadline information in DMS requires each task to be associated not only with a fixed period but also with a specific deadline. The deadline signifies the latest permissible time for a task to complete its execution. The period, on the other hand, represents the interval between successive instances of task activation. This dual consideration of period and deadline allows DMS to make priority assignments that reflect the urgency of task execution. The algorithm aims to strike a balance between the regularity of task execution (as in RMS) and the immediacy implied by the task deadlines.

The priority assignment process in DMS is characterized by a dynamic interplay between task periods and deadlines. Tasks with shorter periods receive higher priority, consistent with RMS principles. However, when comparing tasks with equal periods, DMS employs a secondary criterion based on deadlines. Tasks with earlier deadlines are granted higher priority, emphasizing the importance of timely task completion. This dual-criteria priority assignment ensures that the algorithm not only considers the rate of task execution but also factors in the urgency implied by task deadlines when making scheduling decisions.

The preemptive nature of DMS, akin to RMS, allows higher-priority tasks to preempt the execution of lower-priority tasks. Preemption is a critical feature in real-time systems, enabling the scheduler to promptly respond to tasks with imminent deadlines. In scenarios where a higher-priority task becomes eligible for execution, it can interrupt the execution of a lower-priority task, ensuring that urgent tasks are given the opportunity to execute as soon as they become available. This preemptive capability aligns with the dynamic and responsive nature required in time-sensitive applications.

The simplicity of DMS lies in its adherence to the basic principles of RMS while introducing a nuanced extension with the consideration of task deadlines. The priority assignment process remains transparent and conceptually clear, making it comprehensible for system designers and developers. By building upon the well-established foundation of RMS, DMS inherits the simplicity and predictability that are advantageous in the design and validation of real-time systems. This simplicity facilitates ease of implementation while providing an additional layer of sophistication to prioritize tasks based on both periods and deadlines.

One of the significant advantages of DMS is its enhanced ability to handle tasks with varying timing requirements. In scenarios where tasks have different periods and deadlines, DMS offers a refined priority assignment mechanism that better captures the criticality of task deadlines. Tasks with shorter periods are naturally prioritized, ensuring efficient utilization of resources. Moreover, when faced with tasks of equal periods, the consideration of deadlines allows DMS to distinguish between tasks with varying levels of urgency. This adaptability positions DMS as a valuable extension of RMS in environments where tasks exhibit diverse timing characteristics.

Schedulability analysis in DMS involves assessing whether a set of tasks can be scheduled to meet their deadlines. The analysis accounts for the specific periods and deadlines of tasks, considering both the regularity of task execution and the urgency implied by deadlines. The assessment involves evaluating the utilization of the system's resources in relation to the total computational demands imposed by the tasks. If the system's utilization remains within acceptable limits, considering both periods and deadlines, DMS ensures that all tasks meet their deadlines, making it a valuable tool for real-time systems where timing constraints are paramount.

While DMS introduces enhancements to priority assignment based on task deadlines, it is not without challenges. The dual-criteria prioritization may increase the complexity of the algorithm compared to its predecessor, RMS. The consideration of deadlines introduces additional parameters that must be managed and analyzed during system design. Accurately estimating and predicting task deadlines becomes crucial for effective scheduling decisions. Moreover, the potential for task starvation, a challenge prevalent in other dynamic priority scheduling algorithms, remains an aspect that necessitates attention and careful consideration in the application of DMS.

The application of DMS spans various domains where meeting deadlines is critical, such as avionics, automotive systems, industrial automation, and medical devices. In avionics, where tasks related to navigation, communication, and flight control must adhere to stringent timing requirements, DMS offers an extension of RMS that better aligns with the urgency implied by task deadlines. In automotive systems, particularly in safety-critical functions such as collision avoidance and engine control, DMS can provide a refined scheduling approach that considers both task periods and deadlines. The adaptability of DMS makes it applicable in diverse real-time systems where tasks exhibit varying timing characteristics.

In conclusion, Deadline Monotonic Scheduling (DMS) emerges as a noteworthy extension of the Rate Monotonic Scheduling (RMS) algorithm, introducing a nuanced approach to real-time task scheduling. By incorporating deadline information into the priority assignment process, DMS refines the decision-making mechanism, emphasizing the importance of meeting deadlines in time-sensitive applications. The dual consideration of task periods and deadlines offers a balanced approach that retains the simplicity of RMS while enhancing the algorithm's adaptability to tasks with varying timing requirements. Despite its challenges, DMS represents a valuable tool in the arsenal of scheduling algorithms, contributing to the development of reliable and responsive real-time systems across diverse domains.

Discussing its benefits in scenarios where deadlines are critical.

Deadline Monotonic Scheduling (DMS) unfolds as a beneficial scheduling strategy, particularly in scenarios where meeting deadlines is of paramount importance. The merits of DMS become pronounced in critical real-time systems where timely task completion is not just a preference but an absolute necessity. By building upon the foundation of the Rate Monotonic Scheduling (RMS) algorithm and introducing a nuanced consideration of task deadlines, DMS addresses the inherent challenges posed by tasks with diverse timing requirements. In this discussion, we delve into the distinctive advantages that DMS brings to the fore in environments where deadlines are critical, examining how its prioritization mechanism and adaptability contribute to the reliability and responsiveness of real-time systems.

A fundamental benefit of DMS lies in its enhanced ability to handle tasks with varying timing requirements. In scenarios where tasks exhibit diverse periods and deadlines, DMS distinguishes itself by providing a refined priority assignment mechanism. By considering both the regularity of task execution, as in RMS, and the urgency implied by task deadlines, DMS ensures that the scheduler makes informed decisions. Tasks with shorter periods are prioritized, aligning with RMS principles. However, when faced with tasks of equal periods, the consideration of deadlines becomes pivotal. This nuanced approach allows DMS to prioritize tasks based on their immediacy, ensuring that those with tighter timing constraints receive the attention they require. Consequently, the adaptability of DMS positions it as an invaluable tool in environments where tasks exhibit varying timing characteristics.

The dynamic priority assignment mechanism in DMS is a key element contributing to its effectiveness in scenarios where deadlines are critical. Unlike static priority algorithms, DMS continuously assesses the urgency of each task based on both its period and deadline. The dynamic nature of this prioritization ensures that the scheduling decisions are responsive to changing conditions during runtime. Tasks with more imminent deadlines are granted higher priority, allowing them to be scheduled ahead of tasks with longer deadlines, even if they share similar periods. This dynamic prioritization aligns with the real-world dynamics of critical systems, enabling the scheduler to promptly respond to tasks with urgent timing constraints.

The preemptive nature of DMS further amplifies its benefits in scenarios where deadlines are critical. Preemption allows higher-priority tasks to interrupt the execution of lower-priority tasks, providing a means for urgent tasks to be expedited. In critical real-time systems, where the consequences of missing deadlines can be severe, preemption becomes a crucial feature. The ability of DMS to preempt lower-priority tasks when higher-priority tasks with more imminent deadlines become eligible ensures that the system can respond promptly to the urgency implied by task requirements. This preemptive capability aligns with the dynamic nature of real-time systems and is a cornerstone for maintaining reliability and meeting stringent timing constraints.

The incorporation of deadline information into the priority assignment process enhances the predictability and reliability of DMS in scenarios where deadlines are critical. While RMS relies solely on task periods for priority assignment, DMS introduces a nuanced extension by considering both periods and deadlines. This refinement allows the algorithm to capture the criticality of tasks with tighter timing constraints. Tasks with earlier deadlines are given precedence, reflecting the real-world urgency associated with completing these tasks within specific timeframes. The consideration of deadlines adds a layer of sophistication to the priority assignment process, ensuring that the scheduler makes decisions that align with the importance of timely task completion.

Schedulability analysis in DMS provides a robust means of assessing whether a set of tasks can be scheduled to meet their deadlines. The analysis considers both task periods and deadlines, evaluating the system's utilization in relation to the total computational demands imposed by the tasks. This dual-criteria analysis aligns with the focus of DMS on meeting deadlines and provides a comprehensive assessment of the system's ability to handle critical timing requirements. The analysis aids system designers and developers in ensuring that the real-time system can reliably meet its timing constraints, a crucial aspect in applications where deadlines are critical for system performance and safety.

In scenarios where task characteristics may change during runtime or where accurate predictions of task execution times are challenging, the adaptability of DMS becomes a central advantage. Unlike algorithms that assume known and fixed task periods, DMS accommodates tasks with variable execution times and varying timing requirements. This adaptability is crucial in real-world applications where the predictability of task execution times is challenging, and the system must respond flexibly to dynamic workloads. By dynamically adjusting priorities based on both periods and deadlines, DMS ensures that the scheduling decisions align with the immediate urgency of tasks, contributing to the system's versatility and responsiveness in scenarios where deadlines are critical.

The simplicity of DMS, inherited from its predecessor RMS, remains an advantageous trait in scenarios where deadlines are critical. The priority assignment process in DMS, though nuanced by the consideration of deadlines, retains a clear and transparent logic. Tasks with shorter periods are prioritized, and in cases of equal periods, those with earlier deadlines receive higher priority. This simplicity not only facilitates ease of implementation but also aids in the understanding and validation of real-time systems. In scenarios where meeting deadlines is critical, the straightforward nature of DMS ensures that system designers can readily comprehend and analyze the scheduling decisions, contributing to the reliability and predictability of the system.

Despite its advantages, DMS is not without challenges, and a notable consideration is the potential for task starvation. Task starvation occurs when a low-priority task may never get scheduled if higher-priority tasks with more imminent deadlines continuously arrive. This phenomenon, known as the "starvation problem," can impact the fairness of task execution, especially in scenarios with a constant stream of higher-priority tasks. Addressing and mitigating task starvation remains an ongoing area of research and development in real-time systems using dynamic priority scheduling algorithms like DMS.

In conclusion, Deadline Monotonic Scheduling (DMS) emerges as a beneficial scheduling strategy in scenarios where deadlines are critical. Its refined priority assignment mechanism, dynamic prioritization based on both task periods and deadlines, and preemptive nature contribute to its effectiveness in addressing the challenges posed by tasks with diverse timing requirements. The adaptability of DMS to changing workloads and its ability to meet stringent timing constraints make it a valuable tool in critical real-time systems. The incorporation of deadline information adds a layer of sophistication to the prioritization process, ensuring that the algorithm makes decisions that align with the urgency of task requirements. While challenges such as the potential for task starvation exist, the benefits of DMS in enhancing reliability, responsiveness, and predictability make it a valuable extension of scheduling algorithms in scenarios where meeting deadlines is not just a preference but a critical imperative.

Discussing practical challenges in implementing scheduling algorithms.

Implementing scheduling algorithms poses a myriad of practical challenges that require careful consideration and adept solutions. One of the foremost challenges lies in the need for accurate task execution time estimations. Scheduling algorithms rely heavily on predictions of how long each task will take to execute. In practice, accurately estimating execution times is inherently difficult due to factors such as varying workloads, hardware idiosyncrasies, and the influence of external processes. The dynamic nature of real-time systems further complicates this challenge, as execution times may change during runtime. Consequently, developing robust mechanisms for precise execution time estimation becomes crucial to the effective implementation of scheduling algorithms.

The complexities of resource management present another practical challenge in scheduling algorithm implementation. Real-time systems often involve multiple tasks competing for shared resources, such as CPU time, memory, or communication bandwidth. Balancing these resources to ensure fair and efficient utilization is a delicate task. Contentious scenarios may arise where one task monopolizes resources, leading to potential bottlenecks and performance degradation for other tasks. Striking the right balance and preventing resource contention necessitate sophisticated algorithms and careful design considerations to ensure optimal resource utilization while adhering to the system's timing constraints.

The adaptability of scheduling algorithms to dynamic workloads and changing system conditions introduces a practical challenge in implementation. In real-world scenarios, task characteristics may evolve, and unforeseen events can influence system behavior. Static scheduling algorithms that assume fixed task parameters may struggle to cope with dynamic environments. Dynamic priority scheduling algorithms, while offering adaptability, introduce their own set of challenges, such as the potential for task starvation or excessive pre-emption. Implementing algorithms that strike the right balance between adaptability and predictability becomes crucial to maintaining system stability and responsiveness.

Ensuring fairness and preventing task starvation presents a notable challenge, especially in preemptive scheduling algorithms. Pre-emption allows higher-priority tasks to interrupt the execution of lower-priority ones, ensuring timely processing of critical tasks. However, this mechanism raises concerns about fairness, as lower-priority tasks may be continuously preempted, leading to potential starvation. Addressing this challenge requires implementing mechanisms like priority aging or priority boosting to prevent lower-priority tasks from being indefinitely delayed. Achieving fairness while maintaining the responsiveness of high-priority tasks is a delicate balance that scheduling algorithm implementations must strike.

Synchronization and coordination between tasks present intricate challenges in the implementation of scheduling algorithms. Real-time systems often involve tasks that depend on shared resources or require coordination to achieve their objectives. Coordinating tasks to avoid conflicts and ensuring proper synchronization is a non-trivial task, especially in environments with strict timing constraints. Implementing synchronization mechanisms that prevent race conditions, deadlocks, or priority inversion requires a deep understanding of both the scheduling algorithm and the characteristics of the tasks involved.

Interrupt handling and real-time response add another layer of complexity to scheduling algorithm implementation. Real-time systems must promptly respond to external events, often signaled through interrupts. Efficiently handling interrupts while ensuring timely task execution poses a challenge, as the interrupt service routine (ISR) may preempt the currently running task. Coordinating between the ISR and the main scheduling algorithm to minimize response time introduces complexities that require careful design and thorough testing to ensure the system's real-time responsiveness.

The integration of power management into scheduling algorithms introduces challenges related to energy efficiency. Modern embedded systems often prioritize energy conservation alongside meeting timing constraints. Scheduling algorithms that can dynamically adjust system power states to balance performance and energy consumption require sophisticated implementation. Efficiently transitioning between power states without compromising task deadlines or causing excessive overhead becomes crucial. Balancing the conflicting goals of meeting timing constraints and optimizing energy efficiency adds a layer of complexity to scheduling algorithm implementations in power-constrained environments.

The heterogeneity of hardware platforms and their varying capabilities presents challenges in achieving portability and scalability in scheduling algorithm implementations. Real-time systems may run on diverse hardware architectures with differing computational capabilities, memory hierarchies, and communication architectures. Designing scheduling algorithms that can adapt to this heterogeneity and provide consistent performance across different platforms requires a careful consideration of hardware-specific optimizations and a modular design approach. Achieving portability becomes crucial for the widespread adoption of scheduling algorithms in various real-time applications.

Error handling and fault tolerance introduce additional challenges in the implementation of scheduling algorithms. Real-time systems, especially those deployed in safety-critical domains, must be resilient to faults and errors. Implementing mechanisms for error detection, recovery, and fault tolerance in conjunction with scheduling algorithms requires a comprehensive understanding of the system's criticality. Balancing the need for responsiveness with robust error handling mechanisms is a challenge that necessitates careful consideration during the design and implementation stages.

The validation and verification of scheduling algorithm implementations pose significant challenges. Real-time systems often operate in safety-critical environments, where the consequences of scheduling errors can be severe. Ensuring the correctness of scheduling algorithms under various scenarios and stress conditions requires rigorous testing and validation processes. Developing effective test cases, simulation environments, and formal verification methods is essential to guarantee the reliability and safety of real-time systems employing scheduling algorithms.

The impact of caching and memory hierarchy on scheduling decisions introduces challenges in optimizing performance. Caching effects, memory access times, and cache coherence considerations can influence the execution time of tasks and introduce non-deterministic behavior. Scheduling algorithms must account for these factors to make informed decisions about task prioritization and resource allocation. Optimizing cache utilization while ensuring consistent and predictable task execution times requires a nuanced approach to scheduling algorithm implementation.

In conclusion, implementing scheduling algorithms in real-time systems involves navigating a complex landscape of challenges. Accurate task execution time estimation, resource management, adaptability to dynamic workloads, fairness considerations, synchronization challenges, interrupt handling complexities, power management integration, hardware heterogeneity, error handling and fault tolerance, validation and verification requirements, and considerations of caching and memory hierarchy all contribute to the intricacies of implementation. Successfully addressing these challenges demands a multidisciplinary approach, combining expertise in real-time systems, algorithm design, hardware architecture, and system validation. As real-time systems continue to evolve and find applications in diverse domains, the effective implementation of scheduling algorithms remains a critical aspect in ensuring the reliability, predictability, and responsiveness of these systems.

Analyzing the impact of task arrival patterns on scheduling efficiency.

The efficiency of scheduling algorithms in real-time systems is intricately tied to the patterns of task arrivals, a factor that significantly influences the overall system performance. The analysis of task arrival patterns is essential for understanding how scheduling decisions are made in response to dynamic workloads. In the realm of real-time systems, where tasks often have strict timing constraints, the arrival patterns of tasks play a pivotal role in determining the effectiveness of scheduling algorithms in meeting deadlines and optimizing resource utilization.

One fundamental aspect of task arrival patterns is periodicity. Many real-time systems involve tasks with recurring patterns, where tasks activate at regular intervals. Scheduling algorithms designed for periodic tasks, such as Rate Monotonic Scheduling (RMS), exploit this regularity to make informed decisions about task priorities. RMS, for instance, assigns priorities based on the inverse of task periods, assuming that shorter periods indicate more critical tasks. This assumption aligns with the inherent predictability of periodic task arrival patterns, allowing the scheduler to make proactive decisions that optimize the overall system performance.

However, the real-world scenario often includes a mix of periodic and aperiodic tasks, each with its own set of timing requirements. Aperiodic tasks do not adhere to fixed activation intervals, making their arrival patterns less predictable. The coexistence of periodic and aperiodic tasks introduces challenges in scheduling, as algorithms need to balance the predictability of periodic tasks with the unpredictability of aperiodic tasks. This balance becomes crucial for meeting deadlines and ensuring responsiveness in scenarios where both types of tasks are present.

The distribution of task arrivals over time is another factor influencing scheduling efficiency. Bursty arrival patterns, characterized by clusters of tasks arriving closely together, can strain the scheduling algorithm's ability to meet deadlines. In bursty scenarios, the system may experience peaks in resource demands, leading to potential contention and increased likelihood of task preemption. The challenge lies in adapting the scheduling decisions to accommodate these bursts, ensuring that critical tasks are prioritized during periods of high demand while maintaining fairness and efficiency.

Moreover, considering the stochastic nature of aperiodic task arrivals, probabilistic models become essential for understanding and predicting system behavior. These models take into account statistical properties of task arrivals, allowing for a more nuanced analysis of scheduling efficiency. Probabilistic models provide insights into the likelihood of specific arrival patterns and help in designing scheduling algorithms that are robust to variations in task execution times and unpredictable task arrivals.

The synchronization of task arrivals is another aspect that influences scheduling efficiency. In systems where tasks are interdependent or require coordination, synchronizing their activations becomes crucial for avoiding conflicts and ensuring efficient resource utilization. However, achieving synchronization is a non-trivial task, especially when dealing with a mix of periodic and aperiodic tasks with diverse timing requirements. Scheduling algorithms must be adept at handling dependencies and coordinating tasks to prevent contention and facilitate smooth execution.

In scenarios where tasks have dependencies or communication requirements, the order of task arrivals becomes significant. The timing of when tasks arrive can impact the feasibility of meeting their deadlines and the overall efficiency of the system. Algorithms that consider the order of arrivals and prioritize tasks accordingly enhance the system's ability to meet timing constraints. Task prioritization based on arrival times ensures that tasks with more imminent deadlines receive precedence, aligning scheduling decisions with the urgency implied by task requirements.

The influence of task arrival patterns extends to the preemptive nature of scheduling algorithms. Preemption allows higher-priority tasks to interrupt the execution of lower-priority ones, ensuring timely processing of critical tasks. Task arrival patterns directly affect the frequency and impact of preemptions. In scenarios with frequent task arrivals, the likelihood of preemptions increases, potentially leading to higher overhead and contention. Managing preemptions effectively is crucial for maintaining system responsiveness while avoiding excessive disruption to ongoing tasks.

The interaction between task arrival patterns and scheduling decisions becomes particularly pronounced in dynamic real-time systems, where the workload may change dynamically. The adaptability of scheduling algorithms to varying task arrival patterns is a critical aspect of their effectiveness. Algorithms that can dynamically adjust priorities, allocate resources efficiently, and make informed decisions in response to changing workloads enhance the system's ability to handle the inherent unpredictability of real-world environments.

Task arrival patterns also impact the overall predictability of scheduling algorithms. Predictability is a crucial characteristic in real-time systems, where tasks must complete their execution within specified deadlines. The predictability of scheduling decisions is influenced by the regularity and predictability of task arrivals. Algorithms designed for periodic tasks, such as Earliest Deadline First (EDF), leverage the predictability of task periods to make decisions that optimize the system's overall performance. In contrast, aperiodic task arrivals challenge the predictability of scheduling decisions, necessitating algorithms that can dynamically adapt to unpredictable scenarios.

In scenarios where the timing requirements of tasks are stringent, task arrival patterns directly affect the feasibility of meeting deadlines. The ability of scheduling algorithms to prioritize tasks based on their deadlines becomes crucial in environments where tasks have diverse timing constraints. Algorithms like Deadline Monotonic Scheduling (DMS), which consider both task periods and deadlines in their priority assignment, aim to address the challenges posed by a mix of periodic and aperiodic tasks with varying timing requirements. Task arrival patterns thus become a key factor in determining the effectiveness of priority-driven scheduling algorithms.

The impact of task arrival patterns on scheduling efficiency is further accentuated in systems with limited resources. In resource-constrained environments, effective scheduling becomes paramount for optimizing resource utilization and meeting timing constraints. Task arrival patterns influence the contention for resources, and algorithms must be designed to make judicious decisions that balance the demands of competing tasks. Resource-aware scheduling algorithms consider the availability and allocation of resources in conjunction with task arrival patterns to ensure optimal system performance.

The integration of power management into scheduling decisions adds another layer of complexity influenced by task arrival patterns. In scenarios where power efficiency is a critical concern, algorithms must adapt to task arrivals in a way that minimizes energy consumption while meeting timing constraints. Power-aware scheduling algorithms leverage information about task arrival patterns to dynamically adjust power states, transitioning between high and low power modes to balance performance and energy efficiency. Adapting to the dynamic nature of task arrivals is essential for achieving effective power management in real-time systems.

In conclusion, the impact of task arrival patterns on scheduling efficiency is a multifaceted aspect that profoundly influences the performance of real-time systems. The regularity of periodic tasks, the unpredictability of aperiodic task arrivals, bursty patterns, synchronization requirements, order of arrivals, and their interaction with scheduling decisions collectively shape the challenges and opportunities in designing efficient scheduling algorithms. The adaptability of algorithms to varying workloads, the ability to handle dependencies and communication requirements, and the consideration of power management requirements underscore the importance of understanding and addressing the nuances of task arrival patterns in the development of robust and efficient scheduling strategies. As real-time systems continue to evolve and find applications in diverse domains, the nuanced analysis of task arrival patterns remains a critical avenue for advancing the predictability, reliability, and responsiveness of these systems.

Chapter 5: Challenges and Solutions in Real-Time Systems

Identifying hardware constraints that pose challenges to real-time systems.

Hardware constraints pose substantial challenges to the design and implementation of real-time systems, where timely and predictable responses are paramount. These constraints, rooted in the underlying hardware architecture, significantly impact the system's ability to meet stringent timing requirements, handle dynamic workloads, and ensure reliability. One of the primary hardware constraints is the limited processing power of the central processing unit (CPU). Real-time systems often operate in resource-constrained environments, where the CPU may have finite computational capacity. This limitation becomes a critical factor when scheduling tasks, as the system must judiciously allocate CPU time to meet the timing constraints of tasks with varying priorities.

Memory constraints represent another formidable challenge in real-time systems. The limited availability of random access memory (RAM) imposes restrictions on the amount of data and code that can be stored and accessed during task execution. In scenarios where tasks have substantial memory requirements or when the system needs to handle large datasets, memory constraints can lead to contention and affect the predictability of task execution times. Efficient memory management and optimization techniques become imperative to mitigate the impact of memory limitations on the overall performance of real-time systems.

The communication infrastructure within the hardware architecture introduces additional challenges to real-time systems. In distributed real-time systems or systems with multiple processing units, inter-process communication and data exchange become critical. The latency and bandwidth of communication channels can significantly impact the timeliness of information exchange between tasks or nodes. Ensuring low-latency and high-bandwidth communication is essential for meeting the timing constraints of real-time tasks that rely on timely data sharing and synchronization.

The non-deterministic behavior of hardware components poses a fundamental challenge to real-time systems. Real-time applications require predictable and consistent timing behavior to ensure that tasks complete their execution within specified deadlines. However, inherent non-determinism in hardware, such as variations in CPU execution times, cache effects, and interrupt latencies, can introduce uncertainties in task execution times. Managing and mitigating these non-deterministic factors become critical to achieving the desired level of predictability in real-time systems.

Real-time systems often operate in environments where power consumption is a crucial consideration. Energy-efficient operation is particularly important in embedded systems, battery-powered devices, or applications where minimizing power usage is a key requirement. However, power constraints introduce challenges in balancing the trade-off between performance and energy efficiency. Scheduling decisions must consider not only the timing requirements of tasks but also the impact of those decisions on power consumption. Dynamic power management strategies become essential to adapt the system's power states based on workload characteristics and timing constraints.

The real-time nature of certain applications requires stringent control over the timing and order of hardware events. Hardware interrupt handling, for example, is critical in real-time systems where external events must be promptly and deterministically processed. However, the interrupt handling mechanism introduces challenges related to interrupt latencies and the potential disruption of ongoing tasks. Minimizing interrupt latencies and optimizing interrupt handling routines are crucial for ensuring timely responses to external events without compromising the predictability of task execution.

The limited availability of hardware resources, such as input/output (I/O) devices, can pose challenges to real-time systems. Tasks that rely on I/O operations, such as reading from sensors or writing to actuators, may face contention for access to shared hardware resources. Managing access to I/O devices in a way that ensures timely and predictable responses becomes crucial for real-time applications. The scheduling of tasks involving I/O operations must consider the potential impact on overall system performance and timing constraints.

The variability in clock accuracy and precision across hardware platforms introduces challenges to real-time systems that rely on accurate timing information. Clock drift, jitter, and synchronization issues can affect the consistency of timekeeping in distributed systems or systems with multiple clocks. Achieving synchronized and accurate timekeeping is essential for tasks that depend on precise timing information, such as coordinating events or enforcing temporal dependencies. Hardware constraints related to clock accuracy necessitate careful consideration and calibration to meet the timing requirements of real-time applications.

The limited bandwidth and reliability of communication channels between hardware components can introduce challenges in systems where tasks depend on timely exchange of data. In scenarios where tasks are distributed across multiple nodes or processors, ensuring efficient and reliable communication becomes crucial. Bandwidth limitations can lead to contention, resulting in delays in data transmission. Additionally, communication failures or packet loss can compromise the reliability of real-time systems. Implementing robust communication protocols and error-handling mechanisms is essential to address these challenges and ensure the timely and reliable exchange of information.

The design and implementation of real-time systems must contend with the challenges posed by hardware constraints on external storage devices. Accessing external storage introduces latency and variability in data retrieval times, impacting the predictability of task execution. In scenarios where tasks rely on external data storage, managing the timing of data access and optimizing storage access patterns become critical. Real-time systems must employ strategies to mitigate the impact of external storage constraints on overall system performance and ensure that tasks can meet their timing requirements.

Security considerations add an additional layer of complexity to real-time systems, particularly when they operate in environments where security is a primary concern. Hardware security features, such as encryption and secure boot mechanisms, can introduce overhead that affects the timing behavior of the system. Balancing the need for security with the timing constraints of real-time tasks becomes a delicate trade-off. Implementing security measures without compromising the real-time performance requires careful consideration of hardware constraints and the integration of security mechanisms that align with the specific requirements of the application.

The testing and validation of real-time systems in the presence of hardware constraints pose unique challenges. Hardware-specific behaviors, variations, and potential failures must be thoroughly explored during testing to ensure the reliability and predictability of the system. Real-time systems often operate in safety-critical domains, where the consequences of hardware failures can be severe. Rigorous testing methodologies, including stress testing, fault injection, and scenario-based testing, are essential to validate the robustness of real-time systems under varying hardware conditions.

In conclusion, hardware constraints present a myriad of challenges to the design and implementation of real-time systems. The limited processing power, memory constraints, communication infrastructure, non-deterministic behavior, power considerations, interrupt handling mechanisms, resource availability, clock accuracy, communication channel reliability, external storage access, security considerations, and testing challenges collectively shape the intricacies of developing real-time applications. Addressing these constraints requires a comprehensive understanding of both the hardware architecture and the specific requirements of the real-time application. Efforts to mitigate the impact of hardware constraints on timing predictability, resource utilization, and overall system reliability are essential for ensuring the success of real-time systems in diverse domains.

Discussing strategies to mitigate hardware-induced latencies.

Mitigating hardware-induced latencies is a critical aspect of designing and implementing real-time systems where timely responses are paramount. Hardware-induced latencies can arise from various sources, including CPU execution, memory access, communication channels, interrupts, and external devices. Strategies to address these latencies are multifaceted, encompassing both hardware and software approaches. One fundamental strategy is to optimize the CPU execution path. This involves minimizing the time taken by the CPU to execute instructions, which can be achieved through techniques such as compiler optimizations, code restructuring, and utilizing specialized instruction sets. Additionally, leveraging multi-core architectures can distribute processing loads efficiently, reducing contention and enhancing overall system performance.

Memory access latencies represent a significant contributor to overall system delays. Caches play a pivotal role in mitigating memory-induced latencies by providing faster access to frequently used data. Designing algorithms and data structures that maximize cache locality helps reduce the frequency of cache misses. Furthermore, utilizing memory hierarchy efficiently, including techniques like prefetching and optimizing data access patterns, contributes to minimizing memory-related latencies. In cases where predictable memory access times are crucial, deterministic memory allocators can be employed to manage memory allocation and deallocation with minimal variability.

Communication-induced latencies in distributed real-time systems can be addressed through various strategies. Optimizing communication protocols and employing low-latency network interfaces can help reduce the time required for data exchange between nodes. Moreover, leveraging techniques such as message batching and prioritized communication channels allows for efficient utilization of network resources. The use of Real-Time Ethernet or Fieldbus communication protocols in industrial automation, for instance, exemplifies strategies to minimize communication latencies in time-sensitive applications.

Interrupt handling mechanisms are intrinsic to real-time systems but can introduce latencies if not managed effectively. Minimizing interrupt latencies involves prioritizing and categorizing interrupts based on their urgency and impact. Utilizing interrupt nesting, where higher-priority interrupts preempt lower-priority ones, ensures that critical tasks receive immediate attention. Additionally, employing techniques like interrupt coalescing, where multiple related interrupts are grouped together, reduces the overhead associated with interrupt handling and enhances the predictability of system responses.

External devices, such as sensors and actuators, can introduce latencies due to their inherent response times. Employing hardware-specific optimizations, such as direct memory access (DMA) for efficient data transfer between external devices and memory, reduces the intervention of the CPU and minimizes latencies. Furthermore, choosing hardware components with low response times and integrating dedicated hardware controllers for time-sensitive tasks can enhance the overall responsiveness of the system.

Power management strategies can impact system latencies, especially in scenarios where transitioning between power states introduces delays. Employing dynamic voltage and frequency scaling (DVFS) allows the system to adapt its power state based on workload requirements, optimizing power consumption without compromising performance. However, careful consideration must be given to the transition overhead to ensure that power management decisions align with the real-time constraints of the application.

In scenarios where precise timing and synchronization are critical, clock accuracy becomes a pivotal consideration. High-precision oscillators and clock synchronization protocols, such as the Precision Time Protocol (PTP) in industrial automation, contribute to minimizing clock-induced latencies. Calibration and compensation mechanisms for clock drift can further enhance the accuracy of timing information, ensuring that tasks dependent on precise timekeeping are executed with minimal variability.

The unpredictability of hardware behaviors, such as cache effects and instruction pipeline stalls, can be mitigated through deterministic hardware architectures. Deterministic processors provide guarantees on the timing of instruction execution, minimizing variability in response times. In safety-critical applications, where bounded execution times are crucial, the use of deterministic hardware architectures becomes imperative to ensure that tasks meet their deadlines consistently.

Addressing communication channel reliability is essential to mitigate latencies introduced by potential packet loss or transmission errors. Employing error-checking mechanisms, such as checksums or forward error correction (FEC), enhances the reliability of data transmission. Redundancy in communication paths and the use of fault-tolerant protocols can further ensure that data reaches its destination reliably and with minimal delay, especially in applications where data integrity is critical.

External storage access latencies can be mitigated through various strategies. Employing solid-state drives (SSDs) with lower access times compared to traditional hard disk drives (HDDs) contributes to faster data retrieval. Additionally, optimizing data storage and retrieval patterns, such as utilizing efficient file systems and minimizing the need for random access, can reduce latencies associated with external storage.

Security mechanisms, while crucial, can introduce overhead that impacts system latencies. Employing hardware-accelerated cryptographic algorithms and dedicated security co-processors can offload encryption and decryption tasks, reducing the impact on the CPU and minimizing latencies. Balancing the need for security with the performance requirements of real-time tasks is essential, and hardware-based security features should be chosen judiciously to align with the specific security requirements of the application.

Testing and validation strategies play a pivotal role in identifying and addressing hardware-induced latencies. Rigorous testing, including stress testing and worst-case scenario analysis, allows for the evaluation of system performance under varying hardware conditions. Utilizing hardware-in-the-loop (HIL) testing, where the real-time system is interfaced with hardware components in a simulated environment, enables a comprehensive assessment of latency behavior. Moreover, incorporating fault injection testing helps assess the system's resilience to unexpected hardware failures and uncertainties.

In conclusion, mitigating hardware-induced latencies in real-time systems requires a holistic approach that combines hardware and software strategies. Optimizing the CPU execution path, managing memory access efficiently, addressing communication-induced delays, optimizing interrupt handling mechanisms, leveraging efficient external device interactions, implementing power management strategies, ensuring clock accuracy, utilizing deterministic hardware architectures, enhancing communication channel reliability, optimizing external storage access, balancing security mechanisms, and employing robust testing and validation strategies collectively contribute to minimizing latencies and enhancing the overall responsiveness of real-time systems. As real-time applications continue to evolve and diversify across domains, the effective mitigation of hardware-induced latencies remains a crucial consideration for ensuring the reliability, predictability, and success of these systems.

Addressing challenges arising from uncertainty in task execution times.

Addressing challenges arising from uncertainty in task execution times is a critical aspect of designing and implementing real-time systems. In the realm of real-time computing, tasks are often subject to varying execution times due to factors such as hardware fluctuations, external interferences, or unpredictable changes in the workload. Uncertainty in task execution times can jeopardize the ability of real-time systems to meet stringent timing constraints, leading to potential missed deadlines and degraded system performance. This comprehensive exploration delves into the multifaceted challenges posed by uncertainty in task execution times and the strategies employed to mitigate these challenges.

One of the primary challenges stemming from uncertainty in task execution times is the potential violation of task deadlines. Real-time systems are characterized by the need to complete tasks within predefined time intervals. When the execution times of tasks become uncertain, the risk of exceeding their allocated time slots increases. This violation of deadlines can have cascading effects, impacting the overall predictability and reliability of the system. The challenge lies in devising mechanisms that account for and adapt to the variability in task execution times to ensure that deadlines are consistently met.

To address the challenge of uncertain task execution times, researchers and practitioners have developed scheduling algorithms that integrate adaptability and flexibility. Traditional fixed-priority scheduling algorithms may struggle in the face of unpredictable task execution times, as they assume a deterministic and constant execution duration for each task. In contrast, dynamic priority scheduling algorithms, such as Earliest Deadline First (EDF) or Rate Monotonic Scheduling (RMS), dynamically adjust priorities based on the remaining time to the task's deadline. This adaptability allows the system to accommodate variations in execution times and make scheduling decisions that align with the urgency of impending deadlines.

Another challenge arising from uncertainty in task execution times is the potential for resource contention. In scenarios where multiple tasks compete for shared resources, variability in execution times can lead to unpredictable resource demands. Tasks with longer-than-expected execution times may monopolize resources, causing contention and adversely affecting the performance of other tasks. Mitigating this challenge requires the development of resource-aware scheduling algorithms that consider both the timing constraints and resource utilization patterns. Techniques such as task grouping, resource reservation, and dynamic resource allocation contribute to addressing the impact of uncertainty on resource contention.

Uncertainty in task execution times also introduces challenges in designing effective admission control mechanisms. Admission control is crucial in real-time systems to ensure that tasks are admitted to the system only if their execution can be guaranteed within specified deadlines. However, when execution times are uncertain, accurately estimating the worst-case execution time (WCET) becomes challenging. Overestimating the WCET can lead to underutilization of resources, while underestimating it may result in missed deadlines. Advanced techniques, including probabilistic analysis and statistical profiling, have been explored to enhance the accuracy of WCET estimation and improve the reliability of admission control mechanisms in the face of uncertain execution times.

The adaptability of scheduling algorithms to dynamic execution time variations is a key consideration in addressing uncertainty challenges. While dynamic priority algorithms offer flexibility, they must strike a delicate balance to prevent undesirable phenomena such as task starvation or excessive preemption. Techniques like priority aging, which gradually increases the priority of tasks over time, help prevent long-term starvation. Similarly, priority boosting mechanisms can temporarily elevate the priority of a task that has experienced longer-than-expected execution times, ensuring fair access to resources.

The challenge of uncertainty in task execution times becomes more pronounced in mixed-criticality systems where tasks have varying degrees of importance. Critical tasks with stringent timing requirements must be shielded from the impact of uncertain execution times to ensure the system's safety and reliability. Hierarchical scheduling approaches, such as the partitioned scheduling model, segregate critical and non-critical tasks into separate partitions with dedicated resources. This segregation minimizes the interference from non-critical tasks, mitigating the risk posed by uncertain execution times on critical components of the system.

Effective handling of uncertainty in task execution times necessitates advancements in worst-case execution time analysis. Traditional static analysis techniques, while providing a deterministic view of task execution times, may not capture the dynamic and probabilistic nature of uncertainties. Probabilistic analysis methods, including statistical model checking and simulation-based approaches, offer a more nuanced understanding of the probability distribution of execution times. By considering statistical variations, these methods enable the design of more robust real-time systems that can adapt to a range of potential execution scenarios.

The impact of uncertainty on task execution times extends beyond traditional computing systems to cyber-physical systems (CPS) and the Internet of Things (IoT). In CPS, where real-time tasks interact with physical processes, uncertainty in execution times may result from unpredictable changes in the physical environment. Strategies to address this challenge involve integrating physical models into the scheduling process. Model-based approaches allow real-time systems to anticipate and adapt to variations in the physical environment, enhancing the system's resilience to uncertainty.

In the context of the IoT, where devices with diverse computational capabilities are interconnected, the challenge of uncertain execution times becomes more complex. Edge computing paradigms, which distribute computation closer to the data source, offer potential solutions by reducing the impact of communication latencies and enhancing the predictability of task execution. Fog computing, an extension of edge computing, further facilitates adaptive and decentralized scheduling strategies that can dynamically respond to uncertainties in execution times across a distributed network of devices.

The development of real-time systems that can effectively address uncertainty in task execution times requires advancements in runtime monitoring and feedback mechanisms. Runtime monitoring involves continuously observing the execution behavior of tasks and adapting scheduling decisions based on observed variations. Feedback mechanisms, such as runtime adaptation and dynamic reconfiguration, enable real-time systems to adjust their parameters in response to changing execution time characteristics. These adaptive strategies contribute to the resilience and robustness of real-time systems facing uncertainties.

The integration of machine learning techniques holds promise in addressing the challenges posed by uncertainty in task execution times. Machine learning models can learn from historical execution data to predict future execution times more accurately. Predictive scheduling algorithms, driven by machine learning models, can dynamically adjust priorities based on the learned patterns, enhancing the system's ability to adapt to uncertainties. However, deploying machine learning in real-time systems requires careful consideration of the associated overhead and the need for continuous model refinement to account for evolving execution time patterns.

Furthermore, the concept of probabilistic real-time systems has emerged as a paradigm to explicitly model and manage uncertainty in task execution times. Probabilistic real-time scheduling algorithms consider the probability distribution of task execution times, allowing for more informed scheduling decisions. Techniques such as stochastic task models and probabilistic scheduling analysis contribute to the development of real-time systems that can gracefully handle uncertainties and provide probabilistic guarantees on meeting deadlines.

The challenge of uncertainty in task execution times is closely intertwined with the need for comprehensive testing and validation methodologies. Robust testing strategies, including worst-case scenario testing and stress testing, help uncover the system's behavior under extreme conditions of uncertainty. Furthermore, the use of fault injection techniques allows developers to assess the system's resilience to unexpected variations in execution times and identify potential vulnerabilities. Validating real-time systems under diverse execution scenarios is crucial to ensuring their reliability and predictability in the face of uncertainty.

In conclusion, addressing challenges arising from uncertainty in task execution times requires a multifaceted approach that encompasses advancements in scheduling algorithms, admission control mechanisms, worst-case execution time analysis, mixed-criticality systems, probabilistic modeling, runtime monitoring, machine learning integration, and probabilistic real-time systems. The quest for more adaptive, resilient, and predictable real-time systems in the presence of uncertainty is an ongoing endeavor that demands collaboration between researchers, practitioners, and domain experts. As real-time computing continues to evolve and find applications in diverse domains, the effective mitigation of challenges associated with uncertain task execution times remains essential for ensuring the success and reliability of these systems.

Discussing methods for estimating and guaranteeing task execution durations.

Estimating and guaranteeing task execution durations is a crucial aspect of designing real-time systems, where meeting stringent timing constraints is paramount. The accuracy of these estimates directly influences the system's ability to satisfy deadlines and ensure reliable performance. Various methods and techniques have been developed to address the challenges associated with predicting task execution durations, ranging from static analysis to dynamic runtime monitoring. This comprehensive exploration delves into the diverse methods employed for estimating and guaranteeing task execution durations, examining their strengths, limitations, and applications in the context of real-time systems.

Static analysis methods represent one traditional approach to estimating task execution durations, relying on pre-runtime analysis of code and system characteristics. One widely used technique is Worst-Case Execution Time (WCET) analysis, which aims to identify the maximum time a task can take to complete under any circumstance. WCET analysis involves scrutinizing the program code, examining control flow paths, identifying critical sections, and considering the worst-case effects of processor features, such as caches and pipelines. While static analysis provides deterministic estimates, it often results in pessimistic predictions, assuming worst-case scenarios that may not always materialize in runtime. Nonetheless, WCET analysis serves as a foundational method for establishing upper bounds on task execution durations, contributing to the design of real-time systems with predictable behavior.

Probabilistic methods offer an alternative perspective by acknowledging the inherent uncertainty in task execution durations. Rather than relying on deterministic worst-case estimates, probabilistic models consider the statistical distribution of execution times. Stochastic analysis, a subset of probabilistic methods, leverages statistical techniques to model the probability distribution of execution times and estimate the likelihood of meeting deadlines. This approach allows for more nuanced predictions, providing insights into the variability of task execution durations. Probabilistic methods are particularly relevant in scenarios where deterministic worst-case estimates prove overly conservative, and a more flexible approach that considers likelihoods is desirable.

Model-based methods integrate system modeling into the estimation process, allowing for a more comprehensive understanding of task behavior. By capturing dependencies and interactions between tasks, resources, and environmental factors, model-based approaches can provide more accurate estimates of execution durations. Finite State Machine (FSM) models, Petri nets, and other formalisms help represent the dynamic aspects of real-time systems. Analytical techniques, such as model checking, enable the verification of properties and the exploration of potential execution scenarios. Model-based methods are valuable for systems where interactions between components significantly influence task execution, contributing to more realistic predictions.

Machine learning techniques have gained traction in recent years as a data-driven approach to estimating task execution durations. By leveraging historical data and learning patterns from past executions, machine learning models can make predictions based on observed behavior. Regression models, neural networks, and ensemble methods are applied to learn the relationship between input features (such as task characteristics, system load, or environmental conditions) and task execution durations. The adaptability of machine learning models allows them to capture complex relationships, making them suitable for scenarios where traditional methods struggle to account for dynamic and non-linear factors affecting execution times. However, deploying machine learning in safety-critical systems requires careful validation and consideration of potential model uncertainties.

Runtime monitoring approaches offer a dynamic and adaptive means of estimating task execution durations by observing system behavior during actual execution. Profiling techniques, such as statistical profiling or dynamic instrumentation, collect data on resource usage, cache hits, and other relevant metrics during runtime. By continuously monitoring and updating estimates based on observed behavior, runtime monitoring methods adapt to changing execution conditions. Adaptive strategies, including runtime adaptation and dynamic reconfiguration, enable real-time systems to adjust their parameters in response to evolving execution time characteristics. While runtime monitoring provides real-time insights, it introduces the challenge of overhead, as the monitoring mechanisms themselves consume system resources.

Hybrid methods combine aspects of both static analysis and runtime monitoring to benefit from the strengths of each approach. Hybrid approaches acknowledge the limitations of static analysis in capturing dynamic runtime behavior and the potential inaccuracies of relying solely on runtime monitoring. By integrating both static and dynamic aspects, hybrid methods strive to strike a balance between accuracy and adaptability. Techniques like Measurement-Based Probabilistic Analysis (MBPA) combine statistical profiling with probabilistic modeling to provide more realistic estimates while considering uncertainties inherent in the execution environment. Hybrid methods represent a pragmatic compromise, leveraging the advantages of both static and dynamic analysis to enhance the accuracy of task execution duration estimates.

Real-time operating systems (RTOS) often incorporate specialized mechanisms to facilitate the estimation and guaranteeing of task execution durations. Techniques like time partitioning, where tasks are assigned dedicated time slots, and budget-based scheduling, where tasks are allocated fixed budgets of execution time, contribute to ensuring predictable behavior. RTOS features, such as rate monotonic scheduling or earliest deadline first scheduling, prioritize tasks based on their urgency, aligning scheduling decisions with the temporal requirements of the system. These built-in mechanisms provide a foundation for meeting deadlines and guaranteeing task execution durations in real-time environments, offering a level of determinism and predictability crucial for safety-critical applications.

Mixed-criticality systems introduce additional complexities in estimating and guaranteeing task execution durations due to the co-existence of tasks with varying degrees of criticality. Critical tasks, which demand stringent timing constraints, must be shielded from the potential uncertainties introduced by non-critical tasks. Techniques like time and space partitioning, which segregate critical and non-critical tasks, contribute to ensuring that critical tasks receive dedicated resources and are not adversely affected by uncertainties in the execution times of less critical components. The development of mixed-criticality systems involves carefully balancing the conflicting requirements of critical and non-critical tasks, necessitating sophisticated scheduling and partitioning strategies.

Guaranteeing task execution durations in real-time systems extends beyond estimation methods to encompass mechanisms that ensure the enforcement of timing constraints. Resource reservation techniques, such as the Constant Bandwidth Server (CBS) or the Proportional Share Scheduler (PSS), allocate fixed amounts of resources to tasks, guaranteeing a minimum level of service and preventing resource contention. Techniques like admission control mechanisms assess the feasibility of admitting new tasks into the system based on the available resources and their impact on existing tasks. Real-time systems often employ techniques like deadline monotonic scheduling or earliest deadline first scheduling to ensure that tasks with imminent deadlines receive priority, aligning scheduling decisions with temporal requirements.

Furthermore, temporal partitioning techniques contribute to the guarantee of task execution durations by dividing time into fixed intervals and allocating each partition to specific tasks. This approach ensures that tasks are executed within predefined temporal bounds, mitigating the risk of exceeding allocated time slots. Temporal partitioning is particularly relevant in environments where tasks must coexist without interfering with each other, such as in avionics or automotive systems. By enforcing temporal partitions, real-time systems can achieve temporal isolation, preventing uncertainties in one task from affecting the timing behavior of others.

In conclusion, the estimation and guaranteeing of task execution durations in real-time systems involve a diverse array of methods and techniques, each with its strengths, limitations, and application domains. From traditional static analysis methods like WCET analysis to probabilistic approaches, model-based techniques, machine learning, runtime monitoring, and hybrid methods, the field has seen continual innovation to address the challenges posed by uncertainty in task execution times. Real-time operating systems, mixed-criticality considerations, and mechanisms like resource reservation, admission control, and temporal partitioning contribute to the broader goal of ensuring predictable behavior and meeting stringent timing constraints in safety-critical applications. As real-time systems continue to evolve and find applications in diverse domains, the ongoing quest for more accurate, adaptive, and reliable methods for estimating and guaranteeing task execution durations remains central to the success and dependability of these systems.

Introducing fault tolerance as a critical aspect of real-time computing.

Fault tolerance stands as a critical and indispensable aspect of real-time computing, where the reliability and predictability of systems are paramount. In the context of real-time applications, which often operate in safety-critical domains such as automotive systems, avionics, medical devices, and industrial control systems, the consequences of system failures can be severe and, in some cases, life-threatening. The concept of fault tolerance encompasses a set of strategies, mechanisms, and methodologies designed to ensure that real-time systems can gracefully handle faults, errors, or failures, thereby maintaining their functionality, meeting stringent timing constraints, and ultimately safeguarding human lives and valuable assets.

One of the fundamental pillars of fault tolerance in real-time computing is redundancy. Redundancy involves replicating critical components, tasks, or subsystems within a system to ensure that if one instance fails or deviates from expected behavior, redundant elements can take over seamlessly. Redundancy can be implemented at various levels, including hardware, software, and data. In hardware redundancy, components such as processors, memory modules, or input/output devices are duplicated, allowing the system to continue functioning even if one component fails. In software redundancy, multiple copies of critical software modules or tasks are executed concurrently, and their outputs are compared to detect discrepancies or errors. Data redundancy involves duplicating critical data to safeguard against corruption or loss, ensuring that the system can recover and continue operation in the presence of faults.

Diverse fault tolerance strategies are employed to address different types of faults, ranging from transient errors caused by cosmic rays or electromagnetic interference to permanent faults resulting from hardware degradation or manufacturing defects. Error detection mechanisms play a vital role in identifying faults as they occur. Techniques such as checksums, parity bits, and cyclic redundancy checks (CRC) are utilized to detect errors in data, ensuring the integrity of critical information. Moreover, advanced error detection and correction codes, such as Hamming codes or Reed-Solomon codes, provide more robust protection against errors by not only detecting but also correcting certain types of faults.

In the realm of real-time systems, where timely responses are essential, error detection must be complemented by efficient error recovery mechanisms. Rollback recovery is a prevalent strategy in real-time computing, involving periodically saving the system's state and, in the event of a fault detection, rolling back to a previously consistent state and re-executing from that point onward. This approach ensures that the system can recover from transient faults and continue operation within specified timing constraints. However, in scenarios where a fault results in a permanent error, failover mechanisms come into play. Failover involves switching to a redundant component or subsystem to maintain system functionality. This can be achieved through techniques such as hot swapping, where a faulty component is replaced with a redundant one without shutting down the entire system, ensuring continuous operation.

Checkpointing is another essential technique in fault tolerance, particularly in real-time systems where precise control over the timing and order of events is crucial. Checkpointing involves periodically saving the state of the system, including the values of variables, the program counter, and other relevant information. In the event of a fault or error, the system can revert to a recent checkpoint, minimizing the impact of the fault and facilitating rapid recovery. However, checkpointing introduces challenges in terms of the frequency of checkpoints and the associated overhead, as more frequent checkpoints incur higher computational and storage costs.

Beyond hardware and software redundancies, fault tolerance extends to communication channels in distributed real-time systems. In these environments, where tasks may be distributed across multiple nodes or processors, ensuring the reliable and timely exchange of data is crucial. Replication of critical messages, acknowledgment mechanisms, and protocols like the Reliable Datagram Protocol (RDP) are employed to enhance the fault tolerance of communication channels. Additionally, in systems where data consistency is paramount, techniques such as two-phase commit protocols and quorum-based approaches help maintain consistency even in the presence of node failures or communication errors.

The concept of fault tolerance intertwines with the design and selection of real-time operating systems (RTOS) that underpin many safety-critical applications. RTOS often incorporate features such as task isolation, memory protection, and strict priority-based scheduling to mitigate the impact of faults on system behavior. The use of partitioned scheduling, where critical and non-critical tasks are separated to prevent interference, contributes to fault tolerance in mixed-criticality systems. Furthermore, features like deterministic interrupt handling and reliable inter-process communication mechanisms enhance the ability of RTOS to deliver predictable responses even in the face of faults.

In safety-critical domains like autonomous vehicles or medical devices, where the consequences of failures can be severe, fault tolerance goes beyond traditional redundancy and recovery mechanisms. Advanced techniques such as N-version programming involve developing multiple versions of a critical component by independent teams, and the outputs are cross-validated to identify potential errors. This approach aims to minimize the likelihood of common-mode failures, where multiple redundant components fail in the same way, compromising the effectiveness of redundancy. Diversity-oriented design principles, encompassing diverse hardware architectures, algorithms, and implementation strategies, further contribute to fault tolerance by reducing the likelihood of systematic faults affecting multiple components.

The integration of formal verification techniques is instrumental in the design and validation of fault-tolerant real-time systems. Model checking, theorem proving, and formal specifications enable rigorous analysis of system properties, ensuring that critical safety and timing requirements are met. Formal methods facilitate the identification of potential design flaws, error propagation paths, and vulnerabilities to specific fault scenarios. Additionally, runtime monitoring and anomaly detection techniques provide a continuous assessment of system behavior, allowing for the early detection of deviations from expected norms and triggering appropriate fault tolerance mechanisms.

In scenarios where human intervention is possible, fault tolerance extends to human-machine interaction and user interfaces. Human factors, including the design of user interfaces, training protocols, and error recovery procedures, play a pivotal role in mitigating the impact of faults caused by human errors. Well-designed user interfaces that provide clear feedback, alert users to potential issues, and facilitate rapid decision-making contribute to fault tolerance by enabling effective human intervention in critical situations.

The growing prevalence of real-time systems in the context of the Internet of Things (IoT) and cyber-physical systems introduces new dimensions to fault tolerance challenges. In these distributed and interconnected systems, faults may propagate across devices, networks, and sensors. Adaptive fault tolerance strategies that can dynamically adjust to changing conditions, predict potential faults based on historical data, and prioritize fault mitigation actions become essential. Additionally, in mission-critical applications like smart grids or healthcare systems, the integration of fault-tolerant mechanisms must align with regulatory standards, certification processes, and industry-specific safety norms to ensure compliance and reliability.

In conclusion, fault tolerance stands as a critical and multifaceted aspect of real-time computing, underpinning the resilience and reliability of systems operating in safety-critical domains. The integration of redundancy, error detection and correction mechanisms, rollback recovery, failover strategies, checkpointing, communication channel fault tolerance, and formal verification techniques collectively contribute to the development of fault-tolerant real-time systems. The challenges and considerations in fault tolerance extend beyond the technical realm to encompass human-machine interaction, regulatory compliance, and the evolving landscape of distributed and interconnected systems. As real-time computing continues to advance and find applications in diverse domains, the pursuit of fault-tolerant design principles and methodologies remains imperative to ensure the dependability and safety of these critical systems.

Discussing mechanisms such as redundancy and error detection for fault mitigation.

In the realm of real-time computing, where reliability is paramount and system failures can have severe consequences, fault mitigation strategies are essential to ensure the continued functionality and performance of critical applications. Among these strategies, redundancy stands out as a fundamental mechanism. Redundancy involves duplicating critical components or subsystems within a system to provide backup resources in the event of a failure. This redundancy can be implemented at various levels, including hardware, software, and data, offering a multi-layered approach to mitigating faults.

Hardware redundancy, the most foundational form, entails duplicating essential hardware components to ensure that if one component fails, the redundant counterpart can seamlessly take over. This is particularly crucial in safety-critical applications, such as avionics or medical devices, where hardware failures can have catastrophic consequences. Redundant hardware components, such as processors, memory modules, or input/output devices, operate in parallel, with mechanisms in place to detect discrepancies and switch to the redundant component if a fault is detected. This approach not only enhances reliability but also contributes to fault tolerance, ensuring that the system can continue operation even in the presence of hardware failures.

Software redundancy complements hardware redundancy by duplicating critical software modules or tasks within a system. This redundancy is particularly relevant in scenarios where tasks must execute with precision and meet stringent timing constraints. Multiple copies of the same software task run concurrently, with their outputs compared to detect any discrepancies or errors. If a fault is detected in one instance, the redundant copies can take over to maintain the system's overall functionality. Software redundancy is often employed in real-time systems, where the ability to respond within defined time intervals is critical, and faults must be addressed without compromising the system's timing behavior.

Data redundancy, another facet of fault mitigation, involves duplicating critical data to safeguard against corruption or loss. This redundancy ensures that if one copy of the data is compromised due to a fault, the redundant copy can be used to recover and maintain system integrity. Redundant data storage mechanisms, such as mirrored disks or distributed databases, contribute to fault tolerance by preventing the loss of critical information. In scenarios where data consistency is paramount, such as in financial transactions or industrial control systems, data redundancy plays a pivotal role in mitigating faults and ensuring the reliability of the overall system.

While redundancy provides a robust foundation for fault mitigation, error detection mechanisms are integral to identifying faults as they occur. These mechanisms play a proactive role in continuously monitoring the system's components, detecting errors, and triggering appropriate mitigation strategies. Error detection is particularly critical in scenarios where faults may lead to transient errors, such as those caused by cosmic rays or electromagnetic interference. Techniques such as checksums, parity bits, and cyclic redundancy checks (CRC) are employed to detect errors in data, ensuring the integrity of critical information.

Advanced error detection and correction codes, such as Hamming codes or Reed-Solomon codes, go beyond simple checksums to provide more robust protection against errors. These codes not only detect errors but can also correct certain types of faults, enhancing the system's ability to mitigate the impact of faults on data integrity. In real-time systems, where correctness and reliability are non-negotiable, the integration of error detection and correction mechanisms contributes to maintaining the system's performance even in the face of potential faults.

In the context of communication channels in distributed real-time systems, where tasks may be distributed across multiple nodes or processors, ensuring the reliable and timely exchange of data is crucial. Replication of critical messages and acknowledgment mechanisms are employed to enhance fault tolerance. These mechanisms involve sending duplicate copies of critical messages and receiving acknowledgments to confirm successful reception. If an acknowledgment is not received within a specified timeframe, the system can assume a fault in the communication channel and trigger appropriate mitigation strategies, such as retransmitting the message or switching to redundant communication channels.

Protocols like the Reliable Datagram Protocol (RDP) contribute to fault mitigation by ensuring reliable and ordered delivery of messages, even in the presence of communication errors or node failures. In scenarios where data consistency is paramount, techniques such as two-phase commit protocols and quorum-based approaches help maintain consistency even if some nodes experience faults or communication errors. The integration of fault-tolerant communication mechanisms is particularly relevant in applications such as industrial control systems, where distributed components must coordinate their actions to achieve precise timing and control.

The concept of fault mitigation through redundancy and error detection extends to safety-critical applications, such as autonomous vehicles or medical devices, where the consequences of failures can be severe. N-version programming is a fault mitigation strategy that involves developing multiple versions of a critical component by independent teams. The outputs of these versions are cross-validated to identify potential errors, and the system can rely on a consistent result even if one version experiences a fault. This approach aims to minimize the likelihood of common-mode failures, where multiple redundant components fail in the same way, compromising the effectiveness of redundancy.

Diversity-oriented design principles further contribute to fault tolerance by introducing diversity in hardware architectures, algorithms, and implementation strategies. By avoiding a homogeneous design, diversity-oriented approaches reduce the likelihood of systematic faults affecting multiple components simultaneously. This strategy is particularly relevant in safety-critical applications where faults must be addressed comprehensively, and the impact of a single fault on the entire system must be minimized.

In scenarios where human intervention is possible, fault mitigation extends to human-machine interaction and user interfaces. Human factors, including the design of user interfaces, training protocols, and error recovery procedures, play a pivotal role in mitigating the impact of faults caused by human errors. Well-designed user interfaces that provide clear feedback, alert users to potential issues, and facilitate rapid decision-making contribute to fault tolerance by enabling effective human intervention in critical situations.

The growing prevalence of real-time systems in the context of the Internet of Things (IoT) and cyber-physical systems introduces new dimensions to fault mitigation challenges. In these distributed and interconnected systems, faults may propagate across devices, networks, and sensors. Adaptive fault tolerance strategies that can dynamically adjust to changing conditions, predict potential faults based on historical data, and prioritize fault mitigation actions become essential. Additionally, in mission-critical applications like smart grids or healthcare systems, the integration of fault-tolerant mechanisms must align with regulatory standards, certification processes, and industry-specific safety norms to ensure compliance and reliability.

In conclusion, mechanisms such as redundancy and error detection serve as foundational pillars of fault mitigation in real-time computing. The integration of redundancy at the hardware, software, and data levels provides backup resources and ensures system functionality in the event of a failure. Concurrently, error detection mechanisms actively monitor the system, identifying faults and triggering appropriate mitigation strategies. These fault mitigation strategies are not only crucial for reliability but also contribute to fault tolerance in safety-critical applications. The challenges and considerations in fault mitigation extend beyond the technical realm to encompass human-machine interaction, regulatory compliance, and the evolving landscape of distributed and interconnected systems. As real-time computing continues to advance and find applications in diverse domains, the ongoing pursuit of fault mitigation mechanisms remains imperative to ensure the dependability and safety of these critical systems.

Exploring power consumption challenges in real-time systems.

Power consumption challenges in real-time systems pose a multifaceted and critical dimension, influencing the design, performance, and sustainability of these systems across various domains. As real-time systems become increasingly pervasive in applications such as embedded systems, Internet of Things (IoT) devices, mobile devices, and mission-critical operations, managing and optimizing power consumption has emerged as a significant concern. This exploration delves into the intricate challenges associated with power consumption in real-time systems, considering the impact on performance, thermal considerations, energy efficiency, and the overarching goal of achieving sustainability in the rapidly evolving landscape of computing technologies.

At the heart of power consumption challenges in real-time systems lies the delicate balance between meeting stringent timing constraints and optimizing energy efficiency. Traditional real-time systems prioritize responsiveness and predictability, often leading to the use of high-performance components that consume significant power. The trade-off between achieving real-time performance and minimizing power consumption becomes particularly pronounced in battery-operated devices, where energy efficiency directly impacts device longevity and usability. Striking the right balance requires innovative approaches in hardware and software design to reconcile conflicting requirements.

One of the primary challenges in real-time systems is the demand for high-performance processors to meet strict deadlines. High-performance processors, while capable of executing tasks quickly, often come with elevated power requirements. As a result, real-time systems face the challenge of selecting processors that can deliver the required performance within acceptable power envelopes. This challenge becomes even more complex in scenarios where tasks have varying degrees of criticality, necessitating dynamic adjustments in processing power based on the urgency of tasks. Techniques such as dynamic voltage and frequency scaling (DVFS) allow real-time systems to adapt processor performance to the current workload, mitigating power consumption while meeting performance requirements.

Thermal considerations play a crucial role in power management, especially in real-time systems where maintaining consistent temperatures is essential for reliability and longevity. Excessive power consumption can lead to elevated temperatures, causing thermal throttling, degradation of components, and potential system failures. Real-time systems in applications like automotive electronics or avionics must contend with harsh environmental conditions, making thermal management a critical aspect of power consumption optimization. Advanced cooling solutions, such as liquid cooling or phase-change materials, contribute to mitigating thermal challenges and enabling sustained performance without compromising reliability.

In battery-operated real-time systems, energy efficiency is paramount to extend the operational lifespan of devices and reduce the frequency of recharging or battery replacement. This challenge is particularly pertinent in applications such as wearable devices, IoT sensors, and mobile computing, where compact form factors limit the size of batteries. Real-time systems must employ energy-aware scheduling algorithms that intelligently allocate processing resources to tasks, taking into account the energy consumption profiles of different components. Additionally, low-power modes, such as sleep or idle states, enable real-time systems to conserve energy during periods of inactivity, contributing to overall energy efficiency.

The heterogeneity of real-time systems, where tasks with diverse computational requirements coexist, presents challenges in optimizing power consumption across different components. In mixed-criticality systems, where tasks have varying levels of importance, balancing the power requirements of critical and non-critical tasks becomes a complex task. Hierarchical scheduling approaches, such as partitioned scheduling, segregate critical and non-critical tasks into separate partitions with dedicated resources. This segregation helps manage power consumption by ensuring that critical tasks receive the necessary resources without being impacted by the power fluctuations of less critical components.

Power management in real-time systems extends beyond the processing units to include peripherals, sensors, and communication modules. In many applications, especially in the IoT, these components often spend considerable time in low-power states to conserve energy. However, transitioning between low-power and active states introduces challenges related to latency and responsiveness, particularly in real-time systems where meeting strict deadlines is imperative. Adaptive power management strategies, coupled with intelligent wake-up mechanisms, aim to strike a balance between energy conservation and responsiveness, ensuring that real-time requirements are met without compromising energy efficiency.

The integration of renewable energy sources, such as solar or kinetic energy harvesting, introduces both opportunities and challenges in real-time systems. While these sources offer the potential for sustainable power, the intermittent nature of renewable energy generation necessitates adaptive power management strategies. Real-time systems must dynamically adjust their operation based on the availability of renewable energy, optimizing task execution and power consumption during periods of abundance or scarcity. Energy-aware scheduling algorithms can play a crucial role in coordinating tasks with renewable energy availability, contributing to the overall sustainability of real-time systems.

The increasing prevalence of real-time systems in edge computing environments introduces new dimensions to power consumption challenges. Edge devices, often deployed in remote or inaccessible locations, may have limited access to continuous power sources. Efficient energy harvesting, storage, and distribution mechanisms become crucial in ensuring the autonomy and reliability of real-time edge systems. Additionally, the edge computing paradigm demands real-time processing capabilities close to data sources, necessitating power-efficient designs to support decentralized computing architectures.

In the context of electric and autonomous vehicles, power consumption is a critical factor influencing range, operational costs, and environmental impact. Real-time systems in vehicular applications must optimize power consumption while meeting stringent safety and timing requirements. Electric vehicles, in particular, rely on efficient power management to maximize the utilization of battery capacity, extending the range and usability of the vehicle. Real-time systems in autonomous vehicles face the additional challenge of processing large volumes of sensor data within tight time constraints, demanding innovative hardware and software solutions to balance performance and energy efficiency.

Advancements in hardware architectures, such as the development of low-power processors, specialized accelerators, and energy-efficient memory technologies, contribute to addressing power consumption challenges in real-time systems. The integration of hardware accelerators for specific tasks, such as signal processing or encryption, enables offloading computationally intensive operations to dedicated components, reducing the overall power footprint. Real-time systems benefit from exploring heterogeneous architectures that leverage the strengths of different components to achieve a more favorable balance between performance and power consumption.

In conclusion, power consumption challenges in real-time systems are intricately intertwined with the need to meet stringent timing constraints, ensure reliability, and optimize energy efficiency. The trade-offs between high-performance processing and low-power operation, coupled with considerations for thermal management, energy harvesting, and the growing prevalence of edge computing, demand holistic approaches to power optimization. Real-time systems must continue to evolve, leveraging innovations in hardware and software design, adaptive power management strategies, and sustainability practices to navigate the complex landscape of power consumption challenges. As these systems find applications in diverse domains, from IoT devices to autonomous vehicles, the pursuit of energy-efficient and sustainable real-time computing remains crucial for shaping the future of technology.

Discussing strategies for optimizing power usage without compromising performance.

Optimizing power usage without compromising performance is a multifaceted challenge that intersects hardware design, software development, and system-level considerations. As technology advances and real-time systems become pervasive across various domains, from embedded devices to data centers, the need to balance performance and power efficiency has become increasingly critical. This discussion explores a range of strategies employed to achieve optimal power usage without sacrificing performance, encompassing innovations in hardware architectures, adaptive power management techniques, energy-efficient algorithms, and the growing importance of sustainability in the design of computing systems.

In the realm of hardware design, the selection and optimization of processing units play a pivotal role in determining the power-performance trade-off. The evolution of microprocessor architectures has seen the emergence of low-power variants, featuring technologies such as advanced power gating, dynamic voltage and frequency scaling (DVFS), and heterogeneous computing. Low-power processors are designed to deliver adequate performance while operating within constrained power envelopes, making them well-suited for energy-efficient real-time systems. Heterogeneous architectures, incorporating specialized accelerators for specific tasks, enable offloading computations to dedicated components, reducing the overall power footprint and enhancing performance in targeted workloads.

Beyond the central processing unit (CPU), optimizing power usage involves scrutinizing other components of the system, including memory modules and input/output devices. Energy-efficient memory technologies, such as low-power DDR (LPDDR) and non-volatile memory (NVM), contribute to minimizing the energy consumption associated with data storage and retrieval. Similarly, the selection of power-efficient sensors, communication modules, and peripherals plays a crucial role in overall power optimization. By adopting components designed with low-power characteristics, real-time systems can achieve a more favorable balance between performance and energy efficiency.

Adaptive power management strategies form a cornerstone in the pursuit of optimal power usage. Dynamic Voltage and Frequency Scaling (DVFS) techniques allow real-time systems to adjust the voltage and frequency of the CPU dynamically based on the workload. During periods of low computational demand, the system can operate at lower frequencies and voltages, reducing power consumption. Conversely, when tasks demand higher performance, the system can scale up to higher frequencies to meet the performance requirements. This adaptive approach ensures that power is allocated judiciously based on the current workload, striking a balance between performance needs and energy efficiency.

Additionally, power gating techniques enable selective shutdown or reduction of power to specific components during idle periods. This approach is particularly effective in battery-operated devices and mobile systems, where tasks are sporadic, and periods of inactivity can be leveraged to conserve power. Power gating extends beyond the CPU to encompass peripheral components, allowing for a fine-grained approach to energy conservation. By intelligently managing power states and transitions, real-time systems can optimize power usage without sacrificing responsiveness during active periods.

Energy-aware scheduling algorithms represent a sophisticated strategy for optimizing power usage in real-time systems. Traditional scheduling algorithms focused solely on meeting performance requirements, often neglecting the power implications of task execution. Energy-aware scheduling takes into account the power characteristics of different components and allocates tasks intelligently to minimize overall power consumption. Task consolidation and migration strategies ensure that processing is concentrated on a subset of components, allowing the remaining components to enter low-power states during idle periods. The synergy between task scheduling and power management contributes to sustained performance while achieving energy efficiency.

In mixed-criticality systems, where tasks have varying levels of importance, power optimization strategies must consider the criticality of tasks. Hierarchical scheduling approaches, such as partitioned scheduling, segregate critical and non-critical tasks into separate partitions with dedicated resources. This segregation ensures that critical tasks receive the necessary processing power without being impacted by the power fluctuations associated with less critical components. The hierarchical allocation of resources aligns with the criticality of tasks, enabling optimal power usage in mixed-criticality real-time systems.

Energy-efficient algorithms represent a crucial aspect of power optimization, especially in applications where computational intensity varies over time. Task-specific algorithms that adapt their computational complexity based on input data characteristics can significantly impact power consumption. Machine learning algorithms, for example, can dynamically adjust their model complexity based on the nature of the data, minimizing unnecessary computations and resulting in energy-efficient execution. Tailoring algorithms to the specifics of the workload and the underlying hardware architecture allows real-time systems to harness computational power judiciously, aligning with the principle of optimizing power usage without compromising performance.

The integration of low-power modes, such as sleep or idle states, contributes to overall energy efficiency in real-time systems. During periods of inactivity, components can transition to low-power states, reducing power consumption without entirely shutting down the system. This approach is particularly relevant in battery-operated devices and IoT applications, where periods of activity are interspersed with extended idle periods. Effective management of low-power modes requires a balance between responsiveness and energy conservation, ensuring that the system can swiftly transition from idle to active states when required.

In scenarios where tasks can be executed with varying levels of precision, precision scaling emerges as a viable strategy for power optimization. Precision scaling involves adjusting the level of precision used in computations based on the requirements of the task. For tasks that do not necessitate high precision, reduced precision computation can be employed, resulting in energy savings. Precision scaling is especially relevant in applications where the trade-off between computational accuracy and power consumption is acceptable, such as in multimedia processing or certain signal processing tasks.

The exploration of power optimization strategies extends to the domain of renewable energy integration. Real-time systems that operate on renewable energy sources, such as solar or wind, face the challenge of intermittent energy availability. Adaptive power management mechanisms must dynamically adjust the system's operation based on the availability of renewable energy, optimizing task execution and power consumption during periods of abundance or scarcity. Energy storage solutions, such as batteries or capacitors, play a crucial role in bridging the gaps between energy availability and system demand, enabling sustained operation even in the absence of continuous power sources.

Sustainability considerations have gained prominence in the discourse on power optimization in real-time systems. Beyond the immediate goal of achieving energy efficiency, sustainable computing involves a broader perspective that considers the environmental impact of computing technologies. Designing real-time systems with a focus on minimizing electronic waste, using eco-friendly materials, and adhering to energy-efficient manufacturing processes aligns with the principles of sustainable computing. Additionally, the integration of renewable energy sources, responsible end-of-life disposal practices, and adherence to industry-wide sustainability standards contribute to the overarching goal of creating environmentally conscious real-time systems.

In the context of edge computing, where real-time processing is performed close to data sources, power optimization strategies gain heightened significance. Edge devices, often deployed in remote or inaccessible locations, may have limited access to continuous power sources. Efficient energy harvesting, storage, and distribution mechanisms become crucial in ensuring the autonomy and reliability of real-time edge systems. Furthermore, edge computing demands a reevaluation of traditional computing paradigms, with a focus on lightweight processing, task offloading, and decentralized architectures that optimize power usage while meeting real-time requirements.

Electric and autonomous vehicles represent another frontier where power optimization is integral to operational efficiency. Electric vehicles, reliant on battery capacity, benefit from sophisticated power management strategies that maximize range and usability. Real-time systems in autonomous vehicles must navigate the delicate balance between processing large volumes of sensor data within tight time constraints and optimizing power consumption. Innovative hardware and software solutions, coupled with adaptive power management techniques, are essential for achieving optimal power usage without compromising the safety and performance requirements of vehicular applications.

In conclusion, the strategies for optimizing power usage without compromising performance in real-time systems are diverse and interconnected. The pursuit of optimal power usage involves a holistic approach that spans hardware design, adaptive power management, energy-efficient algorithms, precision scaling, renewable energy integration, sustainability considerations, and tailored strategies for specific application domains. As real-time systems continue to evolve and find applications in an increasingly diverse range of domains, the ongoing exploration and implementation of these strategies remain crucial for shaping the future of energy-efficient and high-performance computing. The delicate balance between meeting real-time constraints and optimizing power usage represents an ongoing challenge and an opportunity for innovation in the dynamic landscape of computing technologies.

Discussing adaptive strategies to dynamically adjust to changing conditions.

Adaptive strategies, rooted in the ability to dynamically adjust to changing conditions, constitute a fundamental paradigm in various domains, ranging from technology and business to ecology and human behavior. The essence of adaptability lies in the capacity to respond effectively to evolving circumstances, uncertainties, and challenges. This discussion explores the diverse facets of adaptive strategies, encompassing their applications in technology, organizational dynamics, ecological systems, and the broader context of human endeavors. Understanding how adaptive strategies operate in dynamic environments provides insights into the resilience, sustainability, and success of systems and entities.

In the realm of technology, adaptive strategies play a pivotal role in shaping the behavior and performance of systems. Dynamic Voltage and Frequency Scaling (DVFS) exemplify an adaptive approach in computing systems, allowing processors to dynamically adjust their voltage and frequency based on workload requirements. This enables systems to balance the trade-off between performance and energy efficiency, optimizing resource utilization under varying computational demands. Adaptive strategies extend beyond individual components to entire systems, where load balancing algorithms dynamically distribute computational tasks among processing units to ensure efficient utilization and responsiveness in the face of changing workloads.

In the context of artificial intelligence and machine learning, adaptive strategies are inherent in algorithms that can learn and evolve based on new data. Machine learning models, such as neural networks, employ adaptive learning techniques to adjust their internal parameters in response to changing patterns in data. This adaptability enables the models to improve their performance over time, making them well-suited for applications ranging from image recognition and natural language processing to autonomous decision-making systems. The ability to dynamically adjust to new information positions adaptive strategies as a cornerstone in the development of intelligent and responsive technologies.

Organizational dynamics represent another domain where adaptive strategies are essential for navigating the complexities of a rapidly changing environment. In the face of market fluctuations, technological advancements, and socio-economic shifts, organizations must cultivate adaptability to remain competitive and sustainable. Agile methodologies, rooted in adaptive principles, have become prevalent in software development and project management. Agile frameworks, such as Scrum, emphasize iterative and flexible approaches, allowing teams to adapt to evolving project requirements, customer feedback, and changing priorities, fostering a culture of continuous improvement and responsiveness.

Beyond project management, adaptive strategies are central to organizational structures and leadership models. The concept of adaptive leadership recognizes that effective leaders must possess the capacity to respond nimbly to challenges, uncertainties, and diverse perspectives. Adaptive leaders foster a culture of learning and experimentation, encouraging teams to iterate on solutions and adapt to evolving circumstances. This approach is particularly relevant in industries characterized by rapid innovation, disruptive technologies, and shifting market landscapes, where adaptability is not merely advantageous but imperative for long-term success.

Ecological systems provide a rich context for understanding adaptive strategies in the natural world. The concept of ecological resilience encompasses the ability of ecosystems to adapt and recover from disturbances, whether natural or anthropogenic. Biodiversity itself is an adaptive strategy, as diverse ecosystems are often more resilient to changes in environmental conditions. Adaptive traits, such as camouflage in animals or drought-resistant features in plants, enhance the survival chances of species in the face of evolving ecological dynamics. Understanding and preserving adaptive capacities in ecosystems are critical for ecological sustainability and conservation efforts.

The principles of adaptation extend to social systems, where communities and societies develop strategies to cope with changing social, economic, and political landscapes. Resilience in the face of adversity, cultural adaptation to new norms, and the evolution of societal structures are manifestations of adaptive strategies in human societies. In the context of globalization, societies must adapt to the interconnected nature of the world, embracing diversity, and fostering cross-cultural understanding. Adaptive governance models, responsive public policies, and inclusive decision-making processes are essential for addressing the multifaceted challenges that societies encounter in an ever-changing world.

The healthcare domain exemplifies the importance of adaptive strategies in responding to dynamic challenges. The emergence of new diseases, shifts in epidemiological patterns, and the impact of unforeseen events, such as pandemics, necessitate adaptive approaches in healthcare systems. Adaptive healthcare delivery models, such as telemedicine and remote monitoring, have gained prominence, especially in response to the COVID-19 pandemic. The integration of data-driven approaches, including predictive analytics and real-time monitoring, enhances the adaptability of healthcare systems to changing patient needs and public health priorities.

In the context of climate change and environmental sustainability, adaptive strategies are integral to mitigating the impacts of a changing climate. Climate adaptation involves adjusting practices, policies, and infrastructure to reduce vulnerability to climate-related risks. Coastal communities, for instance, may implement adaptive strategies such as building resilient infrastructure to withstand rising sea levels and extreme weather events. Agricultural practices can be adapted to changing climate conditions through the development of drought-resistant crops and precision farming techniques. Adaptive strategies in the realm of environmental conservation focus on preserving biodiversity, protecting ecosystems, and promoting sustainable resource management.

In the educational domain, the evolving landscape of learning paradigms demands adaptive strategies to cater to diverse student needs and accommodate advancements in pedagogy and technology. Adaptive learning technologies leverage data and algorithms to tailor educational experiences to individual learners, providing personalized pathways to mastery. This adaptive approach recognizes the unique strengths, weaknesses, and learning styles of students, fostering an environment where education evolves dynamically to meet the changing demands of a knowledge-driven society.

Technological advancements in the field of robotics and automation exemplify adaptive strategies in the development of machines that can respond intelligently to their environment. Adaptive robotic systems incorporate sensors and algorithms to adjust their behavior based on changing conditions. In industrial settings, adaptive robots can optimize their movements, collaborate with human workers, and reconfigure their tasks in response to variations in production requirements. These adaptive capabilities contribute to the efficiency, flexibility, and safety of robotic systems in dynamic work environments.

The financial sector provides a compelling illustration of adaptive strategies in response to dynamic market conditions. Algorithmic trading algorithms dynamically adjust trading strategies based on real-time market data, adapting to fluctuations in stock prices and market trends. Risk management practices incorporate adaptive models that account for changing economic conditions and emerging financial risks. Financial institutions employ adaptive cybersecurity measures to respond to evolving threats, employing machine learning algorithms that learn and adapt to new attack vectors.

In conclusion, adaptive strategies, characterized by the ability to dynamically adjust to changing conditions, permeate diverse domains, reflecting the resilience and responsiveness inherent in systems, organizations, ecosystems, and human endeavors. From the intricacies of technological systems and organizational structures to the complexities of ecological resilience and societal adaptation, the capacity to adapt is integral to success and sustainability. In an era of rapid change, unpredictability, and interconnected global challenges, the cultivation of adaptive strategies emerges as a cornerstone for navigating the complexities of an ever-evolving world. The lessons learned from adaptive approaches offer insights into the dynamic interplay between innovation, resilience, and the continuous quest for improvement across a spectrum of human activities and systems.

Introducing machine learning applications in predicting and adapting to runtime variations.

Machine learning (ML) applications have emerged as powerful tools in predicting and adapting to runtime variations across diverse domains, offering the potential to enhance the performance, efficiency, and adaptability of systems. The ability of machine learning algorithms to analyze complex patterns, learn from data, and make predictions enables them to play a crucial role in addressing the challenges posed by runtime variations in various dynamic environments. This discussion delves into the applications of machine learning in predicting and adapting to runtime variations, exploring how these techniques are employed to optimize performance, mitigate risks, and contribute to the resilience of systems in the face of changing conditions.

One prominent application of machine learning in predicting and adapting to runtime variations is in the realm of predictive maintenance. In industrial settings, where the performance of machinery and equipment is critical, machine learning models are trained on historical data to predict potential failures or deviations from normal operating conditions. By analyzing patterns in sensor data, machine learning algorithms can identify early indicators of equipment deterioration, wear, or impending failures. This predictive capability enables proactive maintenance interventions, minimizing downtime, reducing maintenance costs, and extending the lifespan of machinery. Through continuous learning and refinement, these models adapt to evolving runtime variations, ensuring their effectiveness in dynamic industrial environments.

In the context of cloud computing and data centers, machine learning finds applications in resource allocation and workload management to cope with varying demands. Machine learning algorithms analyze historical usage patterns, user behavior, and workload characteristics to predict future resource requirements. These predictions inform decisions on dynamically allocating computational resources, optimizing the utilization of servers, and adapting to fluctuations in user demand. By dynamically scaling resources up or down based on real-time demand predictions, cloud providers can enhance efficiency, reduce operational costs, and ensure responsive services, thereby adapting to the dynamic nature of runtime variations in the cloud environment.

Autonomous systems, such as self-driving cars and drones, leverage machine learning for real-time decision-making in response to changing conditions. These systems use ML models trained on diverse datasets to predict and adapt to variations in the environment, including road conditions, traffic patterns, and unexpected obstacles. Machine learning algorithms enable these autonomous systems to continuously learn from their experiences, improving their ability to navigate complex scenarios and adapt to dynamic runtime variations. The predictive capabilities of ML contribute to enhanced safety, reliability, and efficiency in autonomous vehicles, aligning with the demands of real-world, dynamic operating environments.

In the field of finance, machine learning applications are prevalent in predicting runtime variations in stock prices, market trends, and investment risks. ML models analyze historical market data, news sentiment, and macroeconomic indicators to make predictions about future market conditions. Traders and investors leverage these predictions to adapt their investment strategies, manage risks, and optimize portfolio performance. The dynamic and unpredictable nature of financial markets makes machine learning particularly valuable in identifying patterns and trends that human analysts might overlook, enabling timely decision-making and adaptation to changing market conditions.

Machine learning plays a crucial role in the healthcare domain, especially in predicting and adapting to variations in patient health and treatment outcomes. Predictive models built on patient data can anticipate the likelihood of specific medical conditions, complications, or responses to treatments. These models continuously adapt as they receive new patient data, refining their predictions and ensuring relevance in diverse healthcare scenarios. Adaptive machine learning applications in healthcare extend to personalized medicine, where treatment plans are dynamically adjusted based on individual patient characteristics, genetic profiles, and real-time monitoring, leading to more effective and tailored healthcare interventions.

In the context of cybersecurity, machine learning applications contribute to predicting and adapting to runtime variations in the threat landscape. ML models analyze network traffic, user behavior, and historical attack data to identify patterns indicative of cyber threats. These models can predict potential security breaches, malware infections, or anomalous activities, allowing organizations to proactively enhance their cybersecurity defenses. The adaptive nature of machine learning in cybersecurity is particularly valuable in the face of evolving cyber threats, where traditional rule-based approaches may struggle to keep pace with the sophistication and variability of attacks.

Machine learning also finds applications in predicting and adapting to runtime variations in energy management systems. In smart grids, for instance, machine learning algorithms analyze data from various sources, such as weather conditions, energy consumption patterns, and renewable energy generation, to predict fluctuations in energy demand. These predictions enable grid operators to dynamically allocate energy resources, balance supply and demand, and optimize the overall efficiency of the grid. Additionally, machine learning contributes to the adaptive control of distributed energy resources, such as solar panels and energy storage systems, ensuring optimal utilization and responsiveness to changing environmental and grid conditions.

Adaptive machine learning applications are increasingly prevalent in natural language processing (NLP) and language translation systems. Predictive models in NLP analyze linguistic patterns, user queries, and contextual information to anticipate user intent and adapt responses. This adaptability enhances the accuracy and relevance of language processing systems, allowing them to comprehend and respond effectively to varying linguistic styles, colloquialisms, and contextual nuances. Machine translation systems, powered by adaptive algorithms, continually learn from diverse language inputs, improving their ability to provide accurate and contextually relevant translations, even in the face of runtime variations in language use.

In the context of sensor networks and the Internet of Things (IoT), machine learning applications contribute to predicting and adapting to variations in sensor data and environmental conditions. ML models analyze sensor readings to predict equipment failures, environmental changes, or anomalies in device behavior. These predictions enable proactive maintenance, resource optimization, and adaptive responses to changes in the physical environment. Machine learning algorithms also play a role in anomaly detection, identifying deviations from expected patterns in sensor data and triggering timely responses to mitigate potential issues.

Education and e-learning platforms leverage machine learning applications to predict and adapt to variations in student learning behavior and performance. Predictive models analyze student engagement, assessment results, and learning patterns to anticipate individual learning needs. Adaptive learning systems use these predictions to dynamically adjust the difficulty level, content, and pace of educational materials, tailoring the learning experience to the unique requirements of each student. Machine learning in education contributes to personalized learning journeys, adaptive feedback mechanisms, and the continuous improvement of educational content based on real-time insights into student performance.

In the domain of climate science, machine learning applications aid in predicting and adapting to variations in climate patterns and phenomena. ML models analyze vast datasets of climate data, satellite imagery, and atmospheric conditions to make predictions about changes in weather patterns, extreme events, and long-term climate trends. The adaptive nature of machine learning in climate science allows models to continually update their predictions based on new data, contributing to more accurate climate projections and facilitating adaptive strategies in response to the impacts of climate change.

The applications of machine learning in predicting and adapting to runtime variations extend to various other domains, including supply chain management, logistics, gaming, and human-computer interaction. The common thread across these applications is the capacity of machine learning algorithms to analyze data, discern patterns, make predictions, and adapt to changing conditions in real-time. As machine learning continues to advance, the integration of adaptive strategies becomes increasingly sophisticated, contributing to the resilience, efficiency, and responsiveness of systems across diverse fields. The continuous evolution of machine learning applications in predicting and adapting to runtime variations holds promise for addressing the complexities of dynamic environments and shaping a future where intelligent, adaptive systems play a central role in optimizing performance and outcomes.

Chapter 6: Real-Time Communication Protocols

Emphasizing the critical role of communication in achieving synchronization.

Communication serves as the lifeblood of synchronization, playing a pivotal and intricate role in aligning disparate elements, systems, or individuals towards a common objective. The essence of synchronization lies in harmonizing activities, processes, or entities to achieve a unified and coherent state. This discussion explores the multifaceted dimensions of communication and its indispensable role in fostering synchronization across various domains, ranging from technological systems and organizational structures to biological processes and human interactions. As we delve into the critical interplay between communication and synchronization, a nuanced understanding emerges of how effective communication acts as the linchpin for achieving harmony, coordination, and seamless collaboration.

In technological systems, where multiple components must operate in concert, communication serves as the linchpin for achieving synchronization. Consider the intricacies of distributed computing, where individual nodes or processors collaborate to execute tasks. Efficient communication protocols are essential to synchronize these distributed elements, enabling them to share information, coordinate activities, and maintain a consistent state. Whether it's a cluster of servers processing data or a network of interconnected devices in the Internet of Things (IoT), effective communication ensures that each component is aware of the overall system state, facilitating synchronization in the execution of tasks and the exchange of data. Communication protocols, ranging from simple message passing to sophisticated coordination mechanisms, form the backbone of achieving temporal and spatial alignment in distributed technological ecosystems.

In the realm of organizational dynamics, communication emerges as the bedrock for achieving synchronization among diverse teams, departments, and stakeholders. The collaborative nature of modern workplaces demands seamless communication to synchronize efforts and align objectives. Clear and transparent communication channels facilitate the dissemination of information, ensuring that every team member is on the same page regarding goals, timelines, and expectations. Effective communication becomes especially critical in matrix organizations or those with geographically dispersed teams, where achieving synchronization requires a delicate balance of information flow and collaboration. Whether it's through meetings, project management tools, or digital platforms, the articulation and exchange of information enable organizational units to synchronize their activities and contribute cohesively to overarching objectives.

In the biological realm, the intricate dance of cellular processes relies on communication mechanisms to achieve synchronization at various levels. Within a single cell, molecular signals and chemical messengers coordinate activities such as gene expression, metabolism, and cell division. Beyond the individual cell, intercellular communication ensures that tissues, organs, and physiological systems operate in harmony. The nervous system, for example, relies on rapid and precise communication between neurons to synchronize complex activities such as movement, perception, and cognition. Hormonal signaling further contributes to the synchronization of physiological processes, maintaining homeostasis and orchestrating responses to internal and external stimuli. In this biological symphony, communication acts as the orchestrator, allowing disparate elements to synchronize and function as an integrated whole.

Human interactions, both in personal relationships and societal contexts, exemplify the critical role of communication in achieving synchronization. Effective communication is the foundation for understanding, empathy, and cooperation. In personal relationships, the ability to articulate emotions, express needs, and listen actively fosters synchronization of feelings and perspectives. Likewise, in societal structures, communication is instrumental in aligning diverse individuals towards shared values, norms, and collective goals. From interpersonal conversations to mass media and digital platforms, the channels of communication serve as conduits for disseminating information, shaping narratives, and fostering a sense of shared understanding that underpins social cohesion. In democratic societies, for instance, effective communication between citizens, leaders, and institutions is essential for synchronization in decision-making, policy implementation, and the pursuit of common interests.

The role of communication in achieving synchronization extends to the field of music, where musicians must communicate seamlessly to create harmonious compositions. In an orchestra, for instance, the conductor serves as a communicator, guiding musicians through subtle gestures, expressions, and cues to synchronize their playing. Each musician, in turn, communicates with others through their instruments, responding to the conductor's signals and to the auditory cues from fellow performers. The synchronization achieved in a musical performance is a testament to the precision and effectiveness of communication, where non-verbal cues and shared understanding enable a collective interpretation of a musical piece.

In the context of transportation systems, communication is instrumental in achieving synchronization among vehicles, infrastructure, and traffic management systems. Intelligent Transportation

Systems (ITS) leverage communication technologies to enable vehicles to exchange information about their speed, position, and intentions. This communication facilitates coordinated actions such as adaptive traffic signal control, collision avoidance, and congestion management. In autonomous vehicles, communication between vehicles and infrastructure is paramount for achieving synchronized movements and ensuring safety on the road. The seamless interaction between vehicles, traffic lights, and central control systems relies on robust communication protocols to synchronize the flow of traffic and optimize transportation efficiency.

In the realm of sports, particularly team sports, effective communication is a cornerstone for achieving synchronization among players. The coordination of movements, strategies, and tactics necessitates constant communication on the field. Verbal cues, non-verbal gestures, and an intuitive understanding among team members contribute to synchronized plays and successful outcomes. In sports like soccer or basketball, where split-second decisions and coordinated actions are essential, the ability to communicate efficiently becomes a defining factor in achieving synchronization and outperforming opponents. Coaches, too, play a crucial role in orchestrating team dynamics through effective communication, ensuring that players are synchronized in their understanding of game plans and strategies.

Technological advancements have given rise to cyber-physical systems, where the integration of digital and physical components requires precise communication for synchronization. Smart grids, for example, rely on communication networks to synchronize the generation, distribution, and consumption of electrical power. Sensors, actuators, and control systems communicate in real-time to adapt to fluctuations in power demand and supply. The synchronization achieved through communication in smart grids enhances efficiency, resilience, and the integration of renewable energy sources, illustrating how digital communication is transforming traditional physical systems into interconnected, synchronized entities.

The critical role of communication in achieving synchronization is further highlighted in the development and implementation of synchronization protocols in computer networks. In distributed computing, synchronization protocols ensure that multiple processes or nodes coordinate their actions to maintain consistency and order. Time synchronization protocols, such as the Network Time Protocol (NTP), facilitate the alignment of clocks across networked devices, ensuring temporal coherence and coordination. These protocols rely on precise communication mechanisms to exchange timing information and adjust clock settings, showcasing the indispensable role of communication in achieving synchronization in complex computing environments.

In conclusion, the critical role of communication in achieving synchronization permeates diverse domains and scenarios. Whether in technological systems, organizational structures, biological processes, human interactions, or various other contexts, effective communication acts as the catalyst for harmonizing disparate elements towards a common goal. The ability to articulate, exchange, and interpret information lies at the heart of synchronization, enabling coordination, collaboration, and coherence. As we navigate the complexities of interconnected systems and dynamic environments, the emphasis on fostering robust communication becomes paramount, ensuring that the intricate dance of synchronization unfolds seamlessly across a spectrum of human activities and technological landscapes.

Discussing the impact of communication delays on real-time tasks.

Communication delays constitute a critical factor in the realm of real-time tasks, exerting a profound impact on the performance, reliability, and responsiveness of systems across diverse domains. The implications of communication delays become particularly pronounced in scenarios where time-sensitive operations are paramount, such as industrial automation, embedded systems, telecommunications, and mission-critical applications. This discussion explores the multifaceted dimensions of the impact of communication delays on real-time tasks, shedding light on the challenges, mitigating strategies, and the evolving landscape of technologies that seek to address this crucial aspect of temporal constraints in computing systems.

In the context of industrial automation, where real-time control of processes is imperative, communication delays introduce a layer of complexity that can jeopardize the precision and efficiency of operations. Industrial control systems often rely on communication networks to transmit commands from controllers to actuators and sensors. Delays in communication can lead to discrepancies between the intended control signals and the actual response of the controlled systems. In scenarios where tight synchronization is required, such as in robotics or manufacturing processes, even minor delays can result in suboptimal performance, reduced accuracy, and, in some cases, safety hazards. The impact of communication delays extends beyond the immediate operational aspects to the broader efficiency and reliability of industrial processes, influencing production rates, product quality, and overall system resilience.

Embedded systems, prevalent in a myriad of applications from automotive control units to medical devices, face intricate challenges posed by communication delays. In safety-critical environments, such as autonomous vehicles, the coordination of various embedded components relies on timely communication to ensure the proper functioning of perception, decision-making, and actuation subsystems. Delays in transmitting critical data, such as sensor inputs or control commands, can compromise the real-time responsiveness required for safe and reliable operation. Moreover, in medical devices like pacemakers or infusion pumps, where precise timing is crucial, communication delays may lead to suboptimal device performance, potentially endangering patient health. As embedded systems become increasingly pervasive in our daily lives, the impact of communication delays on their real-time capabilities underscores the need for robust design practices and efficient communication protocols.

The telecommunications sector, a cornerstone of modern connectivity, is not immune to the ramifications of communication delays. In telecommunications networks, delays can manifest in various forms, including propagation delays, transmission delays, and processing delays. These delays can influence the quality of service in voice and video communication, impacting real-time applications such as video conferencing or voice-over-IP (VoIP). In scenarios where low-latency communication is paramount, such as online gaming or financial trading platforms, even slight delays can result in perceptible degradation of user experience and financial losses. The push towards the implementation of 5G networks and beyond underscores the industry's recognition of the need to minimize communication delays, emphasizing the importance of ultra-reliable low-latency communication (URLLC) for supporting real-time applications in the evolving landscape of telecommunications.

The impact of communication delays is particularly salient in the domain of cyber-physical systems (CPS), where the integration of computational elements with physical processes demands precise synchronization. In applications like smart grids, where real-time monitoring and control are essential for maintaining grid stability, communication delays can disrupt the coordination between sensors, actuators, and control systems. The consequences extend beyond operational inefficiencies to potential vulnerabilities in the grid's resilience to cyber-attacks. In autonomous vehicles, communication delays can impede the ability of vehicles to interact with each other and the surrounding infrastructure, affecting the coordination necessary for safe and efficient transportation. As CPS continue to proliferate in domains such as smart cities, healthcare, and energy management, the mitigation of communication delays emerges as a key consideration for ensuring the reliable and secure operation of these interconnected cyber-physical systems.

The impact of communication delays in real-time tasks is also evident in the field of financial trading, where split-second decisions can translate into significant financial gains or losses. High-frequency trading (HFT) platforms, characterized by rapid execution of trades in response to market fluctuations, are highly sensitive to communication delays. In electronic trading environments, delays in receiving market data or executing trades can result in missed opportunities or unfavorable outcomes. Financial institutions invest significantly in optimizing the latency of their communication networks, employing techniques such as colocation (placing trading servers in close proximity to exchange servers) and employing low-latency communication protocols to gain a competitive edge in executing real-time transactions. The arms race to reduce communication delays in financial markets underscores the critical role of low-latency communication in maximizing trading efficiency.

Real-time tasks in the context of data-intensive applications, such as real-time analytics or streaming services, are also susceptible to the impact of communication delays. In distributed computing environments where data is processed and analyzed in real-time, delays in transmitting information between nodes can result in a lag in decision-making and insights generation. This is particularly relevant in applications like edge computing, where data is processed closer to the source to minimize latency. Delays in communication between edge devices and central processing units can compromise the real-time nature of analytics, hindering the ability to extract timely insights and respond to changing conditions. The optimization of communication protocols and the deployment of edge computing architectures underscore the ongoing efforts to mitigate the impact of communication delays in data-intensive real-time applications.

Mitigating the impact of communication delays involves the deployment of efficient communication protocols and technologies tailored to the specific requirements of real-time tasks. In industrial automation, the adoption of real-time communication protocols such as Profinet, EtherCAT, or Time-Sensitive Networking (TSN) aims to minimize communication delays and enhance synchronization in distributed control systems. These protocols prioritize low-latency communication, deterministic behavior, and temporal synchronization, addressing the unique challenges posed by real-time tasks in industrial settings. Moreover, advancements in wireless communication technologies, such as 5G and Wi-Fi 6, offer the potential to reduce latency and improve the reliability of communication in industrial wireless networks, further mitigating the impact of delays.

In embedded systems, especially those deployed in safety-critical applications, the design of communication interfaces and protocols plays a crucial role in managing delays. Real-time operating systems (RTOS) with deterministic scheduling capabilities are often employed to ensure that critical tasks are executed within specified time constraints. Additionally, the use of fieldbus protocols in automotive systems or healthcare devices, such as Controller Area Network (CAN) or FlexRay, facilitates real-time communication with low latency. The integration of advanced communication technologies, including time-triggered Ethernet or FlexRay, enables the synchronization of communication schedules, minimizing the impact of delays on real-time tasks in embedded systems.

Telecommunications networks are evolving to address the challenges posed by communication delays, particularly in the transition to 5G and the exploration of future communication technologies. The architecture of 5G networks, with its emphasis on low-latency communication and high data rates, aims to support a diverse range of real-time applications. The deployment of edge computing in conjunction with 5G further reduces communication distances and, consequently, latency, enhancing the real-time capabilities of applications such as augmented reality, virtual reality, and autonomous systems. As the telecommunications industry continues to innovate, the development of communication technologies that prioritize low-latency communication becomes instrumental in meeting the demands of real-time tasks across various use cases.

In cyber-physical systems, research and development efforts focus on communication protocols and strategies to mitigate the impact of delays. Time-sensitive networking (TSN) standards, which enhance the determinism and synchronization of communication in industrial networks, are being integrated into cyber-physical systems to reduce latency. The adoption of fog and edge computing models in CPS aims to distribute computation and decision-making closer to the physical processes, minimizing the need for long-distance communication and mitigating the impact of delays on real-time control and monitoring. These advancements underscore the interdisciplinary nature of addressing communication delays, involving not only communication protocols but also system architectures and computing paradigms.

Financial trading platforms employ a myriad of strategies to mitigate the impact of communication delays on real-time transactions. Colocation services, which provide proximity to exchange servers, enable high-frequency traders to minimize the physical distance that signals must travel, reducing transmission delays. Direct market access (DMA) further streamlines the communication path between traders and exchanges, minimizing the time taken to execute trades. Additionally, the use of specialized network protocols, such as the Financial Information eXchange (FIX) protocol, prioritizes low-latency communication to facilitate rapid order execution. The optimization of network infrastructure, coupled with advancements in hardware and software, reflects the financial industry's commitment to minimizing communication delays in real-time trading environments.

In the realm of data-intensive real-time applications, the deployment of edge computing architectures is gaining prominence as a strategy to mitigate the impact of communication delays. By processing and analyzing data closer to the source, edge computing reduces the distance data must travel, minimizing latency and enhancing the real-time capabilities of applications. Edge computing also facilitates the distribution of computing resources, allowing for parallel processing and efficient communication between edge devices. Moreover, the adoption of stream processing frameworks, such as Apache Kafka or Apache Flink, enables the real-time analysis of data streams, reducing the time between data generation and actionable insights. These approaches exemplify the evolving landscape of technologies aimed at addressing communication delays in data-intensive real-time applications.

The impact of communication delays on real-time tasks is a multifaceted challenge that spans various domains, each with its unique requirements and considerations. The evolving landscape of communication technologies, protocols, and system architectures reflects the ongoing efforts to mitigate these delays and enhance the real-time capabilities of diverse applications. As computing systems become more interconnected, data-driven, and time-sensitive, the optimization of communication becomes integral to unlocking the full potential of real-time tasks, whether in industrial automation, telecommunications, embedded systems, or other domains where temporal constraints are paramount. The pursuit of efficient communication strategies, coupled with advancements in networking, computing, and system design, continues to shape the landscape of real-time computing and underscores the importance of managing communication delays for the seamless execution of time-critical operations.

Introducing message queues as a mechanism for asynchronous communication.

Message queues represent a fundamental mechanism in the realm of distributed systems, serving as a cornerstone for enabling asynchronous communication among various components. In the intricate landscape of modern computing, where systems are often composed of diverse, loosely-coupled services, the need for effective communication mechanisms becomes paramount. This discussion delves into the multifaceted dimensions of message queues, exploring their role, principles, advantages, and applications. From the foundational concepts to the practical implementations, the journey through message queues unfolds, shedding light on their significance in fostering decoupled, scalable, and resilient distributed architectures.

At its core, a message queue is a form of communication infrastructure designed to facilitate the exchange of information between different parts of a system in an asynchronous manner. Unlike synchronous communication, where components interact in real-time and are tightly coupled, asynchronous communication through message queues allows components to operate independently, sending and receiving messages at their own pace. This decoupling of components is a key characteristic of message queues, offering flexibility and scalability in the design of distributed systems.

The fundamental principle underlying message queues revolves around the concept of message-oriented communication. In this paradigm, information is encapsulated into discrete units known as messages. A message typically contains data or commands and is placed into a queue, a data structure that follows the First-In-First-Out (FIFO) principle. As messages are enqueued, they wait for processing until the receiving component, often referred to as a consumer, retrieves and handles them. This decoupling of message producers and consumers allows for asynchronous communication, where the timing and pace of message exchange are not synchronized.

Message queues find applications in a myriad of scenarios, addressing challenges encountered in distributed systems, microservices architectures, and beyond. One primary application is in the domain of load balancing, where tasks or requests are distributed among multiple processing units. By employing message queues, systems can efficiently distribute incoming workloads to available workers, ensuring a balanced and scalable approach to resource utilization. This load balancing mechanism becomes particularly crucial in scenarios where the demand for processing fluctuates, enabling systems to dynamically adapt to changing conditions.

Another significant application of message queues is in managing communication between microservices, a prevalent architectural pattern in modern software development. Microservices, which encapsulate functionalities as independent services, often need to communicate with one another to fulfill complex business processes. Message queues provide a way for microservices to exchange information without creating direct dependencies, fostering loose coupling and enabling each microservice to evolve independently. This decoupled communication model aligns with the principles of microservices architecture, promoting scalability, maintainability, and resilience.

Scalability is a key attribute of message queues, allowing systems to handle increasing loads by efficiently distributing tasks or messages among multiple processing units. This scalability is achieved through the parallelism inherent in asynchronous communication. As messages are enqueued, multiple consumers can process them concurrently, preventing bottlenecks and facilitating efficient utilization of computing resources. The horizontal scalability afforded by message queues becomes crucial in scenarios where the demand for processing varies dynamically, enabling systems to scale up or down based on workload fluctuations.

The decoupling provided by message queues contributes to system resilience by isolating components and mitigating the impact of failures. In scenarios where a component or service experiences temporary unavailability or slowdown, messages continue to be enqueued, ensuring that the system can recover gracefully once the affected component resumes normal operation. This fault-tolerant characteristic enhances the overall reliability of distributed systems, making message queues a valuable tool in building robust architectures.

Reliability and durability are essential attributes of message queues, ensuring that messages are not lost even in the face of system failures. Many message queue systems offer features such as persistence, where messages are stored on disk to survive system restarts. This durability ensures that critical information is not lost during transient failures, contributing to the overall integrity of distributed systems. Additionally, acknowledgment mechanisms in message queues allow consumers to confirm the successful processing of messages, providing a means to handle potential errors or reprocess messages if necessary.

The publish-subscribe (pub-sub) pattern is a powerful paradigm facilitated by message queues, enabling the broadcasting of messages to multiple subscribers. In a pub-sub model, a component, known as a publisher, sends messages to a specific channel or topic. Multiple subscribers, interested in messages related to that channel or topic, receive and process the messages independently. This pattern supports the creation of dynamic and flexible communication architectures, where components can subscribe to relevant topics and react to messages without direct knowledge of the message producers.

Diving into the architectural aspects, message queues can be categorized into two primary models: point-to-point (P2P) and publish-subscribe (pub-sub). The point-to-point model involves a single sender (producer) and a single receiver (consumer) for each message. In this model, messages are directed to specific queues, and each message is consumed by a single recipient, ensuring that the message is processed only once. The publish-subscribe model, on the other hand, supports one-to-many relationships. Messages published to a specific topic are broadcasted to all subscribers interested in that topic, allowing multiple components to independently consume relevant messages.

RabbitMQ, Apache Kafka, and Amazon Simple Queue Service (SQS) are examples of popular message queue systems, each with its unique strengths and use cases. RabbitMQ, based on the Advanced Message Queuing Protocol (AMQP), excels in scenarios requiring high throughput and flexibility. It supports various messaging patterns, including point-to-point and publish-subscribe, and provides features such as message acknowledgment, routing, and persistence. Apache Kafka, designed for high-throughput distributed data streams, is particularly suitable for scenarios involving real-time analytics and event sourcing. Its log-based architecture ensures durability and scalability, making it well-suited for handling large volumes of data. Amazon SQS, a fully managed message queue service provided by AWS, offers simplicity and ease of integration. It scales automatically to accommodate varying workloads and provides features such as message retention, dead-letter queues, and encryption.

One of the notable message queue systems is RabbitMQ, known for its flexibility, reliability, and support for multiple messaging patterns. RabbitMQ implements the AMQP protocol, a widely adopted standard for message-oriented middleware. In RabbitMQ, messages are exchanged between producers and consumers through a broker, a central entity responsible for routing messages to the appropriate queues. Producers send messages to exchanges, which act as routing mechanisms, directing messages to specific queues based on predefined rules. Consumers, in turn, subscribe to queues and retrieve messages for processing.

Apache Kafka, often categorized as a distributed streaming platform rather than a traditional message queue, stands out for its unique architecture and capabilities. Kafka is designed to handle high-throughput streams of data in a fault-tolerant and scalable manner. It organizes messages into topics, and producers publish messages to specific topics. Consumers, organized into consumer groups, subscribe to topics and process messages independently. Kafka's log-based storage and distributed nature make it well-suited for scenarios requiring real-time analytics, event sourcing, and continuous data streams.

Amazon Simple Queue Service (SQS), a fully managed message queue service provided by Amazon Web Services (AWS), simplifies the integration of distributed components within the cloud environment. SQS supports both standard queues, offering at-least-once delivery, and FIFO (First-In-First-Out) queues, providing exactly-once delivery. Standard queues are suitable for scenarios where occasional duplicate messages are acceptable, while FIFO queues ensure the order and uniqueness of messages. SQS automatically scales to accommodate varying workloads and provides features such as message retention, dead-letter queues for handling failed messages, and server-side encryption for data security.

The principles of message queues extend beyond individual systems, finding applications in the orchestration of workflows and the coordination of activities in larger distributed systems. Workflow management systems often leverage message queues to decouple various steps in a process, allowing components to progress independently while ensuring that the overall workflow advances seamlessly. This orchestration pattern is especially prevalent in cloud-based architectures, where components or microservices collaborate to fulfill complex business processes, and each step in the process is represented by messages exchanged through queues.

In the context of event-driven architectures, message queues play a central role in enabling components to react to events and changes in the system. Events, such as user actions, system alerts, or data updates, can trigger the generation and propagation of messages through queues. Subscribers interested in specific events can independently consume relevant messages, allowing components to react to changes without direct dependencies on one another. This decoupled and event-driven paradigm aligns with the principles of scalability, flexibility, and responsiveness in distributed systems.

The adoption of containerized and serverless architectures has further emphasized the significance of message queues in managing communication between microservices and components. Containers, orchestrated by platforms like Kubernetes, benefit from the loose coupling facilitated by message queues, allowing individual containers or services to scale independently and communicate asynchronously. Serverless computing, characterized by ephemeral function execution in response to events, relies on message queues to trigger functions, enabling event-driven and scalable architectures without the need for maintaining persistent server instances.

In conclusion, message queues stand as a foundational mechanism for asynchronous communication in the dynamic landscape of distributed systems. Their ability to decouple components, facilitate scalable communication, and ensure fault tolerance makes them integral to the design of modern, resilient architectures. From load balancing and microservices communication to event-driven workflows and the orchestration of cloud-based systems, message queues provide a versatile and robust solution to the challenges posed by the complexities of contemporary computing. As technology continues to evolve, the principles and applications of message queues are poised to play a pivotal role in shaping the future of distributed, scalable, and responsive systems.

Discussing the benefits of publish-subscribe models in decoupled communication.

The publish-subscribe (pub-sub) model stands as a versatile and powerful paradigm in the realm of distributed systems, offering a wealth of benefits that revolve around the core concept of decoupled communication. This discussion delves into the multifaceted advantages of the pub-sub model, exploring its impact on scalability, flexibility, resilience, and overall system architecture. From its fundamental principles to real-world applications, the merits of the publish-subscribe model emerge as a cornerstone in fostering loosely-coupled and responsive communication in modern computing environments.

At its essence, the pub-sub model introduces a level of abstraction to communication, breaking away from the tight coupling traditionally associated with direct point-to-point interactions. In a pub-sub system, components are categorized into publishers and subscribers. Publishers, responsible for generating messages or events, do not have direct knowledge of the subscribers. Instead, they publish messages to channels or topics without specifying who the recipients are. Subscribers, on the other hand, express interest in specific channels or topics and receive relevant messages without needing to know the identity of the publishers. This decoupling of message producers and consumers lies at the heart of the pub-sub model's benefits.

Scalability emerges as a primary advantage of the pub-sub model, driven by its ability to efficiently handle diverse and dynamic workloads. In traditional point-to-point communication, as the number of participants increases, the intricacies of direct connections and dependencies can lead to scalability challenges. The pub-sub model addresses this by introducing a broadcast-like mechanism where messages are disseminated to all interested parties. This approach allows the system to scale horizontally, accommodating a growing number of both publishers and subscribers without introducing bottlenecks or degrading performance. The inherent parallelism of pub-sub architectures contributes to their scalability, making them well-suited for environments where the demand for communication can vary dynamically.

Flexibility is another hallmark benefit of the pub-sub model, offering a dynamic and adaptable communication pattern that aligns with the ever-changing nature of distributed systems. In traditional point-to-point communication, adding or removing components often necessitates modifications to existing connections, potentially leading to system-wide disruptions. In contrast, the pub-sub model provides a more modular and flexible architecture. New components can seamlessly join the system as subscribers to relevant channels, receiving messages without requiring explicit connections to publishers. Likewise, components can be removed or replaced without affecting the overall system, as long as they adhere to the established message format and channels. This flexibility facilitates the evolution and maintenance of distributed systems, allowing them to easily accommodate changes in component structure and functionality.

Resilience is inherent in the pub-sub model, providing a robust mechanism for handling faults and ensuring the continued operation of distributed systems in the face of failures. The decoupling of components means that the failure of one part of the system does not necessarily disrupt the entire communication flow. If a subscriber encounters a failure or becomes temporarily unavailable, the pub-sub system can gracefully continue delivering messages to other subscribers without direct impact. Similarly, if a new subscriber is introduced to the system, it can seamlessly start receiving relevant messages without the need for explicit connections or awareness from existing components. This resilience to faults enhances the overall reliability and availability of distributed systems employing the pub-sub model.

One of the distinguishing features of the pub-sub model is its support for dynamic and event-driven architectures. Events, representing changes in the system state or significant occurrences, can be seamlessly integrated into pub-sub systems. Publishers generate events, which are then broadcasted to all interested subscribers. This event-driven paradigm is particularly valuable in scenarios where real-time responsiveness and adaptability are crucial. For example, in financial systems, market data changes or trading events can be communicated to various components through a pub-sub mechanism, enabling timely reactions and decision-making. This event-driven nature aligns with the needs of modern applications that require responsiveness to changing conditions and efficient handling of dynamic, unpredictable events.

The pub-sub model contributes significantly to the creation of loosely-coupled architectures, where components operate independently without direct knowledge of each other. This loose coupling fosters autonomy among system components, allowing them to evolve independently and promoting modular development practices. Components can be developed, updated, or replaced without requiring extensive coordination with other parts of the system. This separation of concerns enhances the maintainability and extensibility of distributed systems, facilitating parallel development efforts and reducing the risk of unintended side effects when making changes. The pub-sub model's support for loose coupling aligns with the principles of microservices architectures and distributed systems design.

Security and access control are areas where the pub-sub model introduces advantages by providing a centralized point for managing subscriptions and enforcing policies. In a pub-sub system, administrators can define access controls at the level of channels or topics, determining which subscribers are allowed to receive messages on specific subjects. This centralized control enhances security by preventing unauthorized access to sensitive information. Additionally, access controls can be dynamically adjusted to accommodate changes in system requirements or security policies. The centralized management of subscriptions and permissions simplifies the enforcement of security policies, offering a unified approach to securing communication channels in complex distributed systems.

Real-world applications of the pub-sub model span a diverse range of domains, each benefiting from its distinctive characteristics. In financial systems, where rapid reaction to market changes is essential, the pub-sub model facilitates the dissemination of market data to various components responsible for trading, risk management, and analytics. Similarly, in telecommunications, the pub-sub model supports the efficient delivery of messages such as call events, status updates, or notifications to subscribers interested in specific communication channels. The ability to broadcast messages to multiple subscribers in real-time aligns with the demands of these dynamic and data-intensive industries.

In the context of Internet of Things (IoT) and sensor networks, the pub-sub model provides an effective means of managing the flow of data from sensors to various processing components. Sensors act as publishers, generating data events, while analytics engines or monitoring systems act as subscribers interested in specific types of sensor data. This decentralized and scalable communication pattern allows IoT systems to efficiently handle a large number of sensors, each producing diverse data streams. The pub-sub model's adaptability to changing sensor configurations and data types suits the dynamic nature of IoT environments.

The integration of the pub-sub model with cloud computing architectures further exemplifies its versatility and applicability. Cloud-based services often utilize the pub-sub paradigm for managing asynchronous communication between components, allowing services to scale independently and handle diverse workloads efficiently. For example, cloud-based event-driven architectures leverage pub-sub systems to coordinate activities across microservices, respond to triggers, and handle events such as user interactions or data updates. This adaptability to cloud environments aligns with the principles of scalability, flexibility, and responsiveness crucial in modern cloud-based applications.

Despite its numerous advantages, the pub-sub model also introduces challenges that require careful consideration. The potential for message loss or duplication, especially in scenarios involving unreliable networks or transient failures, necessitates the implementation of mechanisms such as acknowledgment and deduplication to ensure message integrity. Additionally, the order of message delivery may not be guaranteed, introducing challenges in scenarios where the sequential processing of events is crucial. These challenges, however, can be addressed through the use of advanced pub-sub systems and the incorporation of additional features to enhance reliability and ordering guarantees.

In conclusion, the publish-subscribe model stands as a paradigm that transcends traditional communication patterns, offering a wealth of benefits that address the complexities of modern distributed systems. Its contributions to scalability, flexibility, resilience, and event-driven architectures make it a valuable tool in designing loosely-coupled, responsive, and adaptable systems. From financial systems and telecommunications to IoT environments and cloud computing, the pub-sub model's versatility finds application across diverse domains, shaping the landscape of distributed computing. As technology continues to evolve, the principles and advantages of the publish-subscribe model remain instrumental in navigating the challenges and opportunities presented by the dynamic and interconnected nature of contemporary computing environments.

Exploring the Precision Time Protocol for achieving precise time synchronization.

The Precision Time Protocol (PTP) stands as a sophisticated and powerful mechanism designed to address the critical need for precise time synchronization in distributed systems, where accurate temporal alignment among devices is paramount. This exploration delves into the intricacies of PTP, unraveling its principles, architecture, and applications. From its foundational concepts to real-world implementations, the journey through PTP unfolds, shedding light on its significance in industries ranging from telecommunications and finance to industrial automation.

At its core, PTP aims to synchronize the clocks of devices within a network with high accuracy, ensuring that they share a common understanding of time. This precision is particularly crucial in scenarios where events must be coordinated with utmost accuracy, such as in financial trading, telecommunications, power grids, and industrial automation. Unlike traditional clock synchronization protocols, PTP goes beyond millisecond-level accuracy, striving for sub-microsecond and even nanosecond precision. The demand for such precision arises from the increasing reliance on distributed systems and the need for temporal consistency across geographically dispersed devices.

PTP operates on the basis of a master-slave architecture, where one device acts as the master clock, and others synchronize their clocks to it as slaves. The master clock broadcasts synchronization messages to the slaves, allowing them to adjust their clocks accordingly. The communication between devices occurs over the network, and PTP employs a combination of hardware timestamps and sophisticated algorithms to minimize clock offset and achieve high levels of accuracy. This combination of hardware and software precision distinguishes PTP from traditional clock synchronization methods.

The principles governing PTP's functionality revolve around the concept of a Grandmaster clock, which serves as the primary reference for time in the network. The Grandmaster clock typically possesses a highly stable and accurate time source, often derived from satellite-based Global Navigation Satellite Systems (GNSS) like GPS. The Grandmaster broadcasts synchronization messages, known as Sync messages, to the slave devices. These messages contain information about the master's perception of time, allowing the slaves to adjust their clocks with precision.

PTP leverages the exchange of multiple types of messages to achieve accurate clock synchronization. In addition to Sync messages, PTP employs Follow-Up messages, which convey additional information about the master's clock state, and Delay Request and Delay Response messages, which aid in calculating the network propagation delay. The protocol's reliance on a combination of message types and timestamps contributes to its ability to achieve sub-microsecond and nanosecond-level synchronization.

The accuracy of PTP is heavily influenced by the implementation of timestamping mechanisms in both hardware and software. Hardware timestamping involves capturing the exact time at which a packet enters or exits a network interface. This direct interaction with the network card ensures that timestamping occurs at a precise moment, minimizing the influence of operating system latencies. PTP-aware network interface cards (NICs) are designed to support such hardware timestamping, contributing to the overall accuracy of PTP-based synchronization.

The software component of PTP involves algorithms that process the collected timestamps to calculate clock offsets and adjust the local clocks accordingly. PTP employs the Best Master Clock Algorithm (BMCA) to select the most accurate clock in the network as the Grandmaster. The BMCA considers factors such as clock stability, precision, and the quality of the time source. Once the Grandmaster is determined, PTP uses a proportional-integral-derivative (PID) controller to adjust the clocks of slave devices. This controller considers the difference between the master's time and the local time, as well as the rate of change of this difference, to finely adjust the slave's clock.

PTP offers two operational modes: one-step and two-step. In the one-step mode, slaves calculate the offset and adjust their clocks based on a single Sync message from the master. This mode is suitable for networks with low latency and stable communication paths. In the two-step mode, the master sends a Sync message followed by a Follow-Up message containing additional timing information. Slaves use both messages to calculate the offset and adjust their clocks. This mode is more resilient to network variations and is often employed in scenarios where communication delays may fluctuate.

In practical terms, PTP finds wide-ranging applications across industries where precise time synchronization is paramount. In financial trading, where split-second decisions can result in significant gains or losses, PTP ensures that trading platforms, algorithms, and market data systems operate with synchronized clocks. The nanosecond-level precision of PTP is crucial for aligning transactions and maintaining the integrity of timestamps in financial systems. The protocol's ability to handle clock synchronization in geographically dispersed data centers contributes to the seamless execution of high-frequency trading strategies.

Telecommunications is another domain where PTP plays a pivotal role, particularly in the evolution from traditional circuit-switched networks to modern packet-switched networks. PTP ensures precise synchronization in the delivery of voice and data services, supporting technologies like Long-Term Evolution (LTE) and 5G. The synchronization of base stations, switches, and network elements is essential for maintaining quality of service, minimizing jitter, and supporting applications that require accurate timing, such as voice over IP (VoIP) and video streaming.

In power systems and smart grids, PTP facilitates the coordination and control of distributed energy resources, grid monitoring, and demand-response mechanisms. The synchronization of devices in substations, phasor measurement units (PMUs), and energy management systems is critical for maintaining grid stability, optimizing energy distribution, and responding to dynamic changes in the electrical grid. PTP's ability to synchronize clocks across widely distributed components contributes to the efficiency and reliability of smart grid operations.

In industrial automation and manufacturing, where precision in control systems is paramount, PTP ensures synchronized operations across devices such as Programmable Logic Controllers (PLCs), sensors, and actuators. This synchronization is vital for coordinating complex processes, maintaining accurate timelines in production lines, and ensuring that automated systems respond to events in a coordinated and timely manner. PTP's nanosecond-level precision aligns with the stringent requirements of modern industrial automation, where real-time control and synchronization are crucial for efficiency and safety.

The adoption of PTP is not limited to specific industries; it extends to any scenario where distributed systems require accurate temporal alignment. PTP's ability to achieve nanosecond-level synchronization is particularly valuable in scientific research, where experiments, data acquisition systems, and instrumentation benefit from precise time coordination. In scenarios where data from multiple sources must be correlated with high accuracy, PTP ensures that timestamps align across diverse devices and sensors.

Despite its numerous advantages, the deployment of PTP comes with challenges and considerations. The reliance on hardware timestamping requires the availability of PTP-compatible network inter-face cards, and the accuracy of synchronization

is influenced by the quality of the time source, such as GNSS signals. The management of PTP in large-scale networks, including the selection of Grandmasters and the configuration of PTP-aware devices, requires careful planning and monitoring. Additionally, the impact of network variations, including latency and jitter, must be considered to achieve optimal synchronization performance.

In conclusion, the Precision Time Protocol stands as a corner-stone in the pursuit of precise time synchronization in distributed systems. Its ability to achieve sub-microsecond and nanosecond-level accuracy distinguishes it as a critical tool in industries where tem-poral alignment is non-negotiable. From financial trading platforms and telecommunications networks to smart grids, industrial automa-tion, and scientific research, PTP's impact spans diverse domains, contributing to the efficiency, reliability, and coordination of distrib-uted systems. As technology continues to advance, and the demands for precision in distributed systems grow, the principles and applica-tions of PTP are poised to play an increasingly vital role in shaping the landscape of synchronized and interconnected systems.

Discussing its application in scenarios where accurate timing is crucial.

The application of the Precision Time Protocol (PTP) extends across a myriad of scenarios where accurate timing is not merely ad-vantageous but critical for the seamless functioning of distributed systems. In financial trading platforms, characterized by rapid trans-actions and split-second decision-making, PTP emerges as a linch-pin for achieving precise time synchronization. The nanosecond-lev-el accuracy afforded by PTP is indispensable in aligning timestamps across trading algorithms, market data feeds, and order execution systems. In this high-stakes environment, where latency discrepan-cies can lead to significant financial implications, PTP ensures that all elements of the trading infrastructure operate with a shared temporal reference, enabling coherent and synchronized actions.

Telecommunications stands as another domain where PTP plays a pivotal role, particularly in the era of evolving communication technologies such as Long-Term Evolution (LTE) and 5G. The synchronization of network elements, base stations, and switches is imperative for maintaining the quality of service and ensuring the efficient delivery of voice and data services. PTP's precision is instrumental in minimizing jitter, optimizing network performance, and supporting applications that demand accurate timing, such as Voice over IP (VoIP) and video streaming. In the dynamic landscape of telecommunications, where networks span vast geographical areas, PTP ensures that devices operate cohesively, contributing to the reliability and efficiency of modern communication systems.

The deployment of PTP extends its reach into the realm of power systems and smart grids, where the coordination of distributed energy resources and the monitoring of grid dynamics demand accurate temporal alignment. In smart grid operations, PTP synchronizes clocks across devices in substations, phasor measurement units (PMUs), and energy management systems. This synchronization is indispensable for optimizing energy distribution, responding to dynamic changes in the electrical grid, and maintaining grid stability. PTP's ability to achieve nanosecond-level precision ensures that the diverse components of smart grids operate in unison, contributing to the resilience and effectiveness of next-generation power systems.

In the field of industrial automation and manufacturing, PTP finds applications where precision in control systems is paramount. Devices such as Programmable Logic Controllers (PLCs), sensors, and actuators must operate in a coordinated and synchronized manner to ensure the efficiency and safety of automated processes. PTP's nanosecond-level accuracy becomes crucial for maintaining accurate timelines in production lines, coordinating complex processes, and responding to events in real-time. In industries where automation is a cornerstone of operational efficiency, PTP contributes to the synchronization of diverse devices, optimizing the performance of automated systems and supporting the stringent requirements of modern industrial automation.

Scientific research, characterized by experiments, data acquisition systems, and instrumentation, represents another arena where PTP's precise time synchronization capabilities find application. In scientific experiments, where data from multiple sources must be correlated with high accuracy, PTP ensures that timestamps align seamlessly across diverse devices and sensors. Whether in physics experiments, environmental monitoring, or astronomical observations, the precision offered by PTP becomes instrumental in achieving accurate temporal coordination. The ability to synchronize events at the nanosecond level facilitates the correlation of data points, contributing to the accuracy and reliability of scientific research outcomes.

The adoption of PTP is not confined to specific industries; rather, it extends to any scenario where distributed systems demand accurate temporal alignment. In the burgeoning field of Internet of Things (IoT), where interconnected devices communicate and collaborate, PTP ensures that sensors, actuators, and other IoT components operate with a shared understanding of time. This temporal coherence becomes crucial in applications ranging from smart homes and cities to industrial IoT deployments. PTP's ability to synchronize clocks across geographically dispersed IoT devices contributes to the efficiency and reliability of IoT ecosystems, enabling seamless communication and interaction between diverse components.

In the aviation and aerospace industry, where precision is paramount for navigation, communication, and control systems, PTP serves as a cornerstone for achieving accurate time synchronization. Air traffic control systems, satellite networks, and communication protocols in aerospace applications rely on precise timing to ensure the safety and efficiency of operations. PTP's ability to synchronize clocks with nanosecond-level precision becomes crucial for coordinating air traffic, maintaining communication links, and ensuring the integrity of data in navigation systems. The aviation sector's stringent requirements for timing accuracy align seamlessly with PTP's capabilities, contributing to the reliability and safety of air transportation.

The healthcare sector represents another domain where PTP's application can be transformative. In medical imaging systems, where the synchronization of multiple imaging devices is essential for diagnostic accuracy, PTP ensures that timestamps align precisely. This synchronization becomes critical in procedures such as surgeries, where different devices need to operate cohesively in real-time. PTP's ability to achieve sub-microsecond and nanosecond-level precision contributes to the coordination of medical equipment, enhancing the efficiency and accuracy of diagnostic and therapeutic procedures. Additionally, in scenarios involving distributed healthcare systems and telemedicine, PTP ensures that timestamps align across different components, facilitating the seamless exchange of medical information.

In military and defense applications, where coordination and precision are paramount for mission success, PTP plays a vital role in achieving temporal alignment. Communication systems, radar networks, and command and control centers benefit from PTP's ability to synchronize clocks with high accuracy. In military operations, where split-second decisions can have significant consequences, PTP ensures that disparate components of defense systems operate cohesively, contributing to the efficiency and effectiveness of military operations.

Despite its myriad applications and advantages, the deployment of PTP comes with challenges and considerations. The reliance on a stable and accurate time source, often derived from satellite-based

Global Navigation Satellite Systems (GNSS) like GPS, necessitates the availability of reliable signals. The quality of the GNSS signal directly influences the accuracy of PTP synchronization. In scenarios where GNSS signals may be obstructed or unreliable, alternative time sources or supplementary measures may be required to ensure synchronization accuracy.

The management of PTP in large-scale networks also requires careful planning and monitoring. The selection of a Grandmaster clock, which serves as the primary reference for time in the network, involves considerations such as clock stability, precision, and the quality of the time source. Configuring PTP-aware devices and ensuring that they operate in harmony with the selected Grandmaster is essential for optimal synchronization performance. Additionally, the impact of network variations, including latency and jitter, must be considered to achieve optimal synchronization in dynamic and heterogeneous network environments.

In conclusion, the application of the Precision Time Protocol spans a diverse array of scenarios where accurate timing is not merely a convenience but an absolute necessity. From financial trading platforms and telecommunications networks to smart grids, industrial automation, scientific research, healthcare systems, and defense applications, PTP's impact is far-reaching. Its ability to achieve sub-microsecond and nanosecond-level precision contributes to the efficiency, reliability, and coordination of distributed systems across industries. As technology continues to advance and the demands for precision in temporal alignment grow, the principles and applications of PTP are poised to remain integral in shaping the landscape of synchronized and interconnected systems, ensuring that disparate elements operate in harmony to meet the stringent requirements of modern applications.

Introducing MQTT as a lightweight messaging protocol for real-time communication.

MQTT (Message Queuing Telemetry Transport) stands as a pivotal player in the landscape of real-time communication, heralded for its lightweight design and efficiency. Born out of the need for a protocol that could cater to the demands of constrained environments, MQTT has found widespread adoption in scenarios where minimal overhead, low bandwidth, and reliable messaging are essential. This exploration dives into the fundamental principles, architecture, and applications of MQTT, unraveling the layers of its design that make it a preferred choice for a diverse range of industries and use cases.

At its core, MQTT was conceived as a publish-subscribe messaging protocol, emphasizing simplicity and frugality in its approach. Conceived by Dr. Andy Stanford-Clark of IBM and Arlen Nipper of Arcom in the late 1990s, MQTT initially aimed to facilitate communication between sensors and actuators on oil pipelines. Its architecture reflects a commitment to lightweight design, making it particularly well-suited for resource-constrained devices and networks where bandwidth is at a premium. MQTT operates over the TCP/IP protocol, enabling it to seamlessly integrate into existing network infrastructures while keeping communication overhead to a bare minimum.

The essence of MQTT lies in its publish-subscribe paradigm, a model that decouples message producers (publishers) from message consumers (subscribers). In this paradigm, publishers broadcast messages to specific channels, referred to as "topics" in MQTT terminology, without any knowledge of the identity or existence of subscribers. Subscribers express interest in specific topics and receive messages published to those topics. This decoupling of producers and consumers makes MQTT an inherently scalable and flexible protocol, catering to dynamic and distributed systems.

The lightweight nature of MQTT manifests in its protocol headers, which are designed to be concise, resulting in minimal data overhead. This efficiency is particularly advantageous in scenarios where bandwidth is limited, such as in remote or low-power environments, satellite communications, or Internet of Things (IoT) deployments. The reduced size of MQTT messages not only conserves network resources but also facilitates faster transmission, a crucial aspect in real-time communication where latency is a key consideration.

One of MQTT's key features is its support for Quality of Service (QoS) levels, offering varying degrees of message delivery assurance. The three QoS levels in MQTT are At Most Once (QoS 0), At Least Once (QoS 1), and Exactly Once (QoS 2). QoS 0 ensures that a message is delivered at most once, with no confirmation from the recipient. QoS 1 guarantees that a message is delivered at least once, and the sender may receive acknowledgment from the recipient. QoS 2 ensures that a message is delivered exactly once by using a four-step handshake mechanism. This flexibility in QoS levels allows MQTT to adapt to different communication scenarios, balancing the trade-off between delivery guarantees and communication overhead.

The architecture of MQTT revolves around the concept of a broker, a central entity that facilitates communication between publishers and subscribers. The broker acts as an intermediary, receiving messages from publishers and forwarding them to subscribers interested in the corresponding topics. This centralized broker-based architecture introduces a level of abstraction that simplifies the complexities of point-to-point communication. Multiple publishers and subscribers can connect to the same broker, allowing for a many-to-many communication model without the need for direct connections between every pair of participants. This broker-mediated approach enhances scalability, manageability, and the overall efficiency of communication in MQTT-based systems.

The connection model in MQTT is based on a lightweight session mechanism, allowing clients (both publishers and subscribers) to connect and disconnect dynamically without losing the state of their communication. The stateless nature of MQTT sessions is advantageous in scenarios where devices may experience intermittent connectivity or where frequent disconnections and reconnections are expected. The ability to maintain continuity in communication sessions, even in the face of device mobility or network fluctuations, makes MQTT well-suited for dynamic and unpredictable environments.

In the realm of security, MQTT offers options for secure communication through the use of Transport Layer Security (TLS) or its predecessor, Secure Sockets Layer (SSL). By encrypting the communication between clients and brokers, MQTT ensures the confidentiality and integrity of the messages exchanged. This becomes particularly crucial in applications where sensitive information is transmitted, such as in healthcare, finance, or industrial control systems. The security features of MQTT provide a robust foundation for deploying the protocol in diverse and sensitive use cases.

The lightweight and flexible nature of MQTT positions it as an ideal choice for applications in the Internet of Things (IoT), where a multitude of devices with varying capabilities need to communicate seamlessly. In IoT scenarios, MQTT's publish-subscribe model enables efficient communication between devices, sensors, and actuators. Devices can publish sensor data to specific topics, and other devices or applications interested in that data can subscribe to the corresponding topics. This loose coupling between devices facilitates scalable and modular IoT architectures, allowing for the integration of diverse sensors and actuators without tight dependencies.

MQTT's adoption in the industrial automation sector underscores its suitability for applications where real-time communication is essential. In industrial settings, where sensors, programmable logic controllers (PLCs), and supervisory control and data acquisition (SCADA) systems collaborate, MQTT provides a lightweight and reliable messaging framework. Sensors can publish real-time data to MQTT topics, and control systems can subscribe to these topics, enabling timely decision-making and control in dynamic industrial environments. The protocol's ability to handle communication in constrained networks and its support for QoS levels make it a valuable asset in scenarios where precision and reliability are paramount.

The application of MQTT extends into smart homes and building automation, where the protocol's lightweight design and efficiency align with the requirements of resource-constrained devices. Smart home devices, ranging from temperature sensors to smart thermostats and lighting controls, can communicate seamlessly using MQTT. The decoupled nature of the publish-subscribe model allows for the integration of new devices without necessitating changes to existing communication patterns. MQTT's ability to operate over low-power networks and its support for intermittent connectivity make it an ideal choice for building automation scenarios.

In addition to its applications in constrained environments, MQTT has also found favor in large-scale and mission-critical systems. Social media platforms, messaging services, and real-time collaborative applications leverage MQTT for efficient and scalable message dissemination. The protocol's ability to handle a high volume of messages with low latency makes it well-suited for applications where timely information delivery is crucial. The simplicity and elegance of MQTT's design contribute to its versatility, allowing it to seamlessly integrate into diverse communication architectures.

The popularity of MQTT is further augmented by the existence of open-source implementations, such as Eclipse Mosquitto, which provide robust and extensible broker solutions. This open-source ecosystem encourages the adoption and evolution of MQTT, fostering a collaborative community that contributes to the protocol's ongoing refinement and adaptability. The availability of MQTT libraries for various programming languages and platforms simplifies its integration into diverse applications, making it accessible to a wide range of developers and industries.

Despite its numerous advantages, the deployment of MQTT also brings forth considerations and challenges. The reliance on a central broker introduces a potential single point of failure, necessitating careful design and redundancy mechanisms for critical deployments. Additionally, while the lightweight design of MQTT is advantageous in many scenarios, it may not be the best fit for applications requiring highly structured and complex message formats. The trade-off between simplicity and expressiveness should be carefully evaluated based on the specific requirements of the use case.

In conclusion, MQTT's journey from its origins in telemetry for oil pipelines to its widespread adoption in diverse industries is a testament to its efficiency, simplicity, and adaptability. As a lightweight messaging protocol, MQTT has transcended its initial use case, finding applications in IoT, industrial automation, smart homes, social media, and beyond. Its publish-subscribe model, broker-based architecture, and support for varying QoS levels position it as a versatile solution for real-time communication in constrained and dynamic environments. Whether facilitating communication between sensors in a remote IoT deployment or enabling real-time collaboration in a social media platform, MQTT continues to play a central role in the evolving landscape of efficient and scalable messaging protocols.

Discussing its efficiency in scenarios with constrained bandwidth and unreliable networks.

The efficiency of MQTT (Message Queuing Telemetry Transport) in scenarios characterized by constrained bandwidth and unreliable networks is a testament to its lightweight design and adaptive capabilities, making it a preferred choice in diverse applications ranging from remote IoT deployments to industrial automation and beyond. In these challenging environments, where the availability of network resources is limited and communication links may be prone to disruptions, MQTT's fundamental principles and features come to the forefront, addressing the unique requirements posed by constrained bandwidth and unreliable connectivity.

At the core of MQTT's efficiency lies its minimalist protocol design, meticulously crafted to minimize data overhead. In scenarios where bandwidth is a precious resource, every bit of transmitted data becomes significant. MQTT addresses this by employing compact protocol headers that carry essential information without unnecessary embellishments. The concise nature of MQTT messages reduces the burden on the network, enabling faster transmission and efficient utilization of available bandwidth. This design philosophy aligns seamlessly with the needs of environments where data transmission must be streamlined, and the cost of communication must be minimized.

The publish-subscribe model that MQTT embraces further contributes to its efficiency in bandwidth-constrained scenarios. By decoupling message producers (publishers) from message consumers (subscribers), MQTT eliminates the need for direct connections between every pair of communicating devices. Instead, devices communicate through a central broker, which acts as an intermediary responsible for routing messages to the appropriate recipients. This broker-mediated approach reduces the number of direct connections, facilitating a many-to-many communication model without the need for a point-to-point connection for every possible interaction. In environments with limited bandwidth, the reduction in direct connections and associated communication overhead enhances efficiency.

Moreover, MQTT's publish-subscribe paradigm allows for a scalable and modular architecture. In scenarios where the number of devices and sensors may vary dynamically, MQTT accommodates this variability seamlessly. New devices can enter the network and start publishing or subscribing to topics without necessitating changes to the existing communication infrastructure. This adaptability is particularly advantageous in IoT deployments, where the number and types of devices may evolve over time. MQTT's ability to scale without introducing complexity makes it a robust choice for environments where resource constraints are dynamic and unpredictable.

The lightweight session mechanism employed by MQTT further enhances its efficiency in scenarios with unreliable networks and intermittent connectivity. In such environments, devices may experience frequent disconnections or fluctuations in network availability. MQTT's stateless session model allows devices to connect and disconnect dynamically without losing the state of their communication. This resilience to network variations ensures that devices can seamlessly resume communication even after temporary disruptions. The ability to maintain continuity in communication sessions, regardless of the network's reliability, is a crucial aspect of MQTT's efficiency in scenarios where connectivity is uncertain.

Another key feature contributing to MQTT's efficiency in constrained environments is its support for Quality of Service (QoS) levels. These QoS levels provide varying degrees of message delivery assurance, allowing applications to tailor their communication requirements to the specifics of the environment. In scenarios with constrained bandwidth and potential network disruptions, MQTT's QoS levels offer a flexible approach to balancing the trade-off between delivery guarantees and communication overhead.

At Most Once (QoS 0) ensures that a message is delivered at most once, with no acknowledgment from the recipient. While this level of QoS does not provide delivery assurance, it minimizes communication overhead, making it suitable for scenarios where occasional message loss is acceptable. At Least Once (QoS 1) guarantees that a message is delivered at least once, and the sender may receive acknowledgment from the recipient. This level introduces a level of reliability without imposing excessive communication costs. Exactly Once (QoS 2) ensures that a message is delivered exactly once through a four-step handshake mechanism. Although this level introduces more communication overhead, it offers the highest level of delivery assurance. The ability to choose the appropriate QoS level based on the specific requirements of the application enhances MQTT's adaptability in scenarios where bandwidth is constrained and network reliability is variable.

In addition to its bandwidth-efficient design, MQTT's suitability for unreliable networks is underscored by its support for session persistence and Last Will and Testament (LWT) messages. Session persistence allows the broker to retain information about a client's subscriptions and unacknowledged messages even if the client disconnects. When the client reconnects, the broker can restore the session, ensuring that the client receives any messages it missed during the disconnection. This feature is particularly valuable in scenarios where devices may experience frequent connectivity disruptions.

The Last Will and Testament (LWT) feature allows a client to specify a message that the broker should send on its behalf in the event of an unanticipated disconnection. This mechanism is crucial for scenarios where the state of a device or application must be communicated to others in the network even in the absence of an explicit disconnection. For example, in remote environmental monitoring, if a sensor node unexpectedly loses connectivity, it can use the LWT feature to inform the network about the discontinuation of data updates. The combination of session persistence and LWT messages enhances MQTT's reliability and ensures that the protocol remains effective even in environments with unreliable networks.

The security features of MQTT also contribute to its efficiency in scenarios where data integrity and confidentiality are paramount. By supporting Transport Layer Security (TLS) or its predecessor, Secure Sockets Layer (SSL), MQTT enables encrypted communication between clients and brokers. This security layer ensures that sensitive information remains confidential and protected from unauthorized access. In constrained environments where security is a concern, MQTT's ability to provide secure communication without unduly burdening the network aligns with the overarching goal of achieving efficiency.

The efficiency of MQTT in scenarios with constrained bandwidth and unreliable networks finds practical applications across a spectrum of industries. In remote or rural IoT deployments, where devices may operate on low-power networks with sporadic connectivity, MQTT's lightweight design and adaptive features enable seamless communication. Industrial automation, where sensors, actuators, and control systems must collaborate in dynamic environments, benefits from MQTT's ability to operate efficiently over constrained networks. Moreover, in smart cities where sensor networks must transmit data across urban landscapes with varying connectivity, MQTT's adaptability proves invaluable.

In conclusion, MQTT's efficiency in scenarios with constrained bandwidth and unreliable networks is rooted in its minimalist design, publish-subscribe paradigm, lightweight session mechanism, support for QoS levels, and security features. These elements collectively enable MQTT to thrive in environments where network resources are limited, and connectivity may be unpredictable. From IoT deployments in remote areas to industrial automation systems and smart city initiatives, MQTT's ability to provide reliable and efficient communication in challenging conditions cements its role as a versatile and adaptive messaging protocol for the real-time communication needs of the modern interconnected world.

Showcasing case studies of successful real-time communication protocol implementations.

Case studies of successful real-time communication protocol implementations provide valuable insights into the practical applications and impact of these protocols across various industries. Examining instances where communication protocols have been effectively deployed underscores their significance in addressing specific challenges and enhancing operational efficiency. In this exploration, we delve into notable case studies that highlight successful implementations of real-time communication protocols in diverse contexts, shedding light on the tangible benefits and lessons learned from these experiences.

One noteworthy case study in the realm of industrial automation showcases the successful implementation of the OPC UA (Object Linking and Embedding for Process Control Unified Architecture) protocol. In a manufacturing facility with a complex network of programmable logic controllers (PLCs), supervisory control and data acquisition (SCADA) systems, and other devices, the adoption of OPC UA facilitated seamless communication and interoperability. The protocol's ability to standardize data exchange formats and provide a secure, platform-independent framework proved instrumental in integrating heterogeneous devices from different vendors. The implementation resulted in improved data integrity, reduced downtime, and enhanced scalability, allowing for the efficient coordination of various components in the industrial automation ecosystem.

In the healthcare sector, a compelling case study revolves around the adoption of the HL7 (Health Level Seven) protocol for real-time communication in electronic health record (EHR) systems. In a hospital setting, where timely access to patient information is critical, the HL7 protocol played a pivotal role in standardizing data exchange between disparate healthcare systems. By defining a common language for the interchange of clinical and administrative data, HL7 facilitated the seamless integration of electronic health records, laboratory systems, and radiology information systems. This interoperability not only improved the accuracy and accessibility of patient data but also streamlined clinical workflows, contributing to enhanced patient care and operational efficiency.

The MQTT (Message Queuing Telemetry Transport) protocol emerges as a star performer in the Internet of Things (IoT) landscape, as demonstrated in a case study involving a smart city deployment. In a city aiming for sustainable urban development, various IoT devices, such as environmental sensors, smart lighting systems, and waste management sensors, needed to communicate in real time. By implementing MQTT, the smart city achieved efficient and scalable communication between diverse IoT devices, fostering a cohesive and interconnected urban infrastructure. The protocol's lightweight design, support for publish-subscribe communication, and adaptability to constrained networks allowed for the seamless integration of sensors and actuators, contributing to improved resource management, reduced energy consumption, and enhanced overall city livability.

The adoption of the WebSockets protocol in the context of real-time web applications presents another compelling case study. A popular social media platform sought to enhance user engagement by implementing real-time features such as instant messaging and live updates. By leveraging WebSockets, the platform achieved low-latency communication between users and the server, enabling real-time interactions without the need for constant polling. This implementation significantly improved the user experience by providing instantaneous updates, reducing message delivery delays, and enhancing overall responsiveness. The success of this case study highlights the effectiveness of WebSockets in creating dynamic and engaging real-time web applications.

In the finance industry, where split-second decision-making is crucial, the implementation of the FIX (Financial Information eXchange) protocol stands out as a pivotal case study. In a high-frequency trading environment, where rapid execution of financial transactions is paramount, the FIX protocol has become the de facto standard for real-time communication between financial institutions and trading platforms. By streamlining the exchange of trading-related information, such as orders and executions, FIX facilitates seamless communication across a diverse ecosystem of market participants. The protocol's emphasis on efficiency, reliability, and standardization has contributed to the rapid execution of trades, minimized latencies, and enhanced overall liquidity in financial markets.

Another notable case study explores the successful deployment of the CoAP (Constrained Application Protocol) in a smart grid infrastructure. In the context of managing distributed energy resources, such as solar panels and energy storage systems, efficient communication between devices is essential for grid optimization. CoAP, designed specifically for constrained environments, provided a lightweight and energy-efficient solution for facilitating real-time communication between smart grid devices. The protocol's support for resource-oriented communication and its ability to operate over low-power networks contributed to the successful integration of diverse components in the smart grid ecosystem. This implementation resulted in improved energy efficiency, enhanced grid reliability, and better responsiveness to dynamic changes in energy demand and supply.

The adoption of the DDS (Data Distribution Service) protocol in a mission-critical aerospace and defense application offers insights into the protocol's effectiveness in complex and demanding environments. In an air traffic management system, where coordination and communication are paramount for ensuring the safety of air travel, DDS provided a robust and reliable middleware solution. The protocol's ability to support real-time data distribution and its adherence to Quality of Service (QoS) specifications ensured timely and secure exchange of critical information between air traffic control systems, radar networks, and aircraft. The successful implementation of DDS contributed to improved situational awareness, reduced response times, and enhanced overall safety in air traffic management.

In the context of collaborative online gaming, the adoption of the WebSocket protocol has played a pivotal role in delivering real-time and interactive gaming experiences. A popular online multiplayer game sought to overcome the limitations of traditional HTTP communication, which introduced latency and delays in transmitting game state updates. By implementing WebSockets, the gaming platform achieved bi-directional communication between the server and players' devices in real time. This enabled instant updates on player actions, improved synchronization of game state, and reduced latency, ultimately enhancing the overall gaming experience. The success of this case study highlights the importance of low-latency communication in delivering immersive and engaging online gaming environments.

The implementation of the DDS protocol in the context of autonomous vehicles exemplifies its efficacy in enabling real-time communication for critical applications. In an autonomous driving ecosystem, where vehicles must exchange information about their status, intent, and environmental observations, DDS provides a reliable and scalable communication solution. The protocol's ability to support large-scale data distribution, dynamic discovery of participants, and customizable QoS configurations contributes to the seamless coordination of autonomous vehicles on the road. This implementation enhances the safety, reliability, and responsiveness of autonomous driving systems, showcasing the practical impact of real-time communication protocols in shaping the future of transportation.

In the domain of telecommunication networks, the successful implementation of the SIP (Session Initiation Protocol) protocol is pivotal for enabling real-time communication services such as voice and video calls. A case study involving a Voice over Internet Protocol

(VoIP) service provider illustrates the effectiveness of SIP in facilitating call setup, media negotiation, and termination. By adhering to the SIP protocol, the service provider achieved interoperability between different communication devices and networks, allowing users to initiate and receive calls seamlessly across diverse platforms. The protocol's extensibility, support for multimedia communication, and standardized signaling mechanisms contribute to its widespread adoption in the telecommunications industry.

These case studies collectively highlight the diverse applications and impact of real-time communication protocols in addressing specific challenges across industries. Whether optimizing industrial automation processes, enhancing healthcare interoperability, enabling smart city infrastructure, supporting high-frequency trading, managing energy grids, ensuring air traffic safety, delivering immersive gaming experiences, facilitating autonomous driving, or powering telecommunications services, real-time communication protocols play a central role in shaping the efficiency, responsiveness, and reliability of modern interconnected systems. The success stories and lessons learned from these implementations underscore the critical importance of selecting and deploying appropriate communication protocols tailored to the unique requirements of each application domain.

Discussing the considerations in selecting the appropriate protocol for specific applications.

Selecting the appropriate communication protocol for specific applications is a nuanced process that involves careful consideration of various factors to ensure optimal performance, reliability, and compatibility with the unique requirements of the given context. This in-depth exploration delves into the key considerations that guide the decision-making process when choosing a communication protocol, examining the multifaceted aspects that influence the selection and deployment of protocols across diverse domains.

One fundamental consideration in selecting a communication protocol revolves around the nature of the data being exchanged. Different applications demand varying levels of data integrity, reliability, and real-time responsiveness. For example, in applications where precision and accuracy are paramount, such as in industrial automation or healthcare systems, protocols with strong guarantees of data integrity, like OPC UA or HL7, may be preferred. On the other hand, in scenarios where timely updates and real-time communication are critical, as in financial trading or IoT deployments, lightweight and efficient protocols such as MQTT or CoAP may be more suitable. Understanding the specific requirements of the data being transmitted forms the foundational basis for protocol selection.

Scalability emerges as a pivotal consideration, particularly in applications that anticipate growth or fluctuations in the number of connected devices or users. Communication protocols must be able to seamlessly handle an increasing volume of data and participants without sacrificing performance. Protocols like MQTT, with their publish-subscribe architecture, provide an inherently scalable model, allowing devices or users to join or leave the network dynamically. Conversely, protocols like DDS, designed for large-scale distributed systems, offer robust mechanisms for managing data distribution in scenarios with a multitude of participants. The ability to accommodate scalability ensures that the chosen protocol can evolve with the changing demands of the application.

Interoperability plays a crucial role, especially in environments where diverse devices, systems, or platforms need to communicate seamlessly. The selected communication protocol should offer standardized mechanisms for data exchange, ensuring compatibility between components from different vendors or with varying specifications. Protocols such as OPC UA in industrial settings or HL7 in healthcare have gained prominence due to their emphasis on standardization, allowing disparate systems to communicate without friction. The consideration of interoperability becomes particularly pertinent in scenarios where heterogeneity is inevitable, emphasizing the need for protocols that transcend vendor-specific boundaries.

The level of latency acceptable in a given application is a determining factor in protocol selection, especially in contexts where real-time or near-real-time communication is essential. Protocols like WebSockets or MQTT, designed for low-latency communication, find favor in applications such as online gaming or financial trading, where delays can significantly impact user experience or transaction outcomes. Conversely, in scenarios where lower latency is tolerable, protocols like HTTP may suffice, especially for web-based applications where real-time constraints are less stringent. Understanding the specific latency requirements of an application becomes pivotal in aligning the chosen protocol with the performance expectations of the system.

Reliability and fault tolerance considerations come to the forefront, particularly in applications where the consequences of communication failures are severe. Protocols like FIX in financial trading or DDS in mission-critical systems prioritize mechanisms to ensure reliable data delivery and fault recovery. These protocols often incorporate features such as Quality of Service (QoS) levels, session persistence, or redundancy mechanisms to mitigate the impact of communication disruptions. In contrast, applications with more lenient reliability requirements may opt for protocols with lightweight designs, accepting occasional data loss in exchange for reduced communication overhead.

Security emerges as a paramount consideration, especially in applications where sensitive or confidential information is exchanged. Protocols like HTTPS or protocols with built-in security features, such as TLS/SSL in MQTT, prioritize the encryption and authentication of data to safeguard against unauthorized access or tampering. This consideration becomes particularly pertinent in industries like healthcare, finance, or critical infrastructure, where regulatory compliance and data protection are non-negotiable. The choice of a secure communication protocol ensures that the application can withstand potential security threats and adhere to industry-specific compliance standards.

The resource constraints of the devices or systems involved in communication play a pivotal role in protocol selection, particularly in scenarios with limited processing power, memory, or bandwidth. Protocols designed for resource-constrained environments, such as CoAP in IoT or lightweight variants of MQTT, prioritize efficiency and minimal data overhead. These protocols are tailored to operate seamlessly on devices with constrained resources, ensuring that communication does not unduly burden the system. The consideration of resource constraints becomes crucial in applications where devices may vary widely in their capabilities, necessitating a protocol that caters to the lowest common denominator.

The adaptability of a communication protocol to dynamic network conditions is another critical consideration, especially in applications where devices may experience intermittent connectivity or operate in challenging environments. Protocols like MQTT with its lightweight session mechanism or CoAP with support for unreliable networks excel in scenarios where connectivity fluctuations are expected. These protocols allow devices to connect and disconnect dynamically without losing the state of their communication, ensuring seamless operation even in the face of network variations. The ability to adapt to unpredictable network conditions ensures the robustness of communication in scenarios where environmental factors may impact connectivity.

Ease of implementation and developer familiarity contribute significantly to the practicality of a communication protocol in real-world applications. Protocols with well-documented specifications, open-source implementations, and a broad ecosystem of libraries and tools simplify the integration process and reduce development effort. HTTP and WebSockets, being foundational protocols of the web, are widely supported and familiar to developers, making them accessible choices for web-based applications. The availability of comprehensive documentation, community support, and a developer-friendly ecosystem eases the learning curve and accelerates the implementation of the chosen protocol.

Cost considerations, both in terms of implementation and maintenance, play a pivotal role, especially in resource-constrained environments or industries with stringent budget constraints. Protocols that require extensive hardware or software investments may be less viable in scenarios where cost efficiency is paramount. Lightweight and open-source protocols, such as CoAP or MQTT, often present a cost-effective solution, especially in large-scale deployments where minimizing infrastructure costs is essential. The consideration of costs extends beyond initial implementation to ongoing maintenance, ensuring that the chosen protocol aligns with the budgetary constraints of the application.

Evolutionary potential and industry support contribute to the long-term viability of a communication protocol. Protocols that enjoy widespread adoption, industry recognition, and ongoing development efforts are more likely to remain relevant and supported in the long run. Standardization bodies or industry alliances endorsing a protocol, as seen in the cases of OPC UA or HL7, provide assurance of its stability and future enhancements. The consideration of the protocol's long-term roadmap ensures that the chosen communication solution remains compatible with evolving technologies and industry standards, safeguarding the investment in the chosen protocol.

The specific requirements of the application domain, such as regulatory compliance, industry standards, or domain-specific protocols, also influence the selection process. Certain industries, like healthcare or finance, may mandate adherence to specific communication standards due to regulatory requirements. In these cases, the choice of protocol is constrained by the need to comply with established norms and regulations. The consideration of industry-specific requirements ensures that the selected protocol aligns with the broader ecosystem and regulatory landscape of the application domain.

In conclusion, the process of selecting the appropriate communication protocol for specific applications is a multidimensional and context-specific endeavor. The considerations span a spectrum from the nature of the data being exchanged, scalability, and interoperability to latency, reliability, security, and resource constraints. The adaptability of the protocol to dynamic network conditions, ease of implementation, cost considerations, evolutionary potential, and industry support also play pivotal roles in guiding the decision-making process. The careful balancing of these considerations ensures that the chosen communication protocol aligns with the unique requirements of the application, fostering efficient, reliable, and future-proof communication in diverse domains.

Chapter 7: Applications of Real-Time Systems

Showcasing applications of real-time systems in medical devices and patient monitoring.

Real-time systems have revolutionized the landscape of medical devices and patient monitoring, ushering in an era of precision, efficiency, and enhanced healthcare outcomes. This comprehensive exploration delves into the diverse applications of real-time systems in the medical domain, illustrating how these systems contribute to the development of advanced medical devices and the continuous monitoring of patients.

One of the paramount applications of real-time systems in the medical field lies in the development of life-saving devices such as implantable cardiac defibrillators. These sophisticated devices are equipped with real-time monitoring capabilities that continuously assess the patient's heart rhythm. When an abnormal heart rhythm, indicative of a potentially fatal arrhythmia, is detected, the defibrillator can instantaneously deliver a life-saving shock to restore the heart's normal rhythm. The real-time processing capabilities of these devices are critical, as prompt intervention is crucial in preventing sudden cardiac arrest and preserving patient lives.

In the realm of patient monitoring, real-time systems play a pivotal role in the development of wearable devices that provide continuous health tracking. Wearable monitors equipped with sensors for heart rate, blood pressure, and oxygen saturation enable real-time data collection, allowing individuals to monitor their health in everyday scenarios. These devices not only empower individuals to take proactive steps towards their well-being but also offer valuable data for healthcare providers. Real-time data analysis in these wearable devices enhances their effectiveness, providing users and healthcare professionals with immediate insights into changes in health metrics.

The integration of real-time systems into ventilators represents a critical advancement in the care of patients with respiratory conditions, especially in intensive care settings. Ventilators equipped with real-time monitoring capabilities continuously assess the patient's respiratory parameters, adapting the ventilatory support in real-time based on the patient's needs. This dynamic adjustment ensures that the patient receives optimal respiratory support, responding promptly to changes in lung function or oxygenation levels. Real-time monitoring of parameters such as tidal volume, respiratory rate, and oxygen levels allows for precise and personalized ventilator management, contributing to improved patient outcomes.

Real-time systems find application in the field of anesthesia delivery, enhancing the safety and precision of administering anesthesia to patients undergoing surgery. Infusion pumps equipped with real-time monitoring capabilities enable anesthesiologists to closely regulate the delivery of anesthesia agents, adjusting dosages in real-time based on the patient's response. The ability to continuously monitor factors such as heart rate, blood pressure, and oxygen saturation ensures that the patient remains in an optimal state during the surgical procedure. Real-time feedback from these monitoring systems allows healthcare providers to make instant adjustments, mitigating the risks associated with anesthesia administration.

In the context of glucose monitoring for diabetes management, real-time systems have significantly transformed the way individuals track and manage their blood glucose levels. Continuous glucose monitoring (CGM) systems employ real-time sensors to measure glucose levels in interstitial fluid, providing a continuous stream of data to users and healthcare professionals. The real-time feedback from CGM systems enables individuals to make timely decisions regarding insulin dosages, dietary choices, and physical activity, leading to better glycemic control. This technology not only enhances the quality of life for individuals with diabetes but also offers valuable insights for healthcare providers in optimizing treatment plans.

The advent of real-time imaging technologies has revolutionized medical diagnostics, with applications ranging from ultrasound to magnetic resonance imaging (MRI). Real-time ultrasound imaging, for instance, enables healthcare practitioners to visualize dynamic processes within the body in real-time, such as the beating heart or blood flow in vessels. This immediacy in imaging is crucial for guiding medical interventions, enabling physicians to make real-time decisions during procedures like biopsies or catheterizations. Similarly, real-time MRI allows for dynamic imaging of structures and processes, providing valuable insights into the functioning of organs and tissues.

Real-time monitoring is integral to the functioning of patient telemetry systems in hospital environments. These systems use real-time data acquisition and transmission to continuously monitor patients' vital signs, such as electrocardiogram (ECG) waveforms, heart rate, and respiratory rate. The data is transmitted in real-time to central monitoring stations, allowing healthcare professionals to promptly identify and respond to any deviations from normal physiological parameters. This capability is particularly critical in high-acuity settings such as intensive care units, where early detection of abnormalities can lead to timely interventions and improved patient outcomes.

Telemedicine platforms leverage real-time systems to enable remote patient monitoring and virtual consultations. With the integration of real-time video and audio communication, healthcare providers can conduct virtual visits, allowing them to assess patients' conditions, discuss symptoms, and make treatment recommendations in real-time. Remote patient monitoring devices, equipped with real-time sensors, facilitate the collection of vital health data, enabling healthcare professionals to monitor patients' conditions from a distance. This application has gained prominence, especially in situations where physical access to healthcare facilities may be limited or restricted.

Real-time electroencephalogram (EEG) monitoring plays a crucial role in the diagnosis and management of neurological disorders, including epilepsy. EEG systems equipped with real-time processing capabilities continuously record and analyze electrical activity in the brain, allowing healthcare providers to identify abnormal patterns indicative of seizures. The real-time nature of EEG monitoring is essential for capturing and documenting seizure events, enabling timely adjustments to treatment plans and improving the quality of life for individuals with epilepsy.

In the field of robotic-assisted surgery, real-time systems facilitate precise control and feedback for surgeons during minimally invasive procedures. Surgical robots equipped with real-time imaging and navigation capabilities allow surgeons to visualize the surgical site in real-time, enhancing accuracy and reducing the risk of complications. Real-time feedback from the robotic system provides surgeons with a responsive and immersive experience, enabling them to perform complex procedures with enhanced dexterity and precision. This application of real-time systems in surgery represents a paradigm shift in the capabilities and safety of minimally invasive interventions.

Real-time polymerase chain reaction (PCR) technology has become instrumental in molecular diagnostics, particularly in the rapid detection of infectious diseases. Real-time PCR allows for the continuous monitoring of DNA amplification during the reaction, enabling the quantification of target nucleic acids in real-time. This capability is pivotal in diagnosing infections, identifying genetic mutations, and monitoring the progression of diseases. Real-time PCR has been widely employed in applications such as COVID-19 testing, where prompt and accurate results are crucial for public health management.

In the domain of neonatal care, real-time systems play a vital role in monitoring the health and well-being of premature or critically ill infants. Real-time monitoring devices, such as neonatal intensive care unit (NICU) monitors, continuously track parameters like heart rate, respiratory rate, and oxygen saturation in real-time. This constant vigilance enables healthcare providers to detect and address potential complications promptly, ensuring the best possible outcomes for vulnerable neonates. The integration of real-time systems in neonatal care exemplifies their transformative impact on improving the survival and long-term health of premature infants.

The applications of real-time systems extend to the development of smart infusion pumps, which deliver medications to patients in a controlled and precise manner. These pumps incorporate real-time monitoring capabilities to assess factors such as drug concentration, infusion rates, and patient response. The real-time feedback allows for dynamic adjustments to the infusion parameters, reducing the risk of medication errors and enhancing patient safety. In critical care scenarios, where accurate medication delivery is crucial, smart infusion pumps equipped with real-time capabilities play a pivotal role in optimizing therapeutic outcomes.

Real-time systems have found application in remote patient monitoring for chronic conditions such as heart failure. Implantable devices, such as cardiac resynchronization therapy (CRT) devices, continuously monitor the patient's cardiac function and transmit real-time data to healthcare providers. This remote monitoring enables early detection of changes in the patient's condition, allowing for timely interventions and adjustments to treatment plans. The real-time nature of remote patient monitoring enhances the proactive management of chronic diseases, reducing hospitalizations and improving patients' quality of life.

In conclusion, the applications of real-time systems in medical devices and patient monitoring have redefined the landscape of healthcare, ushering in an era of precision, responsiveness, and improved patient outcomes. From life-saving implantable devices to wearable monitors, ventilators, anesthesia delivery systems, and advanced diagnostic tools, real-time systems have permeated every facet of modern healthcare. These applications collectively contribute to a paradigm shift in how healthcare is delivered, emphasizing proactive monitoring, timely interventions, and personalized care. The integration of real-time systems continues to shape the future of medicine, paving the way for innovative technologies that enhance the efficiency, safety, and effectiveness of healthcare delivery across diverse medical domains.

Discussing how real-time capabilities enhance diagnostic accuracy and treatment.

The integration of real-time capabilities into medical diagnostics and treatment represents a transformative leap forward in healthcare, significantly enhancing diagnostic accuracy and treatment outcomes. In this comprehensive exploration, we delve into the multifaceted ways in which real-time capabilities contribute to the precision, immediacy, and effectiveness of diagnostics and treatment across various medical domains.

Real-time imaging technologies have become pivotal in elevating diagnostic accuracy to unprecedented levels. Diagnostic modalities such as real-time ultrasound, magnetic resonance imaging (MRI), and computed tomography (CT) offer dynamic, instantaneous visualization of internal structures and physiological processes. Real-time ultrasound, for instance, enables healthcare practitioners to observe the beating heart, blood flow, and fetal development in real-time, providing a wealth of information for accurate diagnosis. The immediacy and dynamic nature of real-time imaging empower clinicians to identify abnormalities, guide interventions, and make informed decisions during diagnostic procedures. This real-time insight enhances diagnostic accuracy by allowing for the observation of dynamic changes and the immediate identification of critical details that might be missed in static images.

In the realm of pathology, real-time capabilities have revolutionized diagnostic procedures such as intraoperative frozen section analysis. Real-time microscopic imaging systems, coupled with advanced staining techniques, enable pathologists to rapidly assess tissue samples during surgery. This immediate feedback guides surgeons in making critical decisions about the extent of tissue removal or the need for additional procedures. The real-time nature of intraoperative pathology significantly reduces the time between sample collection and diagnosis, expediting the overall treatment process and ensuring that surgical interventions are precisely tailored to the patient's specific pathology.

Real-time polymerase chain reaction (PCR) technology has emerged as a cornerstone in molecular diagnostics, playing a pivotal role in identifying infectious diseases, genetic mutations, and variations in gene expression. The continuous monitoring of DNA amplification during the reaction allows for the quantification of target nucleic acids in real-time. This capability not only accelerates the diagnostic process but also provides quantitative insights into the severity of infections or the abundance of specific genetic markers. Real-time PCR is particularly instrumental in infectious disease management, where prompt and accurate diagnosis is essential for implementing timely treatment strategies and public health interventions.

The integration of real-time capabilities into diagnostic imaging modalities extends to functional imaging techniques, such as positron emission tomography (PET) and functional magnetic resonance imaging (fMRI). Real-time functional imaging allows clinicians to observe changes in tissue perfusion, metabolic activity, and neural responses as they occur. In neuroimaging, real-time fMRI provides a unique window into brain function, enabling the assessment of cognitive tasks and mapping brain activity in real-time during surgical procedures. This real-time feedback enhances diagnostic accuracy by providing immediate insights into functional abnormalities, guiding neurosurgeons in preserving critical brain regions and minimizing postoperative deficits.

Telemedicine platforms, enriched with real-time capabilities, facilitate remote diagnostic consultations and expand access to medical expertise. Through real-time video and audio communication, healthcare providers can conduct virtual consultations, visually assess patients, and discuss symptoms in real-time. This immediacy in remote consultations allows for more accurate assessments of physical appearances, movements, and symptoms, mimicking an in-person clinical encounter. Real-time telemedicine consultations have proven particularly valuable in situations where physical access to healthcare facilities is limited, fostering timely diagnoses, treatment recommendations, and ongoing management of various medical conditions.

The real-time monitoring of physiological parameters is a cornerstone in enhancing diagnostic accuracy and treatment efficacy, especially in critical care settings. Patient telemetry systems equipped with real-time data acquisition capabilities continuously monitor vital signs such as electrocardiogram (ECG) waveforms, heart rate, and oxygen saturation. The immediate transmission of this real-time data to central monitoring stations enables healthcare professionals to promptly detect deviations from normal physiological parameters. In critical situations, such as cardiac arrhythmias or respiratory distress, real-time monitoring facilitates early intervention, improving the chances of successful treatment and patient recovery.

In the context of cardiac care, real-time electrocardiography (ECG) monitoring provides instantaneous insights into the heart's electrical activity. Continuous real-time ECG monitoring is particularly valuable for detecting arrhythmias, ischemic events, or other cardiac abnormalities that may require immediate attention. The real-time nature of ECG monitoring allows for the prompt initiation of interventions such as defibrillation in the case of life-threatening arrhythmias, contributing to improved patient outcomes. Additionally, real-time ECG monitoring is instrumental in diagnosing conditions that manifest intermittently, ensuring accurate detection during episodes of cardiac irregularities.

The application of real-time capabilities in point-of-care testing (POCT) brings diagnostics directly to the patient, minimizing turnaround times and facilitating rapid decision-making. Real-time diagnostic devices, such as handheld analyzers for blood gases, glucose, or infectious diseases, provide immediate results at the patient's bedside. This immediacy is critical in emergency situations, where swift diagnostic assessments guide urgent interventions. Real-time POCT not only expedites the diagnostic process but also enables clinicians to make real-time adjustments to treatment plans based on immediate test results, contributing to more effective and targeted patient care.

The integration of real-time capabilities into wearable health monitoring devices has redefined the landscape of continuous health tracking. Wearables equipped with real-time sensors for heart rate, blood pressure, and oxygen saturation enable individuals to monitor their health in everyday scenarios. The real-time feedback from these devices not only empowers individuals to take proactive steps towards their well-being but also offers valuable data for healthcare providers. Continuous, real-time monitoring allows for the early detection of trends or anomalies in health metrics, facilitating timely interventions and personalized health management.

In the domain of neurology, real-time electroencephalogram (EEG) monitoring is instrumental in diagnosing and managing epilepsy. Continuous real-time EEG recording allows healthcare providers to capture and analyze electrical activity in the brain, providing immediate insights into the occurrence of seizures. The real-time nature of EEG monitoring is essential for documenting the onset, duration, and characteristics of seizures, guiding treatment decisions and medication adjustments. Real-time EEG monitoring significantly enhances diagnostic accuracy by capturing critical information during episodes, leading to more precise and tailored management of epilepsy.

In surgical interventions, real-time imaging and navigation systems empower surgeons with immediate visual feedback, enhancing precision and reducing the risk of errors. Surgical robots equipped with real-time capabilities provide dynamic visualization of the surgical site, allowing surgeons to navigate through complex anatomical structures with heightened accuracy. This real-time feedback is particularly crucial in minimally invasive procedures, where visualization is limited, and precise instrument control is paramount. Real-time imaging and navigation contribute to the accuracy of surgical interventions, ensuring optimal outcomes and minimizing the impact on surrounding healthy tissues.

The real-time capabilities of infusion pumps in anesthesia delivery systems contribute to the precise administration of medications during surgical procedures. These pumps continuously monitor drug infusion rates and patient responses in real-time, allowing anesthesiologists to make immediate adjustments based on the patient's needs. The dynamic nature of real-time monitoring ensures that the patient receives the right dosage of anesthesia agents, minimizing the risk of under- or over-administration. This real-time precision in anesthesia delivery contributes to patient safety and optimized surgical outcomes.

Real-time capabilities play a central role in the field of radiation therapy for cancer treatment. Real-time imaging and monitoring during radiation sessions enable clinicians to verify the accuracy of treatment delivery and make immediate adjustments based on patient positioning or anatomical changes. The dynamic feedback from real-time imaging systems ensures that radiation is precisely targeted to the tumor, minimizing exposure to healthy tissues. This real-time precision in radiation therapy contributes to increased treatment efficacy while reducing the risk of side effects.

In the domain of infectious disease management, real-time capabilities in diagnostic testing are crucial for timely and accurate identification of pathogens. Real-time reverse transcription polymerase chain reaction (RT-PCR) assays, as witnessed in the context of the COVID-19 pandemic, provide rapid and sensitive detection of viral RNA. The immediate results from real-time RT-PCR testing enable swift isolation of infected individuals, contact tracing, and implementation of public health measures. The real-time nature of these diagnostic assays is pivotal in curbing the spread of infectious diseases and guiding public health interventions.

The integration of real-time capabilities in adaptive therapy approaches, such as adaptive radiation therapy and adaptive chemotherapy, allows for dynamic adjustments to treatment plans based on individual patient responses. Real-time monitoring of treatment efficacy and potential side effects enables clinicians to tailor therapeutic interventions in response to the evolving characteristics of the disease and the patient's overall health. This adaptability enhances treatment precision, minimizes the risk of adverse effects, and optimizes therapeutic outcomes.

The utilization of real-time capabilities in telemonitoring and remote patient management has proven instrumental in chronic disease management. Patients with conditions such as heart failure, diabetes, or chronic obstructive pulmonary disease (COPD) benefit from continuous real-time monitoring of vital signs and relevant health metrics. The immediate transmission of this data to healthcare providers enables timely interventions, adjustments to treatment plans, and proactive management of chronic conditions. Real-time telemonitoring enhances diagnostic accuracy by facilitating early detection of exacerbations or changes in health status, leading to timely and targeted interventions.

In conclusion, the incorporation of real-time capabilities into medical diagnostics and treatment represents a paradigm shift in healthcare, offering unprecedented levels of precision, immediacy, and effectiveness. From real-time imaging technologies and molecular diagnostics to continuous monitoring, point-of-care testing, and adaptive therapies, these capabilities have permeated every facet of modern healthcare. The immediate insights provided by real-time systems enhance diagnostic accuracy by capturing dynamic changes and facilitating prompt decision-making in treatment strategies. This transformative impact continues to shape the future of medicine, fostering a new era of personalized, responsive, and data-driven healthcare across diverse medical domains.

Exploring the role of real-time systems in automotive safety and performance.

Real-time systems have emerged as integral components in the automotive industry, playing a pivotal role in enhancing both safety and performance aspects of modern vehicles. This comprehensive exploration delves into the multifaceted applications of real-time systems in the automotive domain, elucidating how these systems contribute to the dynamic landscape of vehicle safety, efficiency, and overall performance.

One of the primary realms where real-time systems make a significant impact is in advanced driver assistance systems (ADAS).

These systems leverage real-time sensors, such as cameras, radar, lidar, and ultrasonic sensors, to continuously monitor the vehicle's surroundings. The real-time processing of data from these sensors enables features like adaptive cruise control, lane-keeping assistance, automatic emergency braking, and collision avoidance systems. By providing immediate feedback and intervention capabilities, real-time ADAS contribute substantially to automotive safety, helping prevent collisions, mitigate the severity of accidents, and enhance overall road safety.

Real-time capabilities also play a crucial role in the deployment of electronic stability control (ESC) systems. These systems continuously monitor various parameters, including wheel speed, steering input, and lateral acceleration. In the event of an impending loss of vehicle control, real-time ESC systems intervene by selectively applying brakes to individual wheels or adjusting engine power. This instantaneous response helps stabilize the vehicle and prevent skidding or rollover incidents, significantly improving overall vehicle safety, especially in challenging road conditions.

The advent of real-time systems extends to the domain of collision avoidance technologies, where the integration of sensors and algorithms enables vehicles to detect and respond to potential collisions in real-time. Forward collision warning (FCW) and automatic emergency braking (AEB) systems use real-time data from sensors to assess the proximity to other vehicles or obstacles. In the event of an imminent collision, these systems provide immediate warnings to the driver and, if necessary, autonomously engage the brakes to prevent or mitigate the impact. This real-time decision-making capability significantly reduces the risk of accidents and enhances overall safety on the road.

Real-time systems contribute to the evolution of autonomous driving technologies, representing a paradigm shift in the automotive industry. In autonomous vehicles, real-time data processing is fundamental to the vehicle's ability to perceive its environment, make decisions, and execute actions. Sensors such as lidar, radar, and cameras continuously capture and process information about the vehicle's surroundings in real-time. Advanced algorithms and artificial intelligence (AI) systems analyze this data, enabling the vehicle to navigate, detect obstacles, and make decisions autonomously. The real-time nature of these systems is critical in ensuring timely responses to dynamic and unpredictable road scenarios, fostering the development of safe and reliable autonomous vehicles.

The integration of real-time capabilities extends to traffic management and control systems, where vehicle-to-everything (V2X) communication plays a central role. Real-time communication between vehicles and infrastructure allows for the exchange of information about traffic conditions, road hazards, and other relevant data. This real-time exchange enables vehicles to make informed decisions, such as adjusting speed or changing routes to optimize traffic flow and enhance overall efficiency. Moreover, real-time V2X communication contributes to the development of cooperative adaptive cruise control (CACC) systems, where vehicles can autonomously adjust their speed based on real-time information from surrounding vehicles, leading to improved traffic flow and reduced congestion.

In the realm of vehicle safety, real-time tire pressure monitoring systems (TPMS) offer immediate feedback on tire pressure status. Real-time sensors in each tire continuously monitor pressure levels, and if a deviation from the recommended pressure is detected, the system promptly alerts the driver. Maintaining optimal tire pressure is crucial for vehicle stability, fuel efficiency, and overall safety. The real-time nature of TPMS ensures that any issues with tire pressure are promptly addressed, preventing potential tire failures and accidents resulting from underinflated or overinflated tires.

Real-time systems contribute significantly to improving vehicle safety during nighttime driving with the implementation of adaptive headlights. These headlights utilize sensors and cameras to detect the presence of other vehicles on the road, as well as the vehicle's speed and steering input. In real-time, the system adjusts the direction and range of the headlights to optimize illumination without causing glare for oncoming drivers. This adaptive feature enhances visibility and safety, especially on winding roads or in situations with varying ambient lighting conditions.

The real-time capabilities of electronic brake-force distribution (EBD) systems play a vital role in optimizing braking performance across all wheels of a vehicle. EBD systems continuously monitor various factors, including vehicle speed, wheel speed, and load distribution. In real-time, the system adjusts the braking force applied to each wheel, ensuring optimal balance and preventing wheel lockup. This real-time optimization enhances overall braking efficiency, stability, and control, contributing to improved vehicle safety.

Real-time systems are instrumental in the implementation of predictive maintenance strategies, enhancing the reliability and performance of vehicles. Sensors and diagnostic systems continuously monitor the condition of critical components, such as the engine, transmission, and brakes, in real-time. By analyzing real-time data and detecting early signs of potential issues, predictive maintenance systems enable timely intervention and preventive measures. This proactive approach reduces the risk of unexpected breakdowns, minimizes downtime, and extends the lifespan of vehicle components, ultimately contributing to enhanced vehicle performance and reliability.

The integration of real-time capabilities extends to the field of energy management in electric and hybrid vehicles. Real-time battery management systems (BMS) continuously monitor the state of charge, temperature, and health of the battery pack. This real-time monitoring ensures optimal performance, efficiency, and longevity of the battery. Additionally, real-time regenerative braking systems capture and convert kinetic energy into electrical energy during deceleration, contributing to improved energy efficiency and extended driving range. The real-time optimization of energy usage enhances the overall performance and sustainability of electric and hybrid vehicles.

Real-time systems are pivotal in the implementation of advanced suspension control systems, such as adaptive air suspension and electronic damping systems. These systems continuously monitor various parameters, including vehicle speed, steering input, and road conditions, in real-time. Based on this data, the suspension system adjusts damping rates and ride height to optimize comfort, stability, and handling. The real-time adaptability of these systems enhances the overall driving experience, especially in dynamic driving conditions or on uneven road surfaces.

In the realm of engine management, real-time systems contribute to optimizing fuel injection, ignition timing, and other parameters for combustion efficiency. Real-time engine control units (ECUs) continuously monitor sensor data, such as throttle position, air-fuel ratio, and engine speed, to make instantaneous adjustments. This real-time optimization enhances fuel efficiency, reduces emissions, and maximizes overall engine performance. Additionally, real-time predictive algorithms contribute to the implementation of cylinder deactivation systems, where specific cylinders are deactivated under light load conditions to conserve fuel, showcasing the multifaceted impact of real-time capabilities on vehicle performance and efficiency.

Real-time systems are instrumental in the implementation of advanced driver monitoring systems (DMS), which continuously assess the driver's attention, alertness, and physiological state in real-time. Through the integration of cameras and sensors, real-time DMS analyze facial expressions, eye movements, and other behavioral cues to detect signs of drowsiness or distraction. In the event of driver fatigue or inattentiveness, real-time DMS provide immediate alerts, enhancing overall safety by mitigating the risk of accidents due to driver impairment.

The integration of real-time systems in vehicle-to-vehicle (V2V) communication systems facilitates cooperative collision avoidance strategies. Real-time exchange of information between vehicles allows for the detection of potential collisions or hazardous situations. In response to real-time data from surrounding vehicles, advanced safety systems can autonomously initiate evasive maneuvers, such as steering or braking, to avoid accidents. This real-time coordination among vehicles contributes to an additional layer of safety, especially in scenarios where traditional sensors may have limitations.

Real-time capabilities are harnessed in the implementation of automated parking systems, where vehicles can autonomously navigate and park in constrained spaces. Real-time sensors, such as ultrasonic sensors and cameras, enable the vehicle to continuously assess its surroundings. The real-time processing of this data allows for precise control during parking maneuvers, ensuring safe and efficient parking without collisions. Automated parking systems exemplify how real-time systems contribute to enhancing convenience, efficiency, and safety in everyday driving scenarios.

In the context of cybersecurity, real-time intrusion detection systems are crucial for protecting connected vehicles from cyber threats. Real-time monitoring of network traffic and communication between vehicle components allows for the immediate detection of anomalous behavior or unauthorized access attempts. The real-time response of cybersecurity systems enables timely interventions to prevent potential cyber-attacks, safeguarding the integrity and security of vehicle systems.

In conclusion, real-time systems have become indispensable in the automotive industry, transforming vehicles into intelligent, responsive entities that prioritize safety, efficiency, and performance.

From advanced driver assistance systems and autonomous driving technologies to predictive maintenance, energy management, and adaptive control systems, the applications of real-time capabilities are diverse and impactful. The integration of these systems not only enhances safety features but also contributes to the overall driving experience, sustainability, and reliability of modern vehicles. As the automotive industry continues to evolve, real-time systems will play an increasingly central role in shaping the future of safe, efficient, and technologically advanced transportation.

Discussing applications in autonomous vehicles and advanced driver assistance systems.

The advent of autonomous vehicles and advanced driver assistance systems (ADAS) represents a paradigm shift in the automotive industry, leveraging cutting-edge technologies to enhance safety, convenience, and overall driving experience. This comprehensive exploration delves into the multifaceted applications of autonomous vehicles and ADAS, elucidating how these technologies are reshaping the landscape of transportation and paving the way for a future of intelligent, connected, and automated mobility.

Autonomous vehicles, colloquially known as self-driving cars, are at the forefront of technological innovation in the automotive sector. The core idea behind autonomous vehicles is to enable a car to navigate and operate without direct human input, utilizing a combination of sensors, cameras, radar, lidar, and advanced algorithms. One of the primary applications of autonomous vehicles lies in addressing safety concerns on the road. The real-time perception and decision-making capabilities of autonomous systems significantly reduce the risk of accidents caused by human errors, such as distracted driving or impaired judgment.

In the realm of urban mobility, autonomous vehicles hold the potential to revolutionize transportation systems by offering efficient, on-demand mobility solutions. The concept of autonomous ride-sharing services envisions fleets of self-driving vehicles providing seamless and convenient transportation for users. This application not only enhances accessibility but also has the potential to reduce traffic congestion, lower emissions, and optimize the utilization of vehicles. Real-time communication and coordination among autonomous vehicles enable dynamic route planning and traffic management, contributing to a more efficient and sustainable urban transportation ecosystem.

The integration of autonomous technology extends to freight and logistics, transforming the landscape of goods transportation. Autonomous trucks, equipped with sophisticated sensors and automation systems, can navigate highways and deliver goods with greater efficiency and reduced operational costs. The real-time monitoring of cargo conditions, traffic, and route optimization ensures timely and secure delivery of goods. Additionally, autonomous drones are being explored for last-mile delivery, providing rapid and precise delivery services in urban and remote areas.

In the context of public transportation, autonomous shuttles and buses are being deployed to augment existing transit systems. These vehicles can operate on predetermined routes or dynamically adapt to changing demand, offering flexible and responsive services. The real-time monitoring of passenger loads, traffic conditions, and environmental variables allows for adaptive scheduling and efficient deployment of autonomous public transit options. This application contributes to enhancing the accessibility and sustainability of urban transportation networks.

Autonomous vehicles are also playing a crucial role in addressing mobility challenges for individuals with disabilities or limited mobility. Autonomous taxis or ride-sharing services equipped with accessibility features can provide a newfound level of independence and convenience for passengers with diverse mobility needs. Real-time communication between the vehicle and passengers, coupled with autonomous navigation, ensures a safe and reliable transportation experience for individuals who may face challenges with traditional modes of transportation.

Advanced Driver Assistance Systems (ADAS) represent a significant evolution in vehicle safety, augmenting human driving capabilities and reducing the likelihood of accidents. These systems leverage a combination of sensors, cameras, radar, and machine learning algorithms to continuously monitor the vehicle's surroundings and assist the driver in real-time. One of the foundational applications of ADAS is Adaptive Cruise Control (ACC), which enables vehicles to automatically adjust their speed based on the distance to the vehicle ahead. This real-time responsiveness enhances highway driving comfort and safety, especially in congested traffic conditions.

Collision avoidance systems, an integral component of ADAS, leverage real-time sensors to detect potential collisions and warn or intervene to prevent accidents. Forward Collision Warning (FCW) systems utilize cameras and radar to monitor the road ahead, providing immediate alerts to the driver if a potential collision is detected. In conjunction with Automatic Emergency Braking (AEB), these systems can autonomously apply the brakes to mitigate or prevent collisions, showcasing the real-time decision-making capabilities of ADAS in critical safety scenarios.

Lane Departure Warning (LDW) and Lane-Keeping Assist (LKA) systems contribute to preventing accidents caused by unintentional lane drifting. Real-time cameras and sensors monitor lane markings, and if the vehicle deviates without signaling, the system provides warnings or gently steers the vehicle back into its lane. This real-time intervention enhances vehicle stability and reduces the risk of collisions due to lane departure incidents.

Blind Spot Detection (BSD) systems utilize real-time sensors to monitor the vehicle's blind spots, providing warnings to the driver if there is a vehicle in the adjacent lane. This application enhances situational awareness and reduces the likelihood of collisions during lane changes. Cross Traffic Alert (CTA) systems, often integrated with rearview cameras, provide real-time warnings when backing out of parking spaces, alerting drivers to approaching traffic from the sides.

In the realm of pedestrian safety, ADAS features such as Pedestrian Detection and Collision Mitigation systems leverage real-time sensors and cameras to identify pedestrians in the vehicle's path. In the event of an imminent collision, these systems can autonomously apply the brakes to mitigate the impact or bring the vehicle to a complete stop. This real-time intervention is instrumental in preventing accidents and enhancing the safety of pedestrians in urban environments.

The integration of ADAS extends to improving visibility and awareness during nighttime driving. Night Vision Assistance systems utilize infrared cameras to detect objects, pedestrians, or animals in low-light conditions. Real-time display of this information on the vehicle's dashboard enhances the driver's ability to identify potential hazards in the dark, contributing to overall safety.

The real-time capabilities of ADAS are exemplified in Traffic Sign Recognition systems, which use cameras to identify and interpret traffic signs. The system can recognize speed limits, stop signs, and other relevant signs, providing real-time alerts to the driver. This application contributes to reducing instances of unintentional traffic rule violations and enhances compliance with road regulations.

In the domain of parking assistance, ADAS features such as Automatic Parking Assist use real-time sensors to detect parking spaces and autonomously control the vehicle's steering during parking maneuvers. This real-time assistance simplifies parking in tight spaces and reduces the stress associated with parallel or perpendicular parking. Additionally, Surround View Camera systems provide a real-time, top-down view of the vehicle's surroundings, aiding the driver in navigating complex parking scenarios.

The integration of ADAS extends to driver monitoring systems, which employ real-time cameras and sensors to assess the driver's attention and alertness. These systems can detect signs of drowsiness or distraction and provide real-time alerts to ensure that the driver remains engaged with the driving task. This application enhances overall safety by mitigating the risks associated with driver fatigue or inattention.

Real-time navigation assistance is a fundamental aspect of ADAS, with features such as Lane Centering and Traffic Jam Assist systems. These systems utilize real-time data from cameras and sensors to keep the vehicle centered within its lane and maintain a safe distance from the vehicle ahead in congested traffic. The real-time adaptation to changing traffic conditions enhances driving comfort and reduces the cognitive load on the driver in complex driving environments.

In conclusion, the applications of autonomous vehicles and advanced driver assistance systems are reshaping the landscape of transportation, emphasizing safety, convenience, and efficiency. The real-time capabilities of these technologies, whether in autonomous navigation, collision avoidance, pedestrian safety, or parking assistance, demonstrate their transformative impact on the driving experience. As the automotive industry continues to innovate, the seamless integration of autonomous and ADAS features promises a future where vehicles are not only intelligent and connected but also capable of adapting in real-time to dynamic road scenarios, fostering a safer and more efficient mobility ecosystem.

Showcasing real-time applications in industrial automation and control systems.

The realm of industrial automation and control systems has witnessed a transformative shift with the integration of real-time applications, ushering in an era of heightened efficiency, precision, and responsiveness in manufacturing processes. This comprehensive exploration delves into the multifaceted applications of real-time technologies in industrial automation, elucidating how these systems optimize operations, streamline production, and contribute to the evolution of smart manufacturing.

One of the foundational applications of real-time technology in industrial automation lies in the realm of Programmable Logic Controllers (PLCs) and Distributed Control Systems (DCS). These systems form the backbone of industrial automation, orchestrating and coordinating diverse processes within manufacturing environments. Real-time processing capabilities empower PLCs and DCS to execute control algorithms with millisecond precision, ensuring that machinery and equipment respond instantly to changing conditions on the factory floor. The result is a seamless and synchronized operation of various components, from sensors and actuators to motors and production lines, enhancing overall system reliability and performance.

Real-time applications play a pivotal role in the implementation of Supervisory Control and Data Acquisition (SCADA) systems, offering comprehensive monitoring, control, and data acquisition capabilities in industrial settings. SCADA systems leverage real-time data from sensors and devices distributed across the production floor, providing operators with instantaneous insights into the status of equipment, processes, and overall production metrics. This real-time visibility enables operators to make informed decisions promptly, optimizing production efficiency, and addressing issues before they escalate. Additionally, the integration of real-time SCADA systems contributes to predictive maintenance strategies, allowing for the early detection of equipment anomalies and potential failures.

In the context of motion control systems, real-time applications enable precise and synchronized movement of industrial machinery and robotics. Whether in assembly lines, material handling systems, or robotic workstations, the real-time coordination of servo drives and motors ensures accurate positioning, speed control, and synchronization. This capability is instrumental in achieving high-throughput production, minimizing cycle times, and maintaining stringent quality standards. Real-time motion control is particularly evident in applications such as CNC machining, where the responsiveness of the system is critical for achieving intricate and precise manufacturing operations.

The integration of real-time technology extends to the field of Human-Machine Interface (HMI) systems, facilitating intuitive and responsive interactions between operators and industrial processes. Real-time HMIs provide operators with instant access to critical information, process variables, and control parameters. The real-time visualization of production data enables operators to monitor and control manufacturing processes effectively. Additionally, real-time alarms and notifications alert operators to deviations or abnormalities, allowing for immediate intervention and corrective actions. This real-time interaction enhances operator situational awareness and contributes to overall system resilience.

Real-time applications are instrumental in the deployment of Industrial Internet of Things (IIoT) platforms, creating interconnected ecosystems where sensors, devices, and machines communicate and share data in real-time. IIoT leverages real-time data analytics to extract valuable insights from the vast amounts of information generated by industrial sensors and equipment. This real-time data analysis enables predictive maintenance, anomaly detection, and optimization of operational parameters. The seamless connectivity and instant data exchange facilitated by real-time IIoT platforms contribute to adaptive and agile manufacturing processes, fostering a dynamic and responsive industrial landscape.

In manufacturing execution systems (MES), real-time applications play a crucial role in coordinating and optimizing production workflows. MES leverages real-time data from various sources, including SCADA, PLCs, and sensors, to track the progress of manufacturing operations in real-time. This instant visibility into the production process enables efficient resource allocation, timely identification of bottlenecks, and adaptive scheduling to meet changing demand. Real-time MES applications contribute to lean manufacturing practices by minimizing waste, optimizing production cycles, and ensuring that production targets are met with precision.

Real-time robotics control systems represent a paradigm shift in industrial automation, enabling the deployment of agile and adaptive robotic solutions. These systems leverage real-time feedback from sensors and vision systems to adjust the trajectory, speed, and actions of robots in response to dynamic manufacturing environments. The real-time adaptability of robotic control systems ensures seamless collaboration between humans and robots on the factory floor, contributing to increased productivity, flexibility, and safety. Applications range from collaborative robot (cobots) assembly lines to autonomous mobile robots navigating through warehouses with real-time path planning and obstacle avoidance.

In the realm of batch processing and recipe management, real-time applications contribute to the optimization and control of complex manufacturing processes. Real-time batch control systems enable precise coordination of multiple ingredients, processing steps, and equipment, ensuring that recipes are executed with accuracy and repeatability. This is particularly crucial in industries such as pharmaceuticals, chemicals, and food production, where stringent quality standards and regulatory compliance require real-time monitoring and control of batch processes.

Real-time energy management systems are instrumental in industrial facilities, where efficient energy usage is paramount for both economic and environmental sustainability. These systems leverage real-time data from sensors and meters to monitor energy consumption patterns, identify inefficiencies, and implement real-time adjustments to optimize energy usage. The ability to respond instantaneously to fluctuations in energy demand or pricing contributes to cost savings and aligns with sustainability goals. Real-time energy management is particularly crucial in industries with variable energy costs and stringent energy efficiency targets.

In the domain of quality control and inspection, real-time applications enhance the precision and accuracy of industrial processes. Real-time vision systems and image processing algorithms enable instant inspection and analysis of products on the production line. The ability to make real-time decisions based on visual data ensures that defective products are identified and rejected promptly, maintaining high-quality standards. This is particularly evident in industries such as automotive manufacturing, electronics, and consumer goods, where real-time quality control is integral to ensuring product integrity and customer satisfaction.

Real-time applications are paramount in ensuring the safety of industrial processes through the implementation of Safety Instrumented Systems (SIS). These systems continuously monitor critical parameters and intervene in real-time to prevent or mitigate potentially hazardous situations. The real-time responsiveness of SIS is essential for safeguarding against equipment failures, process deviations, or unforeseen events that could pose risks to personnel, assets, or the environment. Industries with high-risk processes, such as petrochemical and nuclear, rely on real-time SIS to maintain a secure and controlled operational environment.

The integration of real-time technology extends to advanced process control (APC) systems, where the dynamic optimization of process parameters is achieved in real-time. Real-time APC leverages data from sensors, analyzers, and control systems to continuously adjust process variables, ensuring optimal performance and efficiency. This is particularly evident in industries with complex and interconnected processes, such as refining, chemical production, and metallurgy. Real-time APC contributes to minimizing energy consumption, maximizing yield, and enhancing overall process stability.

In conclusion, real-time applications have become indispensable in the realm of industrial automation and control systems, shaping a new era of smart manufacturing characterized by responsiveness, efficiency, and adaptability. From PLCs and SCADA to IIoT platforms, robotics control, and quality inspection, the integration of real-time technologies permeates every facet of industrial processes. The ability to process and act on data instantaneously contributes to optimizing production, ensuring quality, and enhancing safety in diverse industrial settings. As industries continue to embrace digital transformation, real-time applications will remain at the forefront, driving innovation and unlocking new possibilities for the future of industrial automation.

Discussing how real-time capabilities optimize manufacturing processes and ensure efficiency.

The integration of real-time capabilities into manufacturing processes marks a pivotal advancement in industrial efficiency, transforming traditional production paradigms into dynamic and responsive ecosystems. This comprehensive exploration delves into the multifaceted ways in which real-time technologies optimize manufacturing processes, ensuring precision, adaptability, and overall operational excellence.

At the core of this transformative shift is the utilization of real-time data processing in Programmable Logic Controllers (PLCs) and Distributed Control Systems (DCS). These systems, serving as the nerve center of industrial automation, rely on real-time capabilities to orchestrate and synchronize the myriad components of a manufacturing environment. By processing information with millisecond precision, these controllers enable seamless coordination between sensors, actuators, and production machinery. The result is a finely tuned and synchronized operation that enhances the reliability and performance of manufacturing processes.

Real-time capabilities play a pivotal role in Supervisory Control and Data Acquisition (SCADA) systems, providing an overarching view of the manufacturing landscape. SCADA leverages real-time data from sensors and devices dispersed throughout the production floor, affording operators immediate insights into the status of equipment, processes, and production metrics. This instant visibility allows for timely decision-making, proactive issue resolution, and overall optimization of manufacturing operations. Moreover, real-time SCADA systems contribute to predictive maintenance strategies, ensuring that potential faults are identified and addressed before they impact production.

Motion control systems, vital for precision in manufacturing, benefit significantly from real-time applications. Whether in robotic arms, conveyor systems, or CNC machines, the synchronization of servo drives and motors with real-time precision ensures accurate positioning, speed control, and coordination of movements. This level of real-time adaptability is instrumental in achieving high-throughput production, reducing cycle times, and maintaining stringent quality standards. Real time motion control is particularly evident in applications requiring intricate machining operations, where responsiveness is critical for achieving precise outcomes.

Human-Machine Interface (HMI) systems, enhanced by real-time capabilities, provide operators with instantaneous access to critical information and control parameters. These interfaces facilitate real-time monitoring and control of manufacturing processes, enabling operators to make informed decisions promptly. The integration of real-time alarms and notifications alerts operators to deviations or abnormalities, allowing for immediate intervention and corrective actions. This real-time interaction enhances operator situational awareness and contributes to overall system resilience, especially in scenarios where quick responses are crucial.

The advent of the Industrial Internet of Things (IIoT) has ushered in a new era of connectivity and real-time insights in manufacturing. IIoT platforms leverage sensors and devices to generate vast amounts of real-time data, offering manufacturers the opportunity to extract valuable insights. Real-time data analytics in the IIoT context enable predictive maintenance, performance optimization, and adaptive manufacturing strategies. The seamless connectivity and instant data exchange facilitated by real-time IIoT platforms contribute to agile and responsive manufacturing processes, aligning production with changing demand and operational requirements.

In manufacturing execution systems (MES), real-time applications play a vital role in tracking and optimizing production workflows. MES leverages real-time data from various sources, including SCADA, PLCs, and sensors, to monitor the progress of manufacturing operations in real-time. This immediate visibility enables efficient resource allocation, timely identification of bottlenecks, and adaptive scheduling to meet changing demand. Real-time MES applications contribute to lean manufacturing practices by minimizing waste, optimizing production cycles, and ensuring that production targets are met with precision.

Real-time robotics control systems represent a paradigm shift in manufacturing automation, introducing agility and adaptability to the factory floor. These systems leverage real-time feedback from sensors and vision systems to adjust the trajectory, speed, and actions of robots in response to dynamic manufacturing environments. The real-time adaptability of robotic control systems ensures seamless collaboration between humans and robots, contributing to increased productivity, flexibility, and safety. Applications range from collaborative robot (cobots) assembly lines to autonomous mobile robots navigating through warehouses with real-time path planning and obstacle avoidance.

In the context of batch processing and recipe management, real-time applications contribute to the optimization and control of intricate manufacturing processes. Real-time batch control systems facilitate the precise coordination of multiple ingredients, processing steps, and equipment. This ensures that recipes are executed with accuracy and repeatability, crucial in industries such as pharmaceuticals, chemicals, and food production. The real-time adaptability of batch processing systems allows for immediate adjustments based on real-time data, maintaining quality standards and reducing the likelihood of variations in production outcomes.

Real-time energy management systems are pivotal in manufacturing facilities, where efficient energy usage is a key consideration for both economic and environmental sustainability. These systems leverage real-time data from sensors and meters to monitor energy consumption patterns and identify inefficiencies promptly. Real-time adjustments to optimize energy usage contribute to cost savings and align with sustainability goals. This is particularly crucial in industries with variable energy costs and stringent energy efficiency targets, where real-time energy management systems play a crucial role in achieving operational efficiency.

Quality control and inspection processes in manufacturing benefit significantly from real-time applications, enhancing the precision and accuracy of production outcomes. Real-time vision systems and image processing algorithms enable instant inspection and analysis of products on the production line. The ability to make real-time decisions based on visual data ensures that defective products are identified and rejected promptly, maintaining high-quality standards. This is particularly evident in industries such as automotive manufacturing, electronics, and consumer goods, where real-time quality control is integral to ensuring product integrity and customer satisfaction.

Real-time technologies are paramount in ensuring the safety of manufacturing processes through the implementation of Safety Instrumented Systems (SIS). These systems continuously monitor critical parameters and intervene in real-time to prevent or mitigate potentially hazardous situations. The real-time responsiveness of SIS is essential for safeguarding against equipment failures, process deviations, or unforeseen events that could pose risks to personnel, assets, or the environment. Industries with high-risk processes, such as petrochemical and nuclear, rely on real-time SIS to maintain a secure and controlled operational environment.

Advanced Process Control (APC) systems leverage real-time capabilities to dynamically optimize manufacturing processes. Real-time APC systems utilize data from sensors, analyzers, and control systems to continuously adjust process variables, ensuring optimal performance and efficiency. Industries with complex and interconnected processes, such as refining, chemical production, and metallurgy, benefit from real-time APC in minimizing energy consumption, maximizing yield, and enhancing overall process stability. The real-time adaptability of APC contributes to maintaining optimal conditions in the face of changing production requirements or external factors.

In conclusion, the infusion of real-time capabilities into manufacturing processes represents a paradigm shift, unlocking unprecedented levels of efficiency, adaptability, and precision. From the foundational elements of PLCs and SCADA to the transformative impact of IIoT, robotics control, and energy management, real-time technologies permeate every facet of modern manufacturing. The ability to process and act on data instantaneously ensures optimal production outcomes, responsive decision-making, and heightened safety standards. As industries continue their digital transformation journey, the integration of real-time applications will remain central to shaping the future of manufacturing, where agility and responsiveness are the hallmarks of a thriving and adaptive production ecosystem.

Exploring real-time applications in telecommunications and networked environments.

In the realm of telecommunications and networked environments, the integration of real-time applications has revolutionized the way information is transmitted, processed, and shared. This comprehensive exploration delves into the multifaceted applications of real-time technologies in this domain, elucidating how these systems optimize communication, enhance connectivity, and contribute to the seamless functioning of modern telecommunications networks.

Real-time capabilities play a fundamental role in voice over IP (VoIP) systems, transforming traditional voice communication into digital data packets transmitted over networks. The real-time encoding, transmission, and decoding of audio data enable instantaneous voice communication, mimicking the experience of traditional telephone calls. VoIP applications leverage real-time protocols to ensure low latency and high-quality voice transmission, paving the way for cost-effective and flexible communication solutions. The ubiquity of real-time VoIP applications has reshaped the landscape of telephony, enabling global connectivity with minimal delays.

Video conferencing represents another critical application of real-time technologies, facilitating virtual face-to-face communication in diverse settings. Real-time video conferencing systems leverage advanced codecs and protocols to transmit video and audio data with minimal latency, enabling seamless interactions between geographically dispersed individuals or groups. The integration of real-time features, such as screen sharing and collaborative document editing, enhances the overall effectiveness of virtual meetings. Particularly evident in remote work scenarios, real-time video conferencing has become an essential tool for business communication, collaboration, and remote team engagement.

Real-time data streaming applications have become integral in the delivery of multimedia content over the internet. Streaming services for audio and video content leverage real-time protocols to deliver a continuous and seamless playback experience to end-users. Whether it's music, movies, or live events, real-time streaming applications optimize bandwidth usage and adapt to varying network conditions, ensuring a consistent and high-quality user experience. The prevalence of platforms such as Spotify, Netflix, and YouTube underscores the transformative impact of real-time streaming on the consumption of multimedia content.

The advent of real-time messaging applications has redefined how individuals and businesses communicate in a connected world. Instant messaging platforms, characterized by real-time message delivery, have become ubiquitous for personal and professional communication. These applications leverage real-time protocols to transmit text, multimedia, and even voice messages instantly across devices. The real-time nature of messaging applications fosters quick and efficient communication, whether for casual conversations, team collaboration, or customer support. Platforms like WhatsApp, Slack, and Microsoft Teams exemplify the pervasive influence of real-time messaging in modern communication ecosystems.

Real-time collaboration tools have become indispensable in networked environments, enabling teams to work together seamlessly across geographical boundaries. Shared document editing, simultaneous access to collaborative platforms, and real-time updates contribute to the efficiency and productivity of collaborative workflows. In virtual workplaces, where team members may be distributed globally, real-time collaboration tools create a sense of immediacy and interconnectedness, bridging the physical divide and fostering cohesive teamwork. Applications such as Google Workspace, Microsoft Office 365, and collaborative coding platforms exemplify the impact of real-time collaboration on modern work practices.

The realm of online gaming relies heavily on real-time technologies to create immersive and interactive multiplayer experiences. Real-time multiplayer games leverage low-latency communication protocols to synchronize actions and events across players in real-time. Whether in competitive esports or casual gaming, the instantaneous nature of real-time communication ensures a smooth and responsive gaming experience. The prevalence of online gaming platforms, featuring real-time voice chat, text messaging, and dynamic in-game events, attests to the transformative role of real-time technologies in shaping the gaming landscape.

Real-time monitoring and analytics applications are instrumental in ensuring the optimal performance and security of telecommunications networks. Network administrators leverage real-time monitoring tools to track the status of network components, detect anomalies, and respond to issues promptly. Real-time analytics provide insights into network traffic patterns, enabling proactive capacity planning and resource allocation. Security information and event management (SIEM) systems leverage real-time data analysis to detect and respond to security threats in real-time, contributing to the overall resilience of networked environments.

In the context of Internet of Things (IoT) devices, real-time applications play a crucial role in gathering and processing data from a myriad of interconnected sensors and devices. Real-time telemetry and monitoring allow for immediate responses to changes in environmental conditions, equipment status, or user interactions. Applications ranging from smart home devices to industrial IoT systems leverage real-time communication protocols to enable seamless interaction between devices, creating responsive and interconnected ecosystems. The real-time nature of IoT applications contributes to the efficiency of automated processes, predictive maintenance, and real-time decision-making.

Real-time location-based services have become prevalent in mobile applications, enhancing user experiences through location-aware functionalities. Navigation applications utilize real-time GPS data to provide turn-by-turn directions, traffic updates, and estimated arrival times. Location-based social media features, such as check-ins and location tagging, leverage real-time geospatial data to enhance user engagement and content relevance. The integration of real-time location services not only improves user experiences but also contributes to the development of context-aware applications that adapt to users' locations and preferences.

Telemedicine and remote healthcare services leverage real-time communication technologies to connect patients with healthcare professionals in virtual environments. Real-time video consultations, remote monitoring of vital signs, and instant access to medical information enable healthcare providers to deliver timely and effective care to patients. The immediacy of real-time telemedicine applications is particularly valuable in emergency situations, where rapid communication and decision-making are critical. The widespread adoption of telehealth platforms underscores the transformative impact of real-time technologies on healthcare accessibility and delivery.

Real-time financial transactions have become the norm in the digital era, with online banking, mobile payments, and cryptocurrency transactions relying on real-time processing capabilities. Real-time payment systems enable instant fund transfers, ensuring quick and efficient financial transactions. The integration of real-time fraud detection and security measures contributes to the safety of online financial transactions. Cryptocurrency markets, characterized by real-time trading and price fluctuations, showcase the dynamic nature of real-time applications in the financial sector.

In the context of autonomous vehicles and connected transportation systems, real-time communication is essential for ensuring the safety and efficiency of operations. Vehicle-to-vehicle (V2V) and vehicle-to-infrastructure (V2I) communication leverage real-time protocols to enable instantaneous exchange of information between vehicles and infrastructure components. Real-time traffic management systems provide dynamic route guidance and adapt to changing traffic conditions, contributing to congestion reduction and improved transportation efficiency. The integration of real-time communication in connected transportation systems lays the foundation for intelligent and adaptive mobility solutions.

Real-time customer support and service applications have become integral for businesses across various industries. Live chat, real-time ticketing systems, and instant customer feedback mechanisms enable businesses to provide immediate assistance and address customer inquiries promptly. Real-time customer engagement contributes to customer satisfaction, loyalty, and overall positive brand experiences. Businesses leveraging real-time customer support applications can respond swiftly to customer needs, resolving issues in real-time and building trust in the process.

In conclusion, the exploration of real-time applications in telecommunications and networked environments unveils a rich tapestry of interconnected and responsive systems that shape the way we communicate, collaborate, and interact in the digital age. From VoIP and video conferencing to online gaming, real-time monitoring, and location-based services, the pervasive influence of real-time technologies is evident across diverse domains. As these applications continue to evolve, they not only enhance the immediacy of communication but also redefine the possibilities of connectivity, efficiency, and user experiences in our interconnected world.

Discussing the importance of low-latency communication in ensuring seamless connectivity.

The importance of low-latency communication in ensuring seamless connectivity is paramount in a digital landscape where the speed of data transmission defines the user experience across various domains. Latency, often measured in milliseconds, represents the delay between the initiation of a data transfer and the reception of the corresponding response. In the realm of telecommunications, low-latency communication is instrumental in shaping the efficiency and responsiveness of voice over IP (VoIP) systems. In VoIP, where real-time voice data is transmitted as packets over networks, minimizing latency ensures that conversations unfold with the immediacy expected in traditional telephone calls. The absence of perceptible delays in voice communication is not merely a convenience but a fundamental factor contributing to the natural flow of conversations, the effectiveness of business communications, and the overall quality of user experiences.

Furthermore, the significance of low-latency communication is accentuated in the domain of video conferencing, where real-time visual and auditory synchronization is crucial for facilitating effective virtual meetings. High-latency scenarios can introduce delays in video and audio streams, leading to disruptions, awkward pauses, and an overall suboptimal conferencing experience. The demand for seamless connectivity in video conferencing extends beyond business contexts to encompass education, healthcare, and social interactions, emphasizing the need for low-latency communication to replicate the spontaneity and interactivity of face-to-face engagements in the digital realm.

Real-time data streaming applications, which deliver multimedia content over the internet, rely on low-latency communication to ensure a smooth and uninterrupted playback experience. Whether it's music, movies, or live events, high latency can result in buffering delays and degraded streaming quality, diminishing the user's enjoyment. The competitive landscape of streaming services underscores the industry's recognition of the critical role played by low-latency communication in retaining and attracting users. Platforms that deliver content with minimal latency not only enhance user satisfaction but also position themselves as leaders in an era where instant access to high-quality multimedia content is the expectation.

The advent of real-time messaging applications has reshaped interpersonal communication, and the essence of these platforms lies in the immediacy of message delivery. In the context of instant messaging, where users expect their messages to be transmitted and received without noticeable delays, low-latency communication is fundamental. Whether it's casual conversations, professional correspondence, or time-sensitive information sharing, the near-instantaneous nature of messaging applications contributes to the efficiency of communication. The ubiquity of these platforms in personal and professional settings underscores the pervasive influence of low-latency communication on the modern communication landscape.

Collaboration tools that enable real-time interactions and shared document editing in distributed work environments exemplify another domain where low-latency communication is indispensable. In virtual workplaces, where teams are geographically dispersed, the ability to collaborate seamlessly relies on the instant synchronization of changes made by team members. Low-latency communication ensures that modifications to shared documents, updates to collaborative platforms, and changes to project timelines are reflected in real-time, fostering a dynamic and cohesive teamwork environment. The absence of perceptible delays in collaboration tools contributes to the fluidity of collaborative workflows and enhances overall productivity.

Online gaming, characterized by its multiplayer and interactive nature, places a premium on low-latency communication to deliver a responsive and immersive gaming experience. In multiplayer games, where split-second decisions and actions can determine success or failure, minimizing latency is essential. High-latency scenarios can result in delayed responses to player inputs, creating a disjointed and frustrating gaming experience. The competitive nature of online gaming has propelled the gaming industry to prioritize low-latency communication, with gaming platforms and networks continually striving to optimize responsiveness and minimize delays in real-time interactions.

In the context of real-time monitoring and analytics applications, low-latency communication is critical for providing instantaneous insights into data streams. Network administrators, for instance, rely on real-time monitoring tools to track the status of network components, detect anomalies, and respond to issues promptly. In scenarios where security threats or performance deviations require immediate attention, low-latency communication ensures that the necessary alerts and notifications reach administrators without delay. The significance of low-latency communication in monitoring and analytics extends to various domains, including financial transactions, industrial processes, and critical infrastructure, where timely responses are imperative for maintaining operational integrity.

The realm of Internet of Things (IoT) devices, interconnected in vast networks, leverages low-latency communication to enable swift and responsive interactions between devices. Real-time telemetry and monitoring in IoT applications allow for immediate responses to changes in environmental conditions, equipment status, or user interactions. From smart home devices to industrial IoT systems, the ability of devices to communicate in near real-time enhances the efficiency of automated processes, supports predictive maintenance strategies, and contributes to the overall responsiveness of IoT ecosystems. The seamless and instant exchange of information in IoT scenarios is foundational to unlocking the full potential of interconnected and intelligent devices.

In the domain of telemedicine and remote healthcare services, low-latency communication is a linchpin for delivering timely and effective care. Real-time video consultations, remote monitoring of vital signs, and instant access to medical information rely on low-latency communication to bridge the physical distance between healthcare providers and patients. In emergency situations, where rapid communication and decision-making are critical, low-latency telemedicine applications play a vital role in facilitating timely interventions. The importance of low-latency communication in telemedicine extends beyond routine consultations to scenarios where seconds can make a difference in patient outcomes.

Real-time financial transactions, facilitated by online banking, mobile payments, and cryptocurrency platforms, hinge on low-latency communication to ensure the instant transfer of funds. Real-time payment systems, characterized by low-latency transaction processing, provide users with the ability to make immediate and secure financial transactions. The integration of low-latency communication in online financial services extends to fraud detection and security measures, contributing to the reliability and safety of digital transactions. In the dynamic landscape of financial markets and cryptocurrency trading, where split-second decisions can impact outcomes, low-latency communication is foundational to executing trades and managing portfolios with precision.

The evolution of autonomous vehicles and connected transportation systems underscores the indispensable role of low-latency communication in ensuring the safety and efficiency of operations. Vehicle-to-vehicle (V2V) and vehicle-to-infrastructure (V2I) communication rely on low-latency protocols to enable instantaneous exchanges of information between vehicles and various elements of the transportation infrastructure. Real-time traffic management systems leverage low-latency communication to provide dynamic route guidance, adapt to changing traffic conditions, and optimize traffic flow.

In scenarios where split-second decisions are required, such as collision avoidance or emergency braking, low-latency communication is pivotal for ensuring the responsiveness and effectiveness of connected transportation systems.

In customer support and service applications, where instant assistance and issue resolution are paramount, low-latency communication is a cornerstone. Live chat systems, real-time ticketing platforms, and instant customer feedback mechanisms leverage low-latency communication to enable businesses to respond swiftly to customer needs. The immediacy of low-latency customer support contributes to customer satisfaction, loyalty, and overall positive brand experiences. The real-time nature of customer support applications ensures that queries are addressed promptly, issues are resolved in real-time, and customers feel supported throughout their interactions with a business.

In conclusion, the importance of low-latency communication in ensuring seamless connectivity permeates every facet of the digital landscape. From real-time communication in telecommunications and collaborative tools to online gaming, IoT ecosystems, telemedicine, financial transactions, and connected transportation, the need for low-latency communication is foundational to delivering optimal user experiences. In a world where immediacy and responsiveness define the expectations of users and applications, the role of low-latency communication remains instrumental in shaping the efficiency, effectiveness, and overall quality of interactions in our interconnected and digital-centric environment.

Highlighting the critical role of real-time systems in aerospace and defense applications.

The critical role of real-time systems in aerospace and defense applications is paramount in shaping the capabilities, efficiency, and safety of missions that operate within the complex and dynamic environments of air, land, sea, and space. In the aerospace sector, where split-second decisions and precise control are imperative, real-time systems play a pivotal role in flight control and avionics. Flight control systems, empowered by real-time capabilities, continuously monitor aircraft parameters, sensor inputs, and pilot commands to execute instantaneous adjustments, ensuring stability, responsiveness, and adherence to flight plans. Avionics systems, including navigation, communication, and radar systems, rely on real-time processing to provide accurate and timely information to pilots and ground control, contributing to the overall safety and success of airborne missions.

In the realm of defense applications, real-time systems are integral to the functioning of command and control (C2) systems, which orchestrate the coordination and execution of military operations. Real-time C2 systems facilitate the integration of information from various sources, including sensors, intelligence databases, and surveillance platforms, enabling military commanders to make timely and informed decisions. The responsiveness of real-time C2 systems is essential in rapidly evolving scenarios, allowing for adaptive strategies, swift deployment of resources, and the coordination of diverse military assets. Whether in land-based operations, naval deployments, or air campaigns, real-time C2 systems are the nerve center that ensures the synchronization and effectiveness of defense missions.

The aviation industry's reliance on real-time systems extends to air traffic control (ATC), where the safety and efficiency of global air travel hinge on precise and instantaneous communication and coordination. Real-time air traffic management systems monitor the position and trajectory of aircraft in real-time, providing controllers with immediate insights into airspace congestion, weather conditions, and potential conflicts. The coordination of takeoffs, landings, and mid-air maneuvers relies on real-time communication between pilots and air traffic controllers, contributing to the overall safety and optimization of air traffic. The complexity of modern airspace demands the resilience and responsiveness that real-time systems bring to air traffic control operations.

In the field of satellite communications and space exploration, real-time systems are foundational to ensuring the success of missions that operate in the harsh and unforgiving environment of outer space. Satellite systems, equipped with real-time communication capabilities, enable continuous data transmission between spacecraft and ground control. Real-time telemetry and control systems monitor the health and status of satellites, execute precise orbital maneuvers, and respond to dynamic space conditions, contributing to the longevity and effectiveness of satellite missions. In space exploration missions, where the distances involved necessitate immediate command execution, real-time systems ensure that spacecraft respond promptly to instructions, gather data in real-time, and adapt to unforeseen challenges.

Unmanned Aerial Vehicles (UAVs) or drones, utilized extensively in both defense and civilian applications, leverage real-time systems for navigation, control, and mission execution. Real-time embedded systems in UAVs process sensor data, execute flight control algorithms, and respond to environmental changes, allowing for autonomous and adaptive operation. In defense applications, UAVs equipped with real-time systems play roles in reconnaissance, surveillance, and target acquisition, providing military forces with valuable intelligence in real-time. The responsiveness and agility of real-time systems contribute to the effectiveness and versatility of UAVs in a wide range of mission profiles.

The field of radar systems, crucial for surveillance, tracking, and threat detection, relies heavily on real-time signal processing to operate effectively. Radar systems use real-time algorithms to analyze incoming signals, identify targets, and track their movements. In defense applications, such as missile defense systems, the ability to detect and respond to incoming threats in real-time is essential for intercepting and neutralizing potential risks. The speed of real-time radar processing directly influences the reaction time available to deploy countermeasures and protect against airborne threats, underscoring the critical role of real-time systems in modern defense scenarios.

Cybersecurity and information assurance in aerospace and defense applications demand real-time monitoring and response mechanisms to safeguard critical systems from cyber threats. Real-time intrusion detection systems analyze network traffic patterns in real-time, identifying potential security breaches and triggering immediate responses to mitigate risks. The resilience of defense networks and communication systems relies on the instantaneous detection and isolation of cyber threats, preventing unauthorized access and safeguarding sensitive information. The integration of real-time cybersecurity measures ensures that aerospace and defense systems remain secure, resilient, and capable of withstanding evolving cyber threats.

In the context of electronic warfare (EW) systems, real-time signal processing is fundamental for the detection, analysis, and counteraction of enemy electronic signals. Real-time EW systems analyze the electromagnetic spectrum in real-time, identifying hostile signals and executing rapid countermeasures to disrupt or neutralize adversary communication and radar systems. The agility and responsiveness of real-time EW systems are critical in electronic warfare scenarios, where the ability to adapt to changing signal environments and deploy countermeasures instantaneously determines mission success.

The integration of real-time systems in flight simulation and training applications is essential for preparing pilots and military personnel for complex and high-stakes missions. Real-time simulation systems replicate realistic scenarios, providing trainees with immersive and dynamic environments to hone their skills. Flight simulators, equipped with real-time visual and motion feedback systems, allow pilots to experience various flight conditions, emergency scenarios, and combat situations in a controlled and realistic setting. The ability to simulate real-time responses to diverse situations enhances training effectiveness and ensures that personnel are well-prepared for the challenges they may face in actual aerospace and defense operations.

In the development and testing of aerospace and defense hardware, real-time systems play a crucial role in conducting simulations, validating designs, and ensuring the reliability of critical components. Real-time simulations of aircraft, spacecraft, and weapon systems allow engineers to assess performance, evaluate aerodynamics, and identify potential issues in a virtual environment before physical prototypes are built. Testing and validation processes rely on real-time data acquisition and analysis to verify the functionality and safety of aerospace and defense systems under various conditions. The real-time feedback provided by simulation and testing systems contributes to the iterative refinement of designs, ensuring that aerospace and defense technologies meet stringent performance and safety standards.

In conclusion, the critical role of real-time systems in aerospace and defense applications spans a diverse array of domains, from flight control and avionics to command and control systems, air traffic management, satellite communications, unmanned aerial vehicles, radar systems, cybersecurity, electronic warfare, training simulations, and hardware development. The demands of these applications necessitate the responsiveness, precision, and reliability that real-time systems bring to the forefront. As technology continues to advance and missions become more complex, the integration of real-time systems remains indispensable in ensuring the success, safety, and effectiveness of aerospace and defense operations in the dynamic and challenging environments they operate within.

Showcasing examples in avionics, radar systems, and mission-critical defense operations.

In the realm of avionics, the integration of real-time systems stands as a testament to the technological advancements that have transformed aircraft into highly sophisticated and responsive platforms. Avionics, short for aviation electronics, encompasses a wide array of electronic systems crucial for flight operations. One prominent example is the Flight Control System (FCS), a cornerstone of avionics that relies heavily on real-time processing. The FCS continuously monitors aircraft parameters such as altitude, airspeed, and attitude, processing this data in real-time to make instantaneous adjustments to control surfaces like ailerons, elevators, and rudders. The result is a dynamic and adaptive system that ensures stability, responsiveness, and adherence to flight plans, enhancing both the safety and efficiency of air travel. Real-time avionics systems extend beyond the FCS to include Navigation Systems, Communication Systems, and Collision Avoidance Systems, collectively forming an interconnected suite of technologies that contribute to the overall effectiveness of modern aircraft.

In the domain of radar systems, real-time processing plays a pivotal role in enhancing situational awareness, threat detection, and overall mission success. Radar, an acronym for Radio Detection and Ranging, employs electromagnetic waves to detect and track objects in the surrounding airspace or environment. The implementation of real-time signal processing in modern radar systems allows for instantaneous analysis of incoming signals, enabling the identification and tracking of aircraft, ships, or other potential targets. The significance of real-time capabilities is particularly evident in Airborne Early Warning (AEW) radar systems, which are integral to both military and civilian applications. AEW radar platforms, mounted on aircraft, use real-time processing to provide early warning of potential threats, monitor airspace, and support command and control functions. The ability to process and respond to radar data in real-time enhances the effectiveness of defense and surveillance operations, allowing for swift reactions to changing scenarios and ensuring the protection of airspace.

In mission-critical defense operations, the integration of real-time systems is a linchpin that underpins the success of complex and dynamic military missions. One exemplary illustration is in the domain of Command and Control (C2) systems, where real-time capabilities are central to orchestrating and coordinating military operations across diverse theaters. These systems serve as the nerve center for military commanders, enabling the integration of information from various sources such as intelligence databases, sensors, and surveillance platforms. Real-time C2 systems facilitate rapid decision-making by providing commanders with timely and accurate data, allowing them to adapt strategies, allocate resources, and respond to emerging threats in real-time. Whether in land-based operations, naval deployments, or air campaigns, real-time C2 systems are instrumental in ensuring the synchronization, effectiveness, and success of defense missions.

Within avionics, the role of real-time systems extends to the sophisticated world of Inertial Navigation Systems (INS), which are fundamental for providing accurate and continuous information about an aircraft's position, velocity, and orientation. Inertial Navigation Systems, leveraging accelerometers and gyroscopes, operate in real-time to track the aircraft's movements and changes in direction. The instantaneous nature of real-time processing in INS ensures that pilots receive precise navigation information, even in GPS-denied environments or during rapid maneuvers. This capability is particularly crucial in military aircraft, where the ability to navigate accurately in real-time is essential for mission success, evasion of threats, and maintaining a strategic advantage.

In the realm of radar systems, the implementation of real-time capabilities is notably exemplified by modern Active Electronically Scanned Array (AESA) radars. AESA radars, found in both airborne and ground-based applications, employ an array of individual transmit/receive modules that can be controlled independently. This adaptability, combined with real-time processing, allows AESA radars to dynamically adjust beam direction, frequency, and power in response to changing operational requirements. This enables AESA radars to track multiple targets simultaneously, provide electronic countermeasures, and swiftly adapt to evolving threat scenarios. The real-time nature of AESA radar systems contributes to their effectiveness in both surveillance and combat operations, making them a cornerstone technology in modern defense capabilities.

In the context of mission-critical defense operations, Unmanned Aerial Vehicles (UAVs) equipped with real-time systems showcase the transformative impact of technology on modern warfare. UAVs, commonly known as drones, leverage real-time embedded systems for navigation, control, and mission execution. These systems process sensor data in real-time, enabling autonomous and adaptive flight capabilities. In military applications, UAVs equipped with real-time systems play roles in intelligence, surveillance, reconnaissance (ISR), target acquisition, and even precision strikes. The ability of UAVs to operate in real-time, often in contested or hostile environments, provides military forces with valuable situational awareness and operational flexibility, contributing to the success of defense missions.

The significance of real-time systems in mission-critical defense operations is further underscored by the integration of Unmanned Ground Vehicles (UGVs). UGVs, used for tasks such as reconnaissance, surveillance, and explosive ordnance disposal, rely on real-time systems for autonomous navigation and obstacle avoidance. Real-time processing allows UGVs to adapt rapidly to changing terrain, avoid obstacles in their path, and execute complex missions with precision. In military scenarios, UGVs equipped with real-time capabilities contribute to the reduction of risks to human personnel, providing an invaluable asset for enhancing the effectiveness of defense operations.

In the defense sector, Electronic Warfare (EW) systems exemplify the critical role of real-time signal processing in countering and neutralizing adversary threats. Real-time EW systems analyze electromagnetic signals in the environment, identify potential threats such as enemy radars or communication systems, and execute rapid countermeasures. These countermeasures, ranging from electronic jamming to deception techniques, are implemented in real-time to disrupt or disable hostile electronic systems. The agility and responsiveness of real-time EW systems are essential in contested environments, where the ability to adapt to changing signal landscapes and execute immediate counteractions determines the success of defense operations.

Real-time systems are also integral to the success of missile defense operations, where split-second decisions and responses are imperative for intercepting incoming threats. Missile defense systems leverage real-time processing to detect, track, and intercept ballistic missiles or airborne threats. Radars and sensors provide continuous data feeds to real-time command and control systems, enabling rapid analysis and decision-making. The real-time nature of missile defense systems ensures that interception decisions and firing solutions can be executed with precision, contributing to the defense against strategic and tactical missile threats.

Beyond avionics, radar systems, and defense operations, the importance of real-time systems extends to the testing and validation of critical aerospace and defense hardware. In simulation environments, real-time systems replicate realistic scenarios to assess the performance, reliability, and safety of aircraft, spacecraft, or weapon systems. Engineers use real-time simulations to evaluate aerodynamics, assess system responses under various conditions, and validate the functionality of complex aerospace technologies. The ability to simulate real-time responses contributes to the iterative refinement of designs, ensuring that aerospace and defense hardware meets stringent performance standards before physical prototypes are manufactured.

In conclusion, the examples showcased in avionics, radar systems, and mission-critical defense operations underscore the pervasive influence of real-time systems in shaping the capabilities and success of modern aerospace and defense technologies. From enhancing the precision and responsiveness of flight control systems to revolutionizing the adaptability of radar platforms and contributing to the effectiveness of defense operations, real-time systems have become indispensable in ensuring the safety, efficiency, and strategic advantage in these critical domains. The continued evolution of real-time technologies will undoubtedly play a pivotals role in shaping the future of aerospace and defense, enabling advancements that push the boundaries of what is achievable in the complex and dynamic landscapes of aviation and military operations.

Chapter 8: Future Trends in Real-Time Systems

Exploring the synergy between real-time systems and artificial intelligence.

The synergy between real-time systems and artificial intelligence (AI) represents a convergence of technologies that holds transformative potential across various domains, from industrial automation to healthcare and beyond. Real-time systems, characterized by their ability to process and respond to data with minimal delay, form a foundational infrastructure for a wide range of applications. Simultaneously, artificial intelligence, particularly machine learning algorithms, introduces the capability to learn from data, make predictions, and adapt to changing conditions. The intersection of these technologies gives rise to a dynamic symbiosis, where the responsiveness of real-time systems complements the adaptive intelligence of AI, creating a powerful amalgamation that redefines how systems operate and make decisions in real-world scenarios.

In the realm of industrial automation, the marriage of real-time systems and AI is exemplified in the concept of the Industrial Internet of Things (IIoT). Real-time systems facilitate the continuous monitoring and control of industrial processes, while AI algorithms analyze the vast amounts of data generated by sensors and devices. This synergy enables predictive maintenance, where AI models can forecast equipment failures or performance degradation, allowing for proactive intervention to avoid unplanned downtime. The real-time nature of these systems ensures that decisions based on AI insights are promptly executed, optimizing operational efficiency and contributing to the overall reliability of industrial processes.

Healthcare is another domain where the collaboration between real-time systems and AI holds transformative potential. Real-time monitoring systems in hospitals and clinics provide continuous data streams from patient vitals and medical devices. AI algorithms, trained on large datasets, can analyze this real-time data to detect subtle patterns or anomalies indicative of health issues. In critical situations, where timely intervention is paramount, the synergy between real-time systems and AI enables early detection of abnormalities, triggering immediate alerts for medical personnel. This combination enhances patient care by providing proactive and personalized interventions, showcasing how the fusion of real-time capabilities and AI intelligence can revolutionize healthcare delivery.

In the context of autonomous vehicles, the integration of real-time systems with AI is fundamental for enabling safe and efficient navigation. Real-time sensors such as LiDAR, cameras, and radar generate a constant stream of data about the vehicle's surroundings. AI algorithms process this data in real-time to recognize objects, predict trajectories, and make decisions about navigation and control. The real-time aspect is critical for ensuring rapid responses to dynamic environments, such as detecting and avoiding obstacles or adapting to changing road conditions. The synergy between real-time systems and AI in autonomous vehicles exemplifies a transformative application that has the potential to revolutionize transportation and redefine the future of mobility.

In financial trading, the fusion of real-time systems and AI algorithms has reshaped how investment decisions are made. High-frequency trading (HFT) relies on real-time data feeds and rapid execution capabilities, where AI algorithms analyze market trends and make split-second decisions to execute trades. The synergy between real-time systems and AI in this context is evident in the ability to process massive datasets in real-time, identify complex patterns, and execute trading strategies with minimal latency. This convergence has led to a paradigm shift in financial markets, where the speed and accuracy of decision-making have become critical factors in achieving competitive advantages.

The field of cybersecurity leverages the synergy between real-time systems and AI to address the evolving landscape of cyber threats. Real-time monitoring systems continuously analyze network traffic patterns, system logs, and user behaviors. AI algorithms, trained on historical data, can identify patterns indicative of malicious activities or security breaches. The real-time response capability of these systems allows for immediate detection and mitigation of cyber threats, minimizing the potential impact of attacks. The dynamic and adaptive nature of AI in cybersecurity is well complemented by the instantaneous actions that real-time systems enable, providing a robust defense against the ever-evolving tactics of cyber adversaries.

In the context of smart grids, which are modernizing the energy infrastructure, the synergy between real-time systems and AI plays a crucial role in optimizing energy distribution and consumption. Real-time monitoring of electricity usage, coupled with AI algorithms, enables predictive analytics to forecast demand patterns and potential faults in the grid. This synergy facilitates dynamic adjustments in real-time, such as rerouting power or initiating preventive measures to address issues before they escalate. The result is a more resilient and efficient energy distribution system, where real-time responses guided by AI intelligence contribute to sustainability and reliability.

Real-time systems and AI also converge in the context of smart cities, where the integration of technologies aims to enhance urban living. Real-time data from various sensors, such as traffic cameras, environmental monitors, and IoT devices, form the foundation for AI-driven applications that optimize traffic flow, manage public services, and enhance overall urban planning. For example, real-time traffic data processed by AI algorithms can be used to dynamically adjust traffic signal timings, alleviating congestion and improving commute times. The synergy between real-time systems and AI in smart cities reflects a holistic approach to urban management, where data-driven intelligence guides real-time actions for the benefit of residents and the environment.

The advent of edge computing further amplifies the synergy between real-time systems and AI by bringing computational capabilities closer to the data source. In edge computing, real-time processing occurs at or near the source of data generation, reducing latency and enhancing responsiveness. AI models deployed at the edge can make localized decisions without the need to transmit data to centralized servers. This synergy is particularly beneficial in applications where low latency is crucial, such as in autonomous vehicles, industrial automation, or remote healthcare. The combination of real-time capabilities and AI at the edge empowers a new paradigm of distributed intelligence, enabling smart and responsive systems in a variety of contexts.

The synergy between real-time systems and AI extends into natural language processing (NLP) applications, where real-time language understanding and generation capabilities are harnessed for human-computer interaction. Real-time processing is essential in applications like virtual assistants, chatbots, and voice recognition systems, where immediate responses are expected in natural conversational settings. AI algorithms for NLP, driven by machine learning and neural networks, enable these systems to understand context, infer user intent, and generate human-like responses in real-time. This fusion of real-time language processing and AI-driven natural language understanding is transforming the way people interact with digital interfaces, making technology more accessible and user-friendly.

The convergence of real-time systems and AI is also evident in video analytics applications, where real-time video processing coupled with AI algorithms enhances security, surveillance, and content analysis. Real-time video feeds from cameras are analyzed by AI models that can recognize objects, detect anomalies, and even predict events. In security and surveillance, this synergy enables immediate response to potential threats or incidents, such as recognizing unauthorized access or detecting unusual behavior in crowded spaces. Beyond security, the combination of real-time video analytics and AI has applications in content moderation, facial recognition, and augmented reality, contributing to a diverse range of industries and user experiences.

The symbiotic relationship between real-time systems and AI is increasingly prevalent in robotics, where the fusion of real-time control and AI-driven perception and decision-making results in advanced capabilities. Real-time sensor data, such as from cameras and depth sensors, is processed by AI algorithms to enable robots to perceive their environment, recognize objects, and make decisions in real-time. This synergy is crucial in scenarios where robots need to navigate dynamic environments, collaborate with humans, or perform complex tasks with precision. The integration of real-time control and AI in robotics represents a paradigm shift, expanding the possibilities of automation in various industries, from manufacturing to healthcare and logistics.

In the evolving landscape of Internet of Things (IoT), the integration of real-time systems and AI is instrumental in unlocking the full potential of connected devices. Real-time data from sensors embedded in IoT devices is processed by AI algorithms to derive insights, predict patterns, and optimize system behavior. This synergy enhances the efficiency and responsiveness of IoT applications, ranging from smart homes and wearables to industrial IoT deployments. For example, real-time monitoring of industrial equipment combined with AI-based predictive maintenance can prevent equipment failures and optimize maintenance schedules, contributing to increased operational efficiency.

In the context of healthcare, the synergy between real-time systems and AI is exemplified in the realm of telemedicine and remote patient monitoring. Real-time health monitoring devices, such as wearable sensors or IoT-enabled medical equipment, generate continuous streams of data about patients' vital signs. AI algorithms can analyze this real-time data to detect early signs of health issues, provide personalized insights, and trigger timely interventions. The combination of real-time monitoring and AI-driven analysis enhances the quality of remote healthcare delivery, enabling proactive and patient-centric approaches to healthcare management.

The synergy between real-time systems and AI is also prominent in the domain of gaming, where immersive and interactive experiences are shaped by real-time rendering and AI-driven content generation. Real-time graphics processing ensures that visual elements respond instantly to user inputs, creating a seamless and responsive gaming environment. AI algorithms contribute to dynamic content generation, adapting game scenarios, characters, and challenges based on player behavior and preferences in real-time. This fusion of real-time systems and AI in gaming results in engaging and personalized experiences, pushing the boundaries of what is possible in virtual worlds.

As the synergy between real-time systems and AI continues to evolve, it is evident that their integration is driving advancements across a myriad of applications and industries. The responsiveness of real-time systems and the intelligence of AI together create a powerful paradigm that not only enhances efficiency, safety, and decision-making but also unlocks new possibilities in areas such as automation, healthcare, smart cities, and more. The ongoing collaboration between these technologies is poised to shape the future of computing, where the fusion of real-time capabilities and artificial intelligence opens doors to unprecedented innovation and transformative experiences in the digital age.

Discussing how AI enhances decision-making and adaptability in real-time environments.

Artificial Intelligence (AI) stands at the forefront of transforming decision-making processes and adaptability in real-time environments across diverse domains. One of the key contributions of AI lies in its ability to analyze vast datasets and extract meaningful insights, empowering decision-makers with a depth of information that was previously challenging to attain. In real-time scenarios, such as financial trading, AI algorithms excel at processing market data instantaneously, identifying patterns, and making split-second decisions. The adaptability of AI in this context is evident as it continuously learns from market dynamics, adjusting strategies and responses to evolving conditions. The symbiotic relationship between real-time decision-making and AI-driven adaptability reshapes the landscape of financial markets, where the speed and precision of AI enhance decision-making processes.

In healthcare, AI's impact on real-time decision-making is particularly transformative, with applications ranging from diagnostic assistance to personalized treatment plans. Real-time monitoring of patient data, combined with AI algorithms, enables the rapid analysis of complex medical information. In critical situations, such as emergency rooms or intensive care units, AI aids healthcare professionals by providing immediate insights into patient conditions, flagging anomalies, and suggesting potential diagnoses. The adaptability of AI in healthcare manifests in its ability to continuously learn from diverse patient cases, refining diagnostic accuracy and treatment recommendations over time. The fusion of real-time decision support and AI-driven adaptability has the potential to revolutionize patient care, optimizing outcomes and enhancing the efficiency of health-care systems.

The realm of autonomous vehicles offers a compelling illustration of how AI enhances decision-making and adaptability in real-time environments. Self-driving cars rely on AI algorithms to process data from sensors, cameras, and radar in real-time, enabling them to make split-second decisions about navigation, obstacle avoidance, and traffic interactions. The adaptability of AI in autonomous vehicles is exemplified by its capacity to learn from diverse driving scenarios and adapt strategies based on continuous exposure to real-world conditions. The synergy between real-time decision-making and AI-driven adaptability not only ensures the safety of passengers but also positions autonomous vehicles to navigate complex and dynamic environments with increasing precision.

In industrial automation, AI's role in real-time decision-making is pivotal for optimizing processes and maintaining operational efficiency. Real-time systems equipped with AI algorithms can analyze sensor data from manufacturing equipment, detect anomalies, and make decisions to prevent equipment failures or optimize production schedules. The adaptability of AI in this context allows systems to learn from historical data, adjusting decision parameters to optimize performance and respond to variations in real-time production environments. The marriage of real-time decision-making and AI-driven adaptability in industrial settings contributes to enhanced productivity, reduced downtime, and improved overall operational efficiency.

In the domain of cybersecurity, AI serves as a formidable ally in real-time threat detection and response. Real-time monitoring systems analyze network traffic, system logs, and user behaviors, while AI algorithms identify patterns indicative of potential security breaches. The adaptability of AI in cybersecurity is demonstrated by its ability to evolve alongside emerging threats. Machine learning models continuously learn from new attack vectors, adapting detection mechanisms and response strategies in real-time to counteract evolving cyber threats. The integration of real-time decision-making and AI-driven adaptability fortifies cybersecurity measures, providing organizations with proactive defense mechanisms against the dynamic landscape of cyber threats.

The fusion of AI and real-time decision-making is paramount in the context of disaster response and emergency management. Real-time data from various sources, including sensors, satellites, and social media, can be rapidly analyzed by AI algorithms to assess the severity of a disaster, predict its trajectory, and optimize resource allocation. The adaptability of AI in disaster response is evident in its ability to learn from past incidents, enabling more effective decision-making and coordination in subsequent emergencies. The synergy between real-time decision-making and AI-driven adaptability enhances the resilience of disaster response efforts, facilitating timely interventions and mitigating the impact of crises on communities.

In the field of customer service and engagement, AI-powered chatbots and virtual assistants contribute to real-time decision-making by understanding user queries and providing instant responses. The adaptability of these AI systems is showcased in their ability to continuously improve language understanding and user interaction based on real-time feedback. As they learn from user interactions, AI-driven chatbots adapt their responses to specific queries, improving the overall customer experience. The integration of real-time decision-making and AI-driven adaptability in customer service applications streamlines interactions, increases efficiency, and enhances user satisfaction.

In the dynamic realm of e-commerce, AI plays a crucial role in real-time decision-making to personalize user experiences and optimize product recommendations. Real-time analysis of user behavior, purchase history, and preferences enables AI algorithms to make instant decisions about what products to recommend or highlight. The adaptability of AI in e-commerce is manifested in its ability to learn from user interactions, adjusting recommendations based on changing preferences and emerging trends. The fusion of real-time decision-making and AI-driven adaptability in e-commerce platforms enhances customer engagement, increases conversion rates, and contributes to a more personalized online shopping experience.

The integration of AI in smart cities exemplifies how real-time decision-making and adaptability can enhance urban living. Real-time data from sensors and IoT devices across the city, combined with AI algorithms, enables decision-makers to optimize traffic flow, manage public services, and respond to changing environmental conditions. The adaptability of AI in smart cities is evident in its capacity to learn from historical data, anticipating patterns in energy consumption, transportation, and public services. The synergy between real-time decision-making and AI-driven adaptability contributes to the development of efficient, sustainable, and resilient urban environments.

In military and defense applications, AI's role in real-time decision-making and adaptability is crucial for enhancing situational awareness and optimizing tactical responses. Real-time data from sensors, satellites, and reconnaissance platforms is processed by AI algorithms to assess threats, identify targets, and inform strategic decisions. The adaptability of AI in defense scenarios is demonstrated by its ability to learn from evolving tactics and dynamically adjust responses to emerging threats. The fusion of real-time decision-making and AI-driven adaptability empowers military forces with responsive and intelligent capabilities, contributing to the effectiveness of defense operations.

The convergence of AI and real-time decision-making is instrumental in shaping the future of space exploration. Real-time data from spacecraft and satellites, combined with AI algorithms, enables rapid analysis of celestial phenomena, trajectory adjustments, and mission planning. The adaptability of AI in space exploration is evident in its ability to learn from the vastness of cosmic data, optimizing navigation routes and resource utilization. The synergy between real-time decision-making and AI-driven adaptability in space missions enhances the precision and efficiency of exploration endeavors, opening new frontiers in our understanding of the cosmos.

In the realm of financial services, AI's impact on real-time decision-making is profound, particularly in risk management and fraud detection. Real-time analysis of financial transactions, combined with AI algorithms, allows for the instant identification of unusual patterns or potential fraudulent activities. The adaptability of AI in financial services is showcased in its ability to evolve alongside emerging risks, continuously learning from new fraud tactics and adjusting decision criteria in real-time. The fusion of real-time decision-making and AI-driven adaptability fortifies financial institutions against threats, enhancing the security and integrity of financial transactions.

The synergy between AI and real-time decision-making extends into environmental monitoring and conservation efforts. Real-time data from environmental sensors, satellite imagery, and biodiversity studies can be processed by AI algorithms to assess ecological health, detect deforestation, and predict environmental changes. The adaptability of AI in environmental monitoring is evident in its ability to learn from changing ecosystems, optimizing conservation strategies based on real-time insights. The integration of real-time decision-making and AI-driven adaptability contributes to more effective and responsive conservation initiatives, safeguarding biodiversity and ecological balance.

In the context of educational technology, AI enhances real-time decision-making by personalizing learning experiences for students. Real-time analysis of student performance data, combined with AI algorithms, allows for instant adaptations of teaching materials and approaches based on individual learning styles and needs. The adaptability of AI in education is showcased in its ability to continuously refine personalized learning paths, adjusting to students' progress and challenges in real-time. The fusion of real-time decision-making and AI-driven adaptability in educational technology empowers educators with tools to optimize learning outcomes and cater to the diverse needs of students.

In conclusion, the symbiotic relationship between AI and real-time decision-making is a catalyst for transformative advancements across various sectors. The ability of AI to analyze complex data in real-time, coupled with its adaptability to continuously learn and evolve, reshapes how decisions are made and responses are tailored to dynamic environments. From enhancing healthcare diagnostics to optimizing industrial processes, navigating autonomous vehicles, and fortifying cybersecurity, the fusion of AI and real-time decision-making proves instrumental in driving innovation, efficiency, and adaptability across diverse domains. As these technologies continue to advance, their collaborative potential promises a future where intelligent decision-making in real-time becomes an integral facet of numerous applications, ushering in an era of unprecedented capabilities and possibilities.

Analyzing the role of edge computing in the evolution of real-time systems.

Edge computing has emerged as a pivotal technology in the evolution of real-time systems, reshaping the landscape of computing architecture to meet the demands of modern applications. In the conventional cloud-centric model, data processing and storage occur in centralized servers, often leading to latency issues and bandwidth constraints. The rise of edge computing represents a paradigm shift, decentralizing computation by moving data processing closer to the source of data generation. This proximity reduces latency, enhances response times, and enables real-time decision-making, making it a critical enabler for a spectrum of applications ranging from Internet of Things (IoT) devices to autonomous vehicles.

The core concept of edge computing revolves around distributing computational tasks to the "edge" of the network, which can include devices like routers, gateways, and even end-user devices. This distribution of computing resources strategically positions them in close proximity to where data is generated, minimizing the distance that information needs to traverse for processing. This proximity has profound implications for applications that demand real-time responses, such as industrial automation, healthcare monitoring, and smart city infrastructure.

One of the key advantages of edge computing is its ability to alleviate the burden on centralized cloud servers. By offloading processing tasks to the edge, the demand on network bandwidth is reduced, preventing congestion and enhancing the overall efficiency of the system. This is particularly crucial in scenarios where large volumes of data are generated in real-time, such as in smart factories where sensors continuously monitor and report on various aspects of the production process.

Real-time systems, by definition, require instantaneous decision-making based on the most recent data. Edge computing excels in meeting this requirement by significantly reducing the latency associated with data transmission to distant cloud servers. In applications like autonomous vehicles, where split-second decisions can be a matter of life and death, the low-latency characteristics of edge computing are indispensable. Furthermore, this reduction in latency is not only beneficial for safety-critical applications but also enhances the user experience in areas like augmented reality and online gaming.

The evolution of real-time systems is intricately linked with the proliferation of IoT devices, and edge computing plays a pivotal role in harnessing the potential of these interconnected devices. With the exponential growth of IoT, there is a burgeoning need for processing data at the edge to avoid overwhelming centralized servers. Edge computing facilitates the deployment of intelligent devices that can process and analyze data locally, transmitting only relevant information to the cloud. This not only optimizes bandwidth usage but also enhances the scalability and responsiveness of IoT applications.

Security is a paramount concern in the realm of real-time systems, and edge computing introduces both challenges and opportunities in this regard. While decentralization can enhance security by reducing the attack surface exposed to potential threats, it also necessitates the implementation of robust security measures at the edge. Securing a multitude of edge devices, each with its own set of vulnerabilities, requires a comprehensive and adaptive security framework. Moreover, the distributed nature of edge computing demands a shift from traditional perimeter-based security models to more dynamic and context-aware approaches.

The scalability of real-time systems is a critical factor, especially as the volume of data generated continues to skyrocket. Edge computing provides a scalable solution by distributing computation across a network of edge devices. This scalability is not only beneficial in handling increasing data volumes but also allows for the efficient scaling of computational resources based on the specific requirements of different applications. The ability to scale dynamically is particularly advantageous in scenarios where the demand for computational resources fluctuates, ensuring optimal performance without over-provisioning.

Despite its numerous advantages, edge computing introduces complexities in managing a distributed network of heterogeneous devices. Interoperability challenges arise due to the diverse hardware and software configurations of edge devices. Standardization efforts are underway to address these challenges and establish a common framework that enables seamless communication and collaboration among different edge devices. Achieving interoperability is crucial for the widespread adoption of edge computing, ensuring that devices from different manufacturers can work cohesively within a unified ecosystem.

The integration of edge computing with real-time systems opens up new possibilities for edge analytics. Edge analytics involves processing data locally at the edge, extracting valuable insights, and only transmitting relevant information to the cloud. This not only reduces the amount of data that needs to be transmitted but also enables real-time analytics, allowing organizations to gain immediate insights from their data. Edge analytics is particularly advantageous in applications where rapid decision-making based on current data is imperative, such as in financial trading or emergency response systems.

As edge computing continues to mature, the role of artificial intelligence (AI) becomes increasingly prominent in real-time systems. Edge devices equipped with AI capabilities can perform complex computations locally, enabling advanced analytics and decision-making at the edge. This is particularly beneficial in scenarios where real-time processing is essential, such as in autonomous drones or surveillance systems. The integration of AI at the edge not only enhances the intelligence of individual devices but also contributes to the overall efficiency and responsiveness of the entire system.

Energy efficiency is a critical consideration in the evolution of real-time systems, especially in scenarios where devices operate on battery power. Edge computing offers the advantage of localized processing, reducing the need for data to travel back and forth to centralized servers. This not only minimizes the energy consumption associated with data transmission but also allows edge devices to enter low-power states when not actively processing data. The energy-efficient nature of edge computing makes it an attractive solution for battery-powered devices in IoT applications and other edge scenarios.

While the benefits of edge computing are substantial, there are challenges that need to be addressed to fully unlock its potential. Edge management, including device provisioning, software updates, and security patching, requires efficient mechanisms to handle the distributed nature of edge deployments. Additionally, ensuring data consistency and integrity across a network of edge devices is a non-trivial task that necessitates robust synchronization mechanisms. Standardization efforts in these areas are crucial to establishing best practices and facilitating the seamless integration of edge computing into diverse real-time systems.

In conclusion, the role of edge computing in the evolution of real-time systems is transformative, reshaping the traditional paradigms of computing architecture. Its ability to reduce latency, enhance scalability, improve security, and enable localized decision-making positions edge computing as a cornerstone in the era of interconnected devices and applications. As the technology continues to advance, addressing challenges related to interoperability, security, and management will be imperative for its widespread adoption. The synergy between edge computing, AI, and IoT holds the promise of creating intelligent, responsive, and energy-efficient real-time systems that can meet the dynamic demands of the digital age.

Discussing how edge computing addresses latency challenges in distributed environments.

Edge computing has emerged as a transformative solution to address the inherent latency challenges in distributed environments, offering a paradigm shift from traditional cloud-centric models. The latency challenge is a critical issue in distributed systems where data processing and analysis need to occur with minimal delay. In conventional cloud-based architectures, data travels over networks to centralized servers, introducing latency due to the physical distance and network congestion. Edge computing strategically positions computational resources closer to the data source, effectively reducing the round-trip time for data to travel to and from centralized servers. By minimizing the distance that data needs to traverse, edge computing plays a pivotal role in mitigating latency and enhancing the responsiveness of applications in distributed environments.

One of the primary mechanisms through which edge computing tackles latency challenges is by decentralizing computation. In traditional cloud architectures, all data processing is concentrated in a few remote data centers. This centralized model results in latency as data must travel from the edge devices to these remote locations for processing and then back to the devices for action. Edge computing, on the other hand, distributes computational tasks to the "edge" of the network, which can include devices like routers, gateways, and even end-user devices. This decentralization ensures that data processing occurs in close proximity to where the data is generated, minimizing the time it takes for information to travel between the source and the processing unit.

Furthermore, edge computing leverages the concept of local processing, enabling data to be analyzed and acted upon at the edge devices themselves. This approach is particularly advantageous in scenarios where real-time decision-making is crucial. For example, in autonomous vehicles, the ability to process sensor data locally allows for instantaneous responses, reducing the risk of accidents. By avoiding the need to transmit data to centralized servers for processing, edge computing significantly cuts down on the latency associated with remote data processing, making it an ideal solution for time-sensitive applications in distributed environments.

The reduction in latency achieved through edge computing is not only beneficial for individual devices but also has profound implications for network efficiency and overall system performance. In scenarios where large volumes of data are generated continuously, such as in industrial IoT applications, the decentralized processing capabilities of edge computing prevent network congestion. This optimization of bandwidth usage not only mitigates latency but also ensures that the overall network operates more efficiently, providing a scalable solution for the increasing demands of distributed environments.

The synergy between edge computing and real-time systems is particularly evident in applications where split-second decisions are critical. Take, for instance, healthcare monitoring systems that rely on real-time data from wearable devices. In a cloud-centric model, the delay introduced by transmitting data to a distant server for processing could have serious consequences. Edge computing allows for local processing of health data, enabling immediate analysis and response. This is not only vital for patient care but also showcases how edge computing directly addresses the latency challenges inherent in real-time distributed environments.

An additional aspect contributing to the latency reduction in edge computing is the concept of edge caching. By storing frequently accessed data or content closer to the end-users or devices at the edge of the network, edge caching minimizes the need to retrieve data from distant servers. This results in faster response times as the required information is readily available locally. In content delivery networks (CDNs), for example, edge caching is employed to store and deliver popular content from servers positioned at the network's edge. This not only accelerates content delivery but also reduces the latency experienced by end-users, creating a more responsive and efficient user experience in distributed environments.

Moreover, the integration of edge computing with 5G technology further enhances its capability to address latency challenges. 5G networks provide higher bandwidth and lower latency, making them well-suited for supporting the distributed nature of edge computing deployments. The combination of edge computing and 5G enables the creation of ultra-low latency networks, crucial for applications like augmented reality (AR), virtual reality (VR), and mission-critical IoT. The reduced latency achieved by leveraging 5G infrastructure complements the localized processing capabilities of edge computing, creating a powerful combination for applications demanding real-time responses in distributed environments.

Security concerns often arise when discussing distributed systems, and edge computing introduces new challenges in this domain. However, in addressing latency challenges, edge computing also offers security benefits. By processing data locally at the edge, sensitive information can be kept closer to its source, reducing the risk of data exposure during transit to centralized servers. The localized nature of data processing in edge computing provides an opportunity to implement security measures directly at the edge devices, creating a distributed security architecture that can enhance overall system resilience against cyber threats. This approach aligns with the principle of minimizing the attack surface, as only relevant information needs to be transmitted to centralized servers, reducing the exposure to potential security vulnerabilities during data transmission.

Despite the advantages, challenges remain in the seamless integration of edge computing into distributed environments. Interoperability issues arise due to the diverse set of edge devices and platforms, each with its own specifications and capabilities. Standardization efforts are underway to establish common frameworks that enable interoperability, ensuring that edge devices from different manufacturers can collaborate seamlessly within a distributed network. Overcoming these interoperability challenges is crucial to realizing the full potential of edge computing in addressing latency concerns and ensuring a cohesive and efficient distributed computing ecosystem.

In conclusion, edge computing stands as a pivotal solution in the evolution of distributed environments, specifically addressing the latency challenges inherent in traditional cloud-centric models. By decentralizing computation, enabling local processing, and leveraging edge caching, edge computing significantly reduces the round-trip time for data, enhancing the responsiveness of applications in real-time scenarios. The integration of edge computing with 5G technology further amplifies its impact, creating opportunities for ultra-low latency networks. While challenges like interoperability and security persist, the continued development and adoption of edge computing promise to revolutionize the landscape of distributed computing, offering a more efficient and responsive solution for the diverse applications that demand low-latency performance.

Exploring the potential integration of blockchain technology in real-time systems.

The exploration of integrating blockchain technology into real-time systems represents a compelling avenue that holds the promise of transforming the way we conceive, deploy, and secure these systems. Real-time systems, by their nature, demand instantaneous processing, rapid decision-making, and high levels of reliability. Blockchain, originally developed as the underlying technology for cryptocurrencies like Bitcoin, has evolved beyond its financial roots to emerge as a decentralized and tamper-resistant ledger. The fundamental features of blockchain—decentralization, immutability, transparency, and smart contract functionality—present an intriguing framework for addressing various challenges in real-time systems, ranging from data integrity and security to trust and transparency.

One of the primary attributes that make blockchain technology attractive for integration into real-time systems is its decentralized nature. In conventional real-time systems, a single centralized authority often oversees the processing and storage of data, making the system susceptible to a single point of failure. Blockchain, on the other hand, operates on a decentralized network of nodes, each maintaining an identical copy of the ledger. This decentralization not only enhances the resilience of the system against failures or attacks but also contributes to a more distributed and fault-tolerant architecture. In scenarios where real-time decisions are critical, the decentralized nature of blockchain provides a robust foundation for ensuring continuous operation and minimizing the risk of system-wide failures.

Immutability, a key characteristic of blockchain, ensures that once data is recorded on the ledger, it cannot be altered or tampered with. This feature addresses the challenge of data integrity in real-time systems where the accuracy and trustworthiness of information are paramount. In applications such as supply chain management, healthcare, or financial transactions, where real-time data updates are crucial, the immutability of blockchain ensures that the historical record remains intact and verifiable. This not only enhances the reliability of the information but also establishes a transparent and auditable trail of events, contributing to a higher level of accountability in real-time processes.

Transparency is another pivotal aspect of blockchain that aligns with the requirements of real-time systems. In traditional centralized systems, the lack of transparency can lead to trust issues, especially when multiple entities are involved in a transaction or process. Blockchain's distributed ledger ensures that all participating nodes have visibility into the same set of data, fostering transparency and trust among stakeholders. In supply chain management, for instance, the transparency provided by blockchain enables real-time tracking of products, from manufacturing to delivery, reducing discrepancies and enhancing the overall efficiency of the supply chain.

Smart contracts, self-executing contracts with the terms of the agreement directly written into code, introduce a layer of programmability to blockchain technology. This feature holds significant potential for real-time systems by automating and enforcing predefined rules and conditions. In scenarios where quick and automated responses are essential, smart contracts enable the execution of predefined actions without the need for intermediaries. For instance, in the Internet of Things (IoT) ecosystem, smart contracts could facilitate automated transactions or actions based on real-time data from connected devices. This automation not only accelerates processes but also reduces the dependency on manual intervention, making real-time systems more efficient and responsive.

The integration of blockchain into real-time systems also introduces novel possibilities for enhancing the security and privacy of sensitive data. Cryptographic techniques, such as hashing and encryption, are fundamental to blockchain security. The decentralized and distributed nature of the blockchain network adds an additional layer of protection, making it inherently resistant to certain types of cyber attacks. In real-time systems dealing with sensitive information, such as healthcare records or financial transactions, the security mechanisms inherent in blockchain can fortify data protection measures. The implementation of private or permissioned blockchains further allows for control over who can participate in the network, addressing concerns related to data access and privacy in real-time applications.

While the potential benefits of integrating blockchain into real-time systems are substantial, challenges and considerations must be carefully examined. The scalability of blockchain networks, for example, is a critical factor. In real-time systems that generate large volumes of data, such as those in financial trading or industrial automation, ensuring that the blockchain network can handle the transaction throughput in a timely manner is imperative. Scalability solutions, including off-chain transactions and layer-two solutions, are being actively explored to address these concerns and make blockchain technology more viable for real-time applications.

Interoperability is another challenge, especially in heterogeneous environments where diverse real-time systems may need to interact.

Establishing standardized protocols and frameworks for interoperability is crucial to ensure seamless communication and collaboration between different blockchain implementations and real-time systems. Industry consortia and standardization efforts are underway to define common frameworks that can facilitate interoperability and integration across diverse technology stacks.

Regulatory considerations also play a significant role in the integration of blockchain into real-time systems. The regulatory landscape surrounding blockchain and cryptocurrencies is evolving, and compliance with existing and emerging regulations is essential for widespread adoption. Real-time systems operating in sectors such as finance, healthcare, or energy must navigate regulatory frameworks to ensure that the integration of blockchain aligns with legal requirements and industry standards.

Despite these challenges, various real-world use cases exemplify the successful integration of blockchain into real-time systems. Cross-border payments, for instance, have seen improvements in speed, cost, and transparency through the use of blockchain technology. Real-time settlement of transactions, facilitated by smart contracts and decentralized ledgers, reduces the need for intermediaries and accelerates cross-border financial transactions. In a similar vein, the use of blockchain in supply chain management has demonstrated tangible benefits in enhancing traceability, reducing fraud, and optimizing the efficiency of real-time logistics operations.

In conclusion, the potential integration of blockchain technology into real-time systems marks a paradigm shift in the way we design and implement distributed and mission-critical applications. The decentralized, immutable, transparent, and programmable nature of blockchain aligns well with the requirements of real-time systems, offering solutions to challenges related to data integrity, security, trust, and automation. While challenges like scalability, interoperability, and regulatory compliance persist, ongoing research and development efforts, coupled with industry collaboration, are actively addressing these issues. The successful integration of blockchain into real-time systems holds the promise of creating more secure, transparent, and efficient processes across a spectrum of industries, ultimately shaping the future of decentralized and resilient real-time applications.

Discussing how blockchain enhances security and transparency in time-sensitive transactions.

The integration of blockchain technology into time-sensitive transactions marks a transformative leap forward in the realms of security and transparency. Time-sensitive transactions, characterized by the need for rapid processing and accurate execution within stringent timeframes, encompass various domains such as financial services, supply chain management, and healthcare. Blockchain, originally conceived as the underlying technology for cryptocurrencies like Bitcoin, introduces a decentralized and tamper-resistant ledger that fundamentally reshapes how we approach security and transparency in these critical transactions.

At the core of blockchain's impact on security lies its decentralized nature. Traditional centralized systems, which rely on a single point of control or authority, are vulnerable to single points of failure and become attractive targets for malicious actors. In contrast, blockchain operates on a network of distributed nodes, each maintaining a copy of the same ledger. This decentralization not only mitigates the risk of a single point of failure but also enhances the overall resilience of the system against malicious attacks. In time-sensitive transactions, where rapid and secure processing is imperative, the decentralized architecture of blockchain provides a robust foundation for ensuring the continuous and secure flow of information.

The immutability feature of blockchain is another critical aspect that significantly enhances security in time-sensitive transactions. Once data is recorded on the blockchain, it becomes resistant to tampering or alteration. This immutability is achieved through cryptographic hashing, where each block contains a unique identifier (hash) based on the contents of the previous block. Any attempt to alter the data in a block would necessitate the recalibration of subsequent blocks, an operation computationally infeasible and detectable by the network. In financial transactions, for instance, where the integrity of data is paramount, the immutability of blockchain ensures that transaction records remain secure and unaltered, reducing the risk of fraudulent activities.

Transparency, a fundamental characteristic of blockchain, is particularly advantageous in enhancing trust in time-sensitive transactions. In traditional systems, the lack of visibility into the entire transaction lifecycle can lead to trust issues, especially when multiple parties are involved. Blockchain's distributed ledger ensures that all participants in the network have real-time visibility into the same set of data, fostering transparency and trust among stakeholders. In supply chain management, for example, where the movement of goods requires coordination among multiple entities, the transparency provided by blockchain enables real-time tracking and visibility into the entire supply chain. This not only reduces discrepancies but also instills confidence in the accuracy and authenticity of the information, essential for time-sensitive decision-making.

Smart contracts, a unique feature of blockchain, contribute to the security and automation of time-sensitive transactions. Smart contracts are self-executing contracts with the terms of the agreement directly written into code. They enable the automation of predefined rules and conditions, eliminating the need for intermediaries and reducing the risk of errors or delays in execution. In financial transactions, smart contracts can automate processes such as settlement and clearing, streamlining operations and reducing the time required for transaction finalization. The programmable nature of smart contracts introduces a layer of automation that not only accelerates processes but also ensures that predefined conditions are met, adding a level of security and reliability to time-sensitive transactions.

Blockchain's security mechanisms, including cryptographic techniques, play a pivotal role in protecting sensitive data in time-sensitive transactions. Data stored on the blockchain is encrypted and secured using cryptographic algorithms, ensuring that only authorized parties with the appropriate cryptographic keys can access the information. This enhances the confidentiality of data, a crucial consideration in sectors such as healthcare, where patient records and sensitive information must be securely handled. The cryptographic underpinnings of blockchain contribute to a robust security framework that safeguards data during transmission and storage, mitigating the risk of unauthorized access or data breaches in time-sensitive contexts.

The distributed nature of blockchain networks further adds to the security of time-sensitive transactions. In a decentralized network, each participant has a copy of the entire transaction history, eliminating the need for a central authority to validate transactions. This decentralization reduces the risk of a single point of compromise and ensures that no single entity has control over the entire network. In financial transactions, the elimination of a central authority not only enhances security but also reduces the potential for manipulation or fraud, contributing to the overall trustworthiness of the transaction process.

Private and permissioned blockchains offer an additional layer of security in time-sensitive transactions. While public blockchains are open to anyone, private and permissioned blockchains restrict access to a predetermined set of participants. This controlled access ensures that only authorized entities can participate in the network, addressing concerns related to data privacy and confidentiality. In sectors like finance, where sensitive financial data is involved in time-sensitive transactions, the implementation of private or permissioned blockchains provides a tailored and secure environment for conducting transactions while preserving the benefits of blockchain technology.

Despite the substantial security enhancements offered by blockchain, challenges persist, and considerations must be addressed. Scalability, often cited as a limitation of blockchain networks, is a crucial factor in the context of time-sensitive transactions. As transaction volumes increase, ensuring that the blockchain network can handle the throughput in a timely manner becomes imperative. Ongoing research and development efforts are focused on scalability solutions, including off-chain transactions and layer-two solutions, to make blockchain technology more viable for high-frequency and time-sensitive applications.

Interoperability is another challenge, particularly in scenarios where diverse systems and platforms need to interact in time-sensitive transactions. Establishing standardized protocols and frameworks for interoperability is essential to ensure seamless communication and collaboration between different blockchain implementations and existing systems. Industry consortia and standardization initiatives are actively working towards defining common frameworks that can facilitate interoperability and integration across diverse technology stacks.

Regulatory considerations also play a significant role in the adoption of blockchain technology in time-sensitive transactions. Compliance with existing and emerging regulations is essential to ensure the legality and acceptance of blockchain-based transactions. In sectors like finance and healthcare, where regulatory frameworks are stringent, navigating the legal landscape is critical for widespread adoption and integration of blockchain technology.

Real-world use cases illustrate the successful integration of blockchain into time-sensitive transactions. Cross-border payments, for example, have experienced improvements in speed, cost, and transparency through the use of blockchain technology. The decentralized and secure nature of blockchain facilitates real-time settlement of transactions, reducing the need for intermediaries and accelerating cross-border financial transactions. In healthcare, the secure and transparent sharing of patient data among healthcare providers in real-time is facilitated by blockchain, ensuring that critical medical information is accurate, accessible, and secure.

In conclusion, the integration of blockchain technology into time-sensitive transactions represents a paradigm shift in how we approach security and transparency in critical processes. The decentralized, immutable, transparent, and programmable features of blockchain align well with the requirements of time-sensitive transactions, offering solutions to challenges related to data integrity, security, trust, and automation. While challenges such as scalability, interoperability, and regulatory compliance remain, ongoing efforts in research, development, and collaboration are actively addressing these issues. The successful integration of blockchain into time-sensitive transactions holds the promise of creating more secure, transparent, and efficient processes across a spectrum of industries, ultimately reshaping the future of high-stakes and time-critical transactions.

Analyzing ethical considerations in the deployment of real-time technologies.

The deployment of real-time technologies brings forth a multitude of ethical considerations that necessitate careful analysis and thoughtful integration into our evolving digital landscape. Real-time technologies, ranging from data analytics and artificial intelligence to Internet of Things (IoT) devices, have become integral components of various sectors, including healthcare, finance, transportation, and communication. As these technologies enable instantaneous data processing and decision-making, ethical concerns surrounding privacy, transparency, bias, accountability, and the societal impact of real-time systems come to the forefront.

Privacy stands as a paramount ethical consideration in the deployment of real-time technologies. The continuous stream of data generated by these systems, often in real-time, raises concerns about the collection, storage, and usage of personal information. In the healthcare sector, for instance, the deployment of real-time monitoring devices and health analytics raises questions about the confidentiality of patients' medical data. Striking a balance between the benefits of real-time health insights and the right to privacy requires robust privacy policies, consent mechanisms, and encryption practices to safeguard sensitive information from unauthorized access or misuse.

Transparency is another key ethical consideration in the deployment of real-time technologies. As these systems make split-second decisions impacting individuals and organizations, understanding the algorithms, data sources, and decision-making processes becomes essential. Lack of transparency can lead to a lack of accountability and erode trust in the technology. In financial transactions facilitated by real-time systems, transparency in algorithmic trading is crucial to prevent market manipulation and ensure fair and ethical financial practices. Providing clear explanations of how real-time algorithms operate and the criteria they use for decision-making is vital for building trust and fostering ethical use of these technologies.

Bias in real-time technologies poses a significant ethical challenge, particularly when algorithms exhibit discriminatory behavior. If the data used to train these algorithms contain biases, real-time systems can inadvertently perpetuate and amplify those biases, leading to unfair outcomes. In sectors like law enforcement, where real-time facial recognition systems are deployed, the potential for biased algorithms to disproportionately impact certain demographic groups raises concerns about social justice and equity. Ethical deployment requires continuous monitoring, auditing, and addressing of biases to ensure that real-time technologies are fair and unbiased in their outcomes.

The ethical dimension of accountability is critical in real-time systems where decisions occur rapidly and without human intervention. In applications such as autonomous vehicles, where split-second decisions can have life-or-death consequences, determining accountability in the event of system failure or errors becomes a complex challenge. Ethical considerations demand the establishment of clear lines of responsibility and accountability, with a recognition that real-time systems should be designed to minimize harm and prioritize safety. Implementing mechanisms for accountability, such as robust testing, monitoring, and auditing, is essential to ensure that real-time technologies operate ethically and responsibly.

The societal impact of real-time technologies raises ethical questions about their broader implications on individuals, communities, and global dynamics. In the context of surveillance technologies, such as real-time facial recognition or location tracking, concerns emerge regarding the potential erosion of civil liberties and the right to privacy. Ethical deployment necessitates a careful balance between the societal benefits of enhanced security and the potential risks of mass surveillance, emphasizing the importance of democratic oversight, public discourse, and regulatory frameworks to mitigate the negative societal impacts.

The ethical considerations in real-time technologies extend to issues of consent and user autonomy. As these systems continuously collect and analyze data, individuals may have limited control over how their information is used. In the realm of online services and platforms, real-time data tracking for targeted advertising purposes raises questions about user consent and the right to privacy. Ethical deployment requires transparent communication with users, empowering them with informed choices, and respecting their autonomy over the use of their personal data in real-time systems.

Environmental sustainability emerges as an ethical consideration in the deployment of real-time technologies, especially as the demand for computational power and data processing increases. The energy consumption associated with real-time systems, data centers, and the infrastructure supporting them raises concerns about their environmental impact. Ethical deployment mandates a commitment to sustainable practices, energy efficiency, and the exploration of eco-friendly alternatives to minimize the carbon footprint associated with real-time technologies.

Ethical considerations in real-time technologies also touch upon issues of accessibility and digital divide. As these technologies become pervasive, ensuring equitable access and addressing disparities in technological literacy and access is imperative. Ethical deployment requires efforts to bridge the digital divide, providing equal opportunities for individuals and communities to benefit from the advantages of real-time technologies, without exacerbating existing inequalities.

The ethical framework surrounding real-time technologies also encompasses issues of data ownership and control. As real-time systems generate vast amounts of data, questions arise about who owns this data and how it should be managed. In smart cities, where real-time sensors collect data on urban activities, ethical considerations revolve around citizen rights to control and access their data. Ethical deployment entails establishing clear guidelines on data ownership, user rights, and mechanisms for individuals to have control over how their data is used in real-time systems.

The integration of artificial intelligence (AI) in real-time systems introduces a layer of ethical complexity, particularly concerning accountability and decision-making. In sectors like healthcare, where AI algorithms assist in diagnosis and treatment decisions in real-time, ethical concerns revolve around the transparency of AI-driven decision-making processes. Ensuring that AI systems are explainable, auditable, and accountable becomes critical to maintaining ethical standards and gaining the trust of both practitioners and patients.

The ethical implications of real-time technologies are also intertwined with considerations of cultural sensitivity and inclusivity. Real-time systems that interact with diverse user populations must be designed with cultural awareness to avoid perpetuating stereotypes or causing unintentional harm. In natural language processing, for instance, real-time chatbots or virtual assistants should be programmed to understand and respond to users in culturally sensitive ways. Ethical deployment involves ongoing efforts to recognize and address cultural biases, ensuring that real-time technologies respect and reflect the diversity of users.

In conclusion, the deployment of real-time technologies necessitates a comprehensive analysis of ethical considerations to ensure responsible, fair, and inclusive integration into our societies. Addressing issues of privacy, transparency, bias, accountability, societal impact, consent, environmental sustainability, accessibility, data ownership, and cultural sensitivity is essential to mitigate the potential risks and negative consequences associated with real-time systems. Ethical deployment requires a collaborative effort involving technologists, policymakers, ethicists, and the wider public to establish guidelines, regulations, and practices that prioritize the ethical use of real-time technologies and contribute to a digital landscape that respects individual rights, values, and the collective well-being of society.

Discussing the societal implications of real-time systems in various domains.

The deployment of real-time technologies brings forth a multitude of ethical considerations that necessitate careful analysis and thoughtful integration into our evolving digital landscape. Real-time technologies, ranging from data analytics and artificial intelligence to Internet of Things (IoT) devices, have become integral components of various sectors, including healthcare, finance, transportation, and communication. As these technologies enable instantaneous data processing and decision-making, ethical concerns surrounding privacy, transparency, bias, accountability, and the societal impact of real-time systems come to the forefront.

Privacy stands as a paramount ethical consideration in the deployment of real-time technologies. The continuous stream of data generated by these systems, often in real-time, raises concerns about the collection, storage, and usage of personal information. In the healthcare sector, for instance, the deployment of real-time monitoring devices and health analytics raises questions about the confidentiality of patients' medical data. Striking a balance between the benefits of real-time health insights and the right to privacy requires robust privacy policies, consent mechanisms, and encryption practices to safeguard sensitive information from unauthorized access or misuse.

Transparency is another key ethical consideration in the deployment of real-time technologies. As these systems make split-second decisions impacting individuals and organizations, understanding the algorithms, data sources, and decision-making processes becomes essential. Lack of transparency can lead to a lack of accountability and erode trust in the technology. In financial transactions facilitated by real-time systems, transparency in algorithmic trading is crucial to prevent market manipulation and ensure fair and ethical financial practices. Providing clear explanations of how real-time algorithms operate and the criteria they use for decision-making is vital for building trust and fostering ethical use of these technologies.

Bias in real-time technologies poses a significant ethical challenge, particularly when algorithms exhibit discriminatory behavior. If the data used to train these algorithms contain biases, real-time systems can inadvertently perpetuate and amplify those biases, leading to unfair outcomes. In sectors like law enforcement, where real-time facial recognition systems are deployed, the potential for biased algorithms to disproportionately impact certain demographic groups raises concerns about social justice and equity. Ethical deployment requires continuous monitoring, auditing, and addressing of biases to ensure that real-time technologies are fair and unbiased in their outcomes.

The ethical dimension of accountability is critical in real-time systems where decisions occur rapidly and without human intervention. In applications such as autonomous vehicles, where split-second decisions can have life-or-death consequences, determining accountability in the event of system failure or errors becomes a complex challenge. Ethical considerations demand the establishment of clear lines of responsibility and accountability, with a recognition that real-time systems should be designed to minimize harm and prioritize safety. Implementing mechanisms for accountability, such as robust testing, monitoring, and auditing, is essential to ensure that real-time technologies operate ethically and responsibly.

The societal impact of real-time technologies raises ethical questions about their broader implications on individuals, communities, and global dynamics. In the context of surveillance technologies, such as real-time facial recognition or location tracking, concerns emerge regarding the potential erosion of civil liberties and the right to privacy. Ethical deployment necessitates a careful balance between the societal benefits of enhanced security and the potential risks of mass surveillance, emphasizing the importance of democratic oversight, public discourse, and regulatory frameworks to mitigate the negative societal impacts.

The ethical considerations in real-time technologies extend to issues of consent and user autonomy. As these systems continuously collect and analyze data, individuals may have limited control over how their information is used. In the realm of online services and platforms, real-time data tracking for targeted advertising purposes raises questions about user consent and the right to privacy. Ethical deployment requires transparent communication with users, empowering them with informed choices, and respecting their autonomy over the use of their personal data in real-time systems.

Environmental sustainability emerges as an ethical consideration in the deployment of real-time technologies, especially as the demand for computational power and data processing increases. The energy consumption associated with real-time systems, data centers, and the infrastructure supporting them raises concerns about their environmental impact. Ethical deployment mandates a commitment to sustainable practices, energy efficiency, and the exploration of eco-friendly alternatives to minimize the carbon footprint associated with real-time technologies.

Ethical considerations in real-time technologies also touch upon issues of accessibility and digital divide. As these technologies become pervasive, ensuring equitable access and addressing disparities in technological literacy and access is imperative. Ethical deployment requires efforts to bridge the digital divide, providing equal opportunities for individuals and communities to benefit from the advantages of real-time technologies, without exacerbating existing inequalities.

The ethical framework surrounding real-time technologies also encompasses issues of data ownership and control. As real-time systems generate vast amounts of data, questions arise about who owns this data and how it should be managed. In smart cities, where real-time sensors collect data on urban activities, ethical considerations revolve around citizen rights to control and access their data. Ethical deployment entails establishing clear guidelines on data ownership, user rights, and mechanisms for individuals to have control over how their data is used in real-time systems.

The integration of artificial intelligence (AI) in real-time systems introduces a layer of ethical complexity, particularly concerning accountability and decision-making. In sectors like healthcare, where AI algorithms assist in diagnosis and treatment decisions in real-time, ethical concerns revolve around the transparency of AI-driven decision-making processes. Ensuring that AI systems are explainable, auditable, and accountable becomes critical to maintaining ethical standards and gaining the trust of both practitioners and patients.

The ethical implications of real-time technologies are also intertwined with considerations of cultural sensitivity and inclusivity. Real-time systems that interact with diverse user populations must be designed with cultural awareness to avoid perpetuating stereotypes or causing unintentional harm. In natural language processing, for instance, real-time chatbots or virtual assistants should be programmed to understand and respond to users in culturally sensitive ways. Ethical deployment involves ongoing efforts to recognize and address cultural biases, ensuring that real-time technologies respect and reflect the diversity of users.

In conclusion, the deployment of real-time technologies necessitates a comprehensive analysis of ethical considerations to ensure responsible, fair, and inclusive integration into our societies. Addressing issues of privacy, transparency, bias, accountability, societal impact, consent, environmental sustainability, accessibility, data ownership, and cultural sensitivity is essential to mitigate the potential risks and negative consequences associated with real-time systems. Ethical deployment requires a collaborative effort involving technologists, policymakers, ethicists, and the wider public to establish guidelines, regulations, and practices that prioritize the ethical use of real-time technologies and contribute to a digital landscape that respects individual rights, values, and the collective well-being of society.

Exploring the implications of quantum computing on real-time processing.

Quantum computing, a revolutionary paradigm in computation, holds the promise of reshaping the landscape of real-time processing across various domains. As we delve into the implications of quantum computing on real-time processing, it is essential to understand the foundational principles of quantum mechanics that underpin this transformative technology. Quantum bits or qubits, the basic units of quantum information, leverage the principles of superposition and entanglement, allowing quantum computers to process vast amounts of information simultaneously and surpass classical computing capabilities.

In the realm of real-time processing, one of the foremost implications of quantum computing lies in its potential to exponentially accelerate certain types of computations. Classical computers, relying on bits that exist in either a 0 or 1 state, perform calculations sequentially. Quantum computers, however, exploit superposition to exist in multiple states simultaneously, enabling them to explore a multitude of possibilities in parallel. This parallelism has profound implications for real-time processing, particularly in scenarios where traditional computational power may fall short.

Quantum algorithms, such as Shor's algorithm and Grover's algorithm, exemplify the transformative potential of quantum computing in real-time processing. Shor's algorithm, for instance, demonstrates the ability of quantum computers to efficiently factorize large numbers, a task that poses a significant challenge for classical computers. In the context of cryptography, where the security of widely-used encryption methods relies on the difficulty of factoring large numbers, the advent of quantum computers poses both a threat and an opportunity. While quantum computers could potentially break existing cryptographic protocols, they also pave the way for quantum-resistant cryptography to ensure secure real-time processing in a post-quantum era.

Grover's algorithm, on the other hand, addresses the search problem, offering quadratic speedup compared to classical algorithms. In real-time databases and search applications, the ability of quantum computers to search unsorted databases exponentially faster than classical counterparts introduces a paradigm shift in information retrieval. This has implications for industries reliant on rapid data access, such as finance, where real-time processing of vast datasets is crucial for making informed decisions.

Despite the transformative potential, the practical realization of large-scale, fault-tolerant quantum computers – a necessity for widespread impact in real-time processing – remains a formidable challenge. Quantum coherence, the fragile state that allows qubits to exist in superposition, is susceptible to environmental noise and disturbances. Maintaining coherence over extended periods, known as quantum decoherence, poses a significant hurdle in the development of practical quantum processors. Quantum error correction algorithms and fault-tolerant quantum gates are areas of active research aimed at mitigating the impact of errors on quantum computations.

Quantum supremacy, a milestone achieved when a quantum computer outperforms the most powerful classical computers for a specific task, has been demonstrated by leading quantum computing companies. Google's achievement with its Sycamore processor marked a historic moment, showcasing the ability of quantum computers to perform calculations in minutes that would take classical supercomputers thousands of years. While quantum supremacy does not immediately translate to practical advantages in real-time processing, it signifies the progress made in quantum computing capabilities and sets the stage for exploring applications that could revolutionize real-time computations.

In the domain of optimization problems, quantum computing exhibits particular promise. Real-time optimization, whether in supply chain management, logistics, or financial portfolio management, involves finding the most efficient solutions among a vast number of possibilities. Quantum algorithms, like the Quantum Approximate Optimization Algorithm (QAOA), offer a potential speedup in solving these complex optimization problems. The ability to explore a larger solution space simultaneously can significantly impact industries where real-time decision-making relies on optimizing complex systems.

Real-time simulations, critical in fields such as material science, drug discovery, and climate modeling, stand to benefit from the quantum advantage. Quantum computers excel in simulating quantum systems, providing insights into molecular structures and interactions that classical computers struggle to model accurately. This has implications for drug discovery, where understanding molecular interactions in real time is essential for designing new pharmaceuticals. Quantum simulations could potentially revolutionize our ability to model and predict complex systems with unprecedented accuracy, advancing real-time processing in scientific research and innovation.

Machine learning, a cornerstone of real-time data processing applications, is also poised for transformation through quantum computing. Quantum machine learning algorithms leverage quantum parallelism to explore multiple solutions simultaneously, offering potential advantages in tasks such as pattern recognition and optimization. Quantum-enhanced machine learning has the potential to significantly accelerate the training of complex models, enabling real-time applications in areas like natural language processing, image recognition, and recommendation systems.

Encryption, a fundamental aspect of real-time security protocols, undergoes a paradigm shift in the quantum era. The widely-used public-key cryptographic algorithms, including RSA and ECC, rely on the difficulty of certain mathematical problems for security. Shor's algorithm, a quantum algorithm designed to efficiently factorize large numbers, threatens the security of these algorithms. As quantum computers advance, the cryptographic landscape must evolve to embrace quantum-resistant encryption methods. Post-quantum cryptography, including lattice-based and hash-based cryptographic approaches, is actively explored to ensure the security of real-time communications and data in a quantum-powered future.

Quantum communication, an integral component of quantum computing ecosystems, holds implications for real-time secure communication. Quantum key distribution (QKD), a quantum-secure communication method, leverages the principles of quantum mechanics to enable the secure exchange of cryptographic keys. The phenomenon of quantum entanglement ensures the detection of any eavesdropping attempts, providing a level of security that classical cryptographic methods cannot match. As real-time communication systems evolve, integrating quantum-safe encryption methods becomes imperative to safeguard sensitive information.

The implications of quantum computing extend beyond specific algorithms and applications to the very foundations of computational complexity theory. The classically intractable problems, known as NP-hard problems, may find novel solutions with quantum algorithms. This has profound implications for optimization problems that are prevalent in real-time processing scenarios, potentially unlocking new avenues for solving complex challenges efficiently.

Real-time processing, driven by the convergence of quantum computing and artificial intelligence, introduces novel paradigms for machine learning models. Quantum machine learning algorithms, such as the Quantum Boltzmann Machine and quantum neural networks, explore the intersection of quantum computing and deep learning. These models leverage quantum parallelism to explore vast solution spaces efficiently, potentially outperforming classical counterparts in specific tasks. The synergy between quantum computing and artificial intelligence holds the promise of unlocking new realms of real-time data processing and decision-making capabilities.

Despite the transformative potential, the journey towards practical quantum computing faces formidable challenges. Quantum coherence, quantum error correction, and the development of scalable quantum processors remain active areas of research. Quantum supremacy milestones, while significant, do not yet translate to practical advantages for most real-time processing applications. The path to achieving fault-tolerant, large-scale quantum computers that can consistently outperform classical counterparts remains uncertain.

Ethical considerations also come to the forefront as quantum computing advances. The potential for quantum computers to break existing cryptographic protocols raises concerns about data security and privacy. Additionally, the societal impact of quantum computing on employment patterns, economic structures, and global power dynamics necessitates careful ethical reflections and policy considerations.

In conclusion, the implications of quantum computing on real-time processing are profound and far-reaching. From exponential speedup in specific computations to the transformation of encryption methods and the revolutionizing of optimization problems, quantum computing introduces a new era in computation. The journey towards practical quantum computers is ongoing, with challenges and opportunities intertwining as researchers and industry pioneers strive to unlock the full potential of quantum technologies. The fusion of quantum computing with real-time processing has the potential to redefine the boundaries of what is computationally possible, shaping the future of information processing, communication, and innovation.

Discussing potential breakthroughs and challenges in leveraging quantum principles.

The exploration of quantum principles has opened a frontier of possibilities, holding the potential for breakthroughs that could reshape the landscape of technology, computation, and communication. At the heart of quantum mechanics lies the concept of superposition, where particles can exist in multiple states simultaneously, and entanglement, an intriguing phenomenon where the state of one particle is correlated with the state of another, even if they are spatially separated. These quantum phenomena form the basis of the emerging field of quantum information science, paving the way for transformative breakthroughs and posing formidable challenges.

One of the most anticipated breakthroughs in leveraging quantum principles is the realization of fault-tolerant quantum computing. Building practical quantum computers capable of executing complex algorithms relies on overcoming the inherent fragility of quantum bits or qubits. Quantum coherence, the ability of qubits to exist in superposition, is susceptible to environmental noise and disturbances, leading to quantum decoherence. Developing error correction techniques and creating fault-tolerant quantum gates are critical steps towards building large-scale, reliable quantum processors. Once achieved, fault-tolerant quantum computing has the potential to revolutionize computational power, solving problems that are currently intractable for classical computers, and accelerating breakthroughs in fields like cryptography, optimization, and material science.

Quantum cryptography stands out as a potential breakthrough in leveraging quantum principles for secure communication. Quantum key distribution (QKD), a quantum-secure communication method, harnesses the principles of superposition and entanglement to enable the exchange of cryptographic keys in a way that is theoretically immune to eavesdropping. The phenomenon of quantum entanglement ensures the detection of any attempt to intercept the quantum keys, providing a level of security that classical cryptographic methods cannot achieve. Implementing QKD in real-world communication systems has the potential to transform the landscape of secure communication, safeguarding sensitive information against the threats posed by quantum computers capable of breaking classical encryption methods.

In the realm of quantum computing applications, quantum machine learning emerges as a promising avenue for breakthroughs. Quantum machine learning algorithms leverage the parallelism inherent in quantum computing to process vast amounts of data simultaneously, potentially outperforming classical counterparts in certain tasks. Quantum-enhanced machine learning has the potential to significantly accelerate the training of complex models, offering advantages in areas such as pattern recognition, optimization, and data classification. As breakthroughs in quantum algorithms continue, the synergy between quantum computing and machine learning could usher in a new era of computational capabilities with profound implications for artificial intelligence and data-driven decision-making.

Quantum simulation represents another potential breakthrough with far-reaching implications, particularly in the realm of scientific research and innovation. Quantum computers excel in simulating quantum systems, providing insights into molecular structures, materials, and physical phenomena that classical computers struggle to model accurately. This has profound implications for drug discovery, materials science, and climate modeling. Quantum simulations can unlock a deeper understanding of complex systems, allowing researchers to explore novel materials, design more effective drugs, and gain insights into fundamental scientific questions. The potential breakthroughs in quantum simulation promise to accelerate the pace of scientific discovery and innovation across various disciplines.

However, the journey towards leveraging quantum principles is not without its challenges. One of the formidable obstacles lies in the development of scalable quantum processors. Quantum coherence, while a fundamental aspect of quantum computation, is delicate and easily disrupted by external factors. Maintaining coherence over a sufficient number of qubits for practical computations requires addressing the challenges of quantum error correction, quantum gates, and mitigating the impact of environmental noise. The race towards building scalable quantum processors that can consistently outperform classical computers is an ongoing challenge that involves researchers, engineers, and industry leaders around the globe.

Quantum communication, despite its potential breakthroughs, faces challenges in practical implementation. Creating robust quantum communication networks that can transmit quantum keys over long distances while maintaining quantum coherence poses technical challenges. Overcoming issues related to quantum memory, loss of quantum information during transmission, and synchronization of quantum states in distributed networks is crucial for realizing the full potential of quantum communication. As breakthroughs in quantum communication continue, the integration of quantum-secure communication methods into existing communication infrastructures requires careful consideration of technical, regulatory, and standardization challenges.

Ethical considerations also emerge as a significant challenge in the quest to leverage quantum principles. Quantum computing's potential to break widely-used cryptographic protocols raises concerns about data security and privacy. The development and deployment of quantum-resistant cryptographic methods become imperative to ensure the security of sensitive information in a post-quantum era. Additionally, the societal impact of quantum technologies, including potential shifts in economic structures, employment patterns, and global power dynamics, necessitates ethical reflections and policy considerations to navigate the implications of these breakthroughs responsibly.

The exploration of quantum principles also intersects with environmental considerations. As quantum computers become more powerful, their energy requirements increase, raising questions about the environmental sustainability of large-scale quantum computing operations. Efficient quantum algorithms, eco-friendly quantum hardware, and sustainable practices in quantum computing facilities become crucial for minimizing the environmental impact of breakthroughs in quantum technologies. Striking a balance between advancing quantum capabilities and ensuring environmental sustainability is a challenge that requires ongoing attention in the development and deployment of quantum technologies.

Furthermore, the realization of quantum technologies requires interdisciplinary collaboration and education. Breakthroughs in quantum computing, communication, and simulation demand a workforce with expertise in quantum physics, computer science, engineering, and related fields. Developing educational programs, training initiatives, and fostering collaboration between academia and industry are essential for cultivating the talent needed to advance quantum technologies and overcome the challenges associated with their practical implementation.

In conclusion, the journey of leveraging quantum principles holds the promise of transformative breakthroughs across various domains, from computation and communication to scientific research and machine learning. The realization of fault-tolerant quantum computing, quantum cryptography, quantum machine learning, and quantum simulation could usher in a new era of capabilities with profound implications for technology and innovation. However, challenges related to scalable quantum processors, practical implementation of quantum communication, ethical considerations, environmental sustainability, and interdisciplinary education must be navigated to unlock the full potential of quantum technologies. The pursuit of these breakthroughs requires a collaborative and multidisciplinary effort, combining scientific exploration, engineering ingenuity, and ethical reflections to shape a quantum-powered future responsibly.

| Page